C000002804

PENGUIN TRA

Travels in Nepal

Charles Pye-Smith was born in Huddersfield in 1951. He studied ecology at Newcastle-upon-Tyne and London universities. He is the author of *The Other Nile: Journeys in Egypt, the Sudan and Ethiopia* and *Barcelona* (Penguin 1992), and co-author of three books on environmental matters. He has been a regular presenter of the BBC World Service's programme *Global Concerns*; he also works for television and writes regularly for a variety of national publications.

TRAVELS in NEPAL

THE SEQUESTERED KINGDOM

CHARLIE PYE-SMITH

PENGUIN BOOKS

PENGUIN BOOKS

Published by the Penguin Group
Penguin Books Ltd, 27 Wrights Lane, London W8 5TZ, England
Penguin Books USA Inc., 375 Hudson Street, New York, New York 10014, USA
Penguin Books Australia Ltd, Ringwood, Victoria, Australia
Penguin Books Canada Ltd, 10 Alcorn Avenue, Toronto, Ontario, Canada M4V 3B2
Penguin Books (NZ) Ltd, 182–190 Wairau Road, Auckland 10, New Zealand

Penguin Books Ltd, Registered Offices: Harmondsworth, Middlesex, England

First published by Aurum Press 1988
Published in Penguin Books 1990
5 7 9 10 8 6 4

Photographs supplied by the author
Maps by Richard Natkiel Associates

The author and the publishers are grateful to Faber & Faber Ltd and to Harcourt
Brace Jovanovich, Inc. for permission to reproduce an excerpt from 'Portrait of a
Lady' from *Collected Poems 1909–1962* by T.S. Eliot, copyright 1936 by Harcourt
Brace Jovanovich, Inc., copyright © 1963, 1964 by T.S. Eliot.

Printed in England by Clays Ltd, St Ives plc

For Pat Harris and Cécile Purpora,
with love

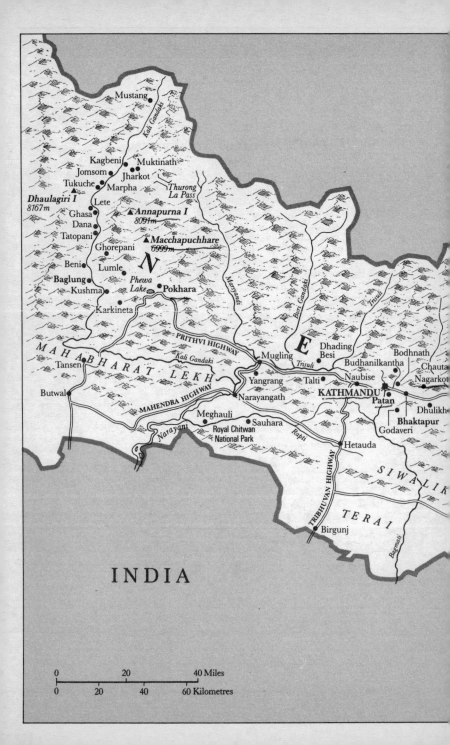

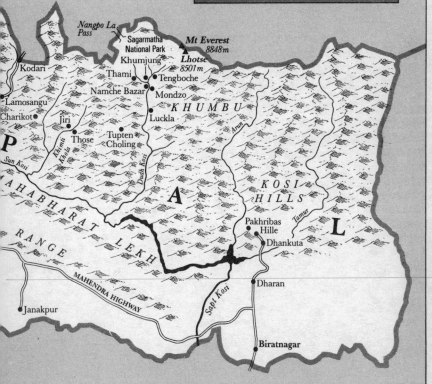

Contents

Illustrations

Perhaps nowhere in Asia is the contrast between a dignified, decaying past and a brash, effervescent present as violent as in Nepal; and one knows that here too eventually, the present will have its shoddy triumph.

Dervla Murphy, *The Waiting Land*

Preface

C HANCE TAKES YOU DOWN a particular street on a particular day at a particular time. Perhaps it is pouring with rain – this book is full of rain – and you are chilled to the marrow; or perhaps the sun shines – Nepal is bathed in light too – and you bask in its warmth whilst all around there are birds singing, people laughing and hooves clattering on dry cobbles. You may meet a lunatic, a beggar, a genius or a monk; a farmer, a politician, a butcher or a porter. Perhaps you come across the ritual sacrifice of a goat: the blood coagulates in the sun like pine resin, or spreads rapidly and fades as the rain sends a pink wash across the temple paving. Or maybe there is a woman breast-feeding, a man kicking a dog, or a child chasing an old bicycle wheel after a bus. Today may be one of those days when the air is heavy and ordurous, as it often is where the untouchables live by the river in Kathmandu; then again, and even there, pleasanter smells may drift by on the breeze: the sweet, charred smell of the dead being burnt; the moist breath of whiskery buffaloes; the heavy musk of a perfumed woman passing, her hips swinging, her calloused toes splayed in the dust.

Travel is a deliciously capricious business, and this account inevitably reflects the vagaries of chance and mood to which every traveller is subject. There are days when one is filled with such love for the world that whatever one comes across seems fine, however foul. Conversely, there are times when one's humour is so black that nothing, however beautiful, can inspire within you feelings of love and generosity. We are continually passing judgment: moments of indifference, which in themselves have a censorious quality, are constantly buffeted by waves of praise and wonder, of condemnation and disgust. A transient existence simply magnifies this process, for one is for ever darting in and out of places. First impressions become final impressions, and as often as not they tell as much about the judge as they do about that which is being judged.

I had harboured a desire to go to Nepal since childhood, and I never doubted that sooner or later I would get there. Nepal has always fascinated people in the West, and especially the British. We have a strong affection for the Gurkha soldiers, without whom many of our wars might have been more attenuated affairs. Hillary and Tensing, the first men to reach the summit of Everest, are household names, and there are few who have not heard of the Sherpas. Scenically and architecturally Nepal is one of the most beautiful countries in the world. It also has the distinction of being one of the few countries in Asia which was never colonized by a European power. Less than forty years ago a way of life persisted here which had scarcely changed since medieval times; Western visitors were few and far between. All this has changed. In 1951 King Tribhuvan abandoned his country's policy of splendid isolation. The twentieth century was belatedly ushered in, and with it came the trappings of high technology, a flood of Western aid workers and a growing number of tourists eager to see for themselves whether Nepal lived up to its romantic reputation.

If this book has any purpose other than the descriptive, it is to assess the impact which foreign aid has had on Nepal. Overrunning a country by force is just one way of influencing what happens within its borders; providing it with loans, grants and technical assistance – the main ingredients of foreign aid – is another. Most people in the West consider foreign aid to be a 'good thing', and our governments are frequently criticized for not giving more of it. The assumption is that aid helps to alleviate poverty. I hope this book goes some way towards showing that often this is not the case.

During the year before I left for Nepal I gazed at a map of the country virtually every day. It was tacked on to the wall above my bath – it still is – and I used to speculate about where I would go once there. My plans, I realized soon after my arrival, were wildly ambitious. It would have required years rather than months to achieve them. The reason for this is quite simple: Nepal is infinitely bigger than it looks. It covers an area little greater than England, and not much more than a quarter that of France, but its topography is such that measuring distances in terms of miles is meaningless. Whilst the thin strip of flat land along the Indian border, the Terai, is reasonably well-served by roads and public transport, most of Nepal is mountainous and accessible only on foot. I had hoped to see much of the country in a matter of a few months; when I look at the map now I realize just how little I saw. I wandered across it as a fly, searching for food, does across a stained-glass window, my feet touching briefly a small fraction of the many panes. One day soon I hope to return, not to the places described here, but to all those valleys and villages which I didn't see.

Seldom have I experienced such warm hospitality as in Nepal, and there are many people I must thank. A very special mention must go to

Preface

Hemanta Mishra and Brot Coburn, two men of admirable good humour and great kindness. Both became firm friends, and the times I spent with them added greatly to my appreciation of the country. I would also like to express my gratitude to the following people, some of whom I have written about and all of whom helped or entertained me in some way: Dipak Gyawali, Deepak Bajracharya, Trailokya Shrestha, Panna Lal Khadge, Sushma Mishra, Didi Thunder, George McBean, Sarah Cameron, Lorna Reid, Sabine Lehmann and Hadda Amir.

Then there are the many people who showed me round the aid projects which I visited, or at least discussed them with me in their offices. I have praised some of the projects, and damned others. I must stress that the opinions expressed here are mine, and they may differ markedly from those of the people listed below. My thanks go to Roger Wells of the British Embassy; Charles Borman and Hem Thapa of Pakhribas Agricultural Centre; Don Gilmour, Andrew Carter and Bob Fisher of the Nepal Australia Forestry Project; Mingma Norbu Sherpa and Bijay Pratap Malla of the King Mahendra Trust for Nature Conservation; Stephen Graham of the Water and Energy Commission Secretariat; Burt Levenson of the United States Agency for International Development; Jeevan Raj Adhikari, principal of Jiri Technical School; Tara Niraula and Mr S. B. Ranjitkar of the Swiss Association for Technical Assistance; Ganesh Gurung of the Centre for Nepal and Asian Studies at Tribhuvan University; Promod Kumar Koirala of the Ministry of Panchayat and Local Development; and Durgesh Man Singh, member of the National Planning Commission.

CP-S
London, 1988

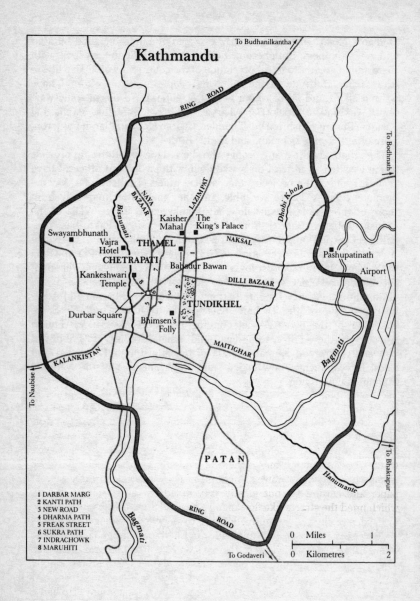

Kathmandu

To Budhanilkantha

RING ROAD

To Bodhnath

NAYA BAZAAR

Bisnumati

LAZIMPAT

Dhobi Khola

Swayambhunath

Kaisher Mahal

The King's Palace

NAKSAL

Pashupatinath

Airport

Vajra Hotel

THAMEL

CHETRAPATI

Bahadur Bawan

Kankeshwari Temple

DILLI BAZAAR

TUNDIKHEL

Durbar Square

Bhimsen's Folly

KALANKISTAN

MAITIGHAR

Bagmati

To Naubise

PATAN

To Bhaktapur

Bagmati

Hanumante

RING ROAD

To Godaveri

1 DARBAR MARG
2 KANTI PATH
3 NEW ROAD
4 DHARMA PATH
5 FREAK STREET
6 SUKRA PATH
7 INDRACHOWK
8 MARUHITI

| 0 | Miles | | 1 |
| 0 | Kilometres | | 2 |

1

Kaleidoscope City

IT SHOULDN'T HAVE RAINED much in early March, but there were many days when it did. The rain would begin a little after two o'clock in the afternoon and continue for an hour or so, occasionally longer. Sometimes it rained at night too. The thunder used to rattle and rumble across the mountains to the north of Kathmandu, and the rain would come straight down, like the stage rain in old black-and-white films. It was a cold, temperate rain and altogether different from the steamier rains which came later with the summer monsoons. This rain made you shiver. Afterwards the street dogs would shake themselves dry and strain their grimacing heads backwards to bite at the fleas and lice. Sometimes they spun round in circles, like the tiger which turned to butter in the *Little Black Sambo* stories. Just watching them made me itch.

The sacred bulls and cows continued to lumber slowly down the streets, oblivious both to the rain, which made their hides glisten, and to the yellow-roofed taxis, which ploughed furrows through the puddles. After a while I got to know some of them individually, much as one does the tramps in one's home town. Sometimes they would try to eat pieces of paper and cardboard, but mostly they dined on the rotten vegetables which lined the streets like flotsam on a beach. Offhand I remember three in particular: two consumptive-looking cows which scavenged around a yellow rubbish skip down a small alley in Chetrapati; and a large, sleepy, hump-backed bull which spent the days on New Road, near a brick dais where policemen would gather to smoke and chatter, either among themselves or to the men who sat cross-legged selling newspapers and shining shoes. I always had my shoes shined by the same boy. He had a profound squint and a wonderful smile. He never did my shoes for less than 10 rupees, although the going rate was seven. When it rained the shoe-shiners would throw their tubes of wax and cream into wooden boxes and head for shelter under a large piple tree or in one of the shop doorways.

It was after one of these March rains that I cycled east towards Pashupatinath. It was late afternoon. The streets were slithery and the air fresh. The road headed out past the King's Palace before disappearing into the shabby suburbs. It fell sharply down to a small river, which it crossed on an iron bridge, then rose again and wound its way between vegetable plots and scattered houses, which were modest yet stately in the way that old mud-brick houses with mellow pantiled roofs often are. Some had fine carved windows on their upper floors, and now that the rain had stopped, old women with leathery faces and heavy gold nose-rings leant on the sills and watched the trickle of people making their way, on foot and cycle, back to their homes beyond Kathmandu.

I crossed the Chinese ring-road and free-wheeled down a steep lane towards the Bagmati River, turning at the bottom of the hill to climb slightly again below an avenue of poplars and eucalyptus. There was such a calmness here that I abandoned my cycle before I reached Pashupatinath and made my way on foot to the riverside. Everything was bathed in a soft, pastel light – the narrow, viscous river; the cremation *ghats;* the temple with its gilded pagoda roofs piled in tiers. There was a watery hint of sun in the cloudy sky, beneath which blurred greys and pale blues and ochres were punctuated by sharply defined splashes of brighter colour: the vermilion *tika* on the foreheads of the Hindu pilgrims; the blood-orange embers of a funeral pyre which was being stoked to completion near a little humped bridge. The family of the deceased sat impassively a few yards away from the pyre, while groups of young men talked idly and quietly, not out of reverence, but because it was that sort of an evening. Even the temple monkeys seemed uncharacteristically subdued. There were people chanting in a building to the south, and outside it a man in cut-off jeans was chopping wood. The air smelt fresh and damp, meaty and woody.

There was still a little light in the sky when I cycled back past the King's Palace. In the bushes behind the high railings mynah birds were making a tremendous noise, much as starlings do in winter when night comes to European cities, and in the tall trees egrets were flapping clumsily on their unkempt, guano-soiled nests. Most of the fruit bats which roosted here during the day had already left for their feeding grounds in the plains to the south of Kathmandu, but a few late risers were still here, waking and stretching slowly like bits of macrami gradually unfolding.

I have never understood by what system or reasoning the French, whose language ascribes gender to all things, decided which countries should be masculine and which feminine. Nepal is masculine and so is the

Himalaya, although the other two great mountain ranges in the world, the Andes and the Alps, are both feminine. Neither do I understand, incidentally, why the mountains which stretch from Afghanistan to Burma, and which give Nepal the appearance of a carelessly slung hammock on relief models of Asia, should be singular rather than plural. I have no opinion one way or the other about Nepal's gender – either would do; and the same goes for all the other countries I have visited, with the exception perhaps of France (yes, it does feel feminine) and Ethiopia (which ought to be masculine, but isn't as far as the French are concerned). None of this matters much, because it is cities – not countries – which deserve to be sexed. There are some which seem overwhelmingly masculine and others whose femininity is so striking that one discovers them with the same relish as one embarks on an *affaire*. In the first category I would put places such as Brussels and Geneva and Lyons. They are besuited cities, smartly dressed but flabby inside, like the overweight businessmen you see sitting in their cafés over long lunches. At best I find myself indifferent to such places; they are unwelcoming and frequently dull. Getting to know them is as easy as talking to a Trappist monk.

When I think of the cities I love, it is as though I am thinking of a good woman; and sometimes it is like thinking of a bad woman. Kathmandu is a mix of the two; never a virgin, but often a tart. From the moment you arrive the city embraces you with a generosity that lifts the heart. Kathmandu is a place where one could spend a lifetime alone without ever being lonely, or at least that is how it struck me as a stranger. It is a city whose inhabitants are obsessed by caste and class, yet Kathmandu, one feels, welcomes the poor and the rich, the wise and the foolish, with equal avidity. Outwardly, it is a very public city. People ablute, evacuate, spit and worship in the streets. They weave and sew in their doorways and they sell vegetables and plastic toys and hardware on the steps of the temples. They kill buffalo on the riverbank at Maruhiti and goats on the bridge which links Kathmandu to Patan. You can buy heroin on the streets and hashish and cocaine; and if you want to change money on the black market you will find the money-changers at every corner in Thamel and down the alleys near Freak Street. People sleep on the streets when they're tired; and under the piple tree at Chetrapati they have their hair cut by men who sit cross-legged and do the job with cut-throat razors. Men play karem board on the streets and in the bus parks; and down by the river – at Pashupatinath and elsewhere – they burn the dead, while in the water there are always pigs scavenging among the rubbish, men digging gravel and often children swimming. This is how Kathmandu greets the stranger; and she reveals so much that for a few days you fool yourself into thinking that you already know her. But every time I came back to Kathmandu after trips into the country I saw a different city. I was looking into the same kaleidoscope, but during each of my absences it had been given a good shake; and on each return the patterns I saw seemed different, more complex and more illusive than before.

The first of the many memories I have of Kathmandu is of the ride out to Pashupatinath. As for the rest, they fall into no particular chronology, and indeed they seem so disparate now that I find it hard to believe that they all belong to the same place and the same short span of a few months. Imagine yourself in a museum which displayed an Egyptian mummy beside a tin of baked beans; Velázquez's 'Saint John of Patmos' next to Warhol's 'Marilyn Monroe'; a Ming vase on the same table as a Woolworth's cup and saucer ... The easiest way to make sense of a place is to remember the faces; then fit the faces to a family, the family to a building, the building to a street.

I always stayed at the Hotel Vajra, which provided me, on the various occasions I returned to the capital after forays into the countryside, with good company and terrible food. It was run by a German woman, Sabine Lehmann, and a Tibetan called Sengpo Lama. Sabine was gargantuan in every sense, a huge woman with a fine hooked nose, a tremendous laugh and a voice of astonishing power and resonance. She had an office in a building across the flowery courtyard from the main hotel and dispensed orders by shouting through her window: you could hear her half a mile away. When I arrived at the Vajra, Sabine was in the process of rehearsing the annual play with a mixed cast of Europeans, Americans, Tibetans and Newars, the latter being the indigenous people of Kathmandu. The play was *Ling Gesar: Episodes of the Superhuman Life of the Tibetan Hero*. Judging from the sounds which shook the building till eleven o'clock every evening, it was a story of horrible violence.

Theatre was Sabine's passion, and it had played a large part in her wanderings. Though outwardly ebullient, she was in many ways modest, and I had some difficulty, even when I knew her well, in prizing from her details of her past. It seems that many years ago – I suppose she was about forty by now – she and a group of friends in San Francisco had built a boat called *The Hericlatus*. They called themselves the 'Theatre of All Possibilities', and the boat took them to many places around the world. First they went to Mexico, where they settled for a while at Santa Fe. There they built *dobi* houses and met Ed Bass, the man who became their patron. Later they sailed through the Panama Canal, down the coast of South America, then across to Bombay, where they looked for a building in which they could set up a theatre. They didn't find one, but they did meet a Tibetan who suggested they should come to Kathmandu. Hence the Vajra.

The Vajra was one of the few buildings of any merit to have gone up in the tourist-inspired building boom. Most of the modern hotels were ugly in the extreme, none more so than the most expensive, the Everest Sheraton, the Annapurna and the Oberoi. The Vajra's architects had done their best to create a building which looked oriental. The doors and windows had been designed and carved by Newar craftsmen, Tibetan frescos had been painted on the ceilings, the roofs were tiled and pagoda-like, and bells hung from the eaves and tinkled in the breeze, just as they do on the city's temples. Its rooms, which were simple and pleasant, looked down over a walled garden.

The Vajra was part of a network of projects around the world, all of which had been paid for by Mr Bass, a Texan whose financial resources appear almost unlimited – he is one of four brothers whose interests include oil fields and Disneyland. All the projects had, in Sabine's words, 'an ecological bent', and all had theatre groups attached to them. In Texas, there was the Caravan of Dream. In Arizona, there was Sunspace Ranch, where scientists had created something called 'Biosphere II', a large bubble containing marshes, forests, grasslands and room for half a dozen people to live. Other projects were under way in France, Australia and Puerto Rico. The theatres in the network were known as Studio 1 (Texas), Studio 3 (London), Studio 7 (Vajra) and so forth. There was plenty of gossip about the group, much of it malicious. Some said they were a cult; others that they intended to launch themselves into space, far away from this beastly earth, in a Biosphere capsule. Newspapers and magazines, many of which have run features on Sunspace Ranch, nearly always refer to Mr Bass as 'a philanthropist'. I don't think he is. Philanthropy implies an interest in the general welfare of mankind. Mr Bass is simply a rich man who spends his money as he wishes. To spend $1 million on a hotel which houses a few Thespians and caters for visitors like me, when a few minutes' walk away there are people living in the depths of misery, is not the action of a philanthropist.

As for the guests, they were a mixed bunch, and mostly unmemorable. Among the exceptions was Charles Thomas, a quietly spoken, very thin, three-quarters bald American in his early fifties. He had a wide, flattish, chiselled face and when he was silent, or sitting alone, its unblinking immobility conspired with his pallid complexion to give him the appearance of a marble bust; the sort of face which one felt should be dusted rather than washed. In conversation the mask fell away. He could be witty, charming, infuriating and insulting, all within a short space of time. Charles had been coming to the Vajra, on and off, for four years, and he had become as much a part of the hotel as its heavy wooden furniture. He avoided direct sunlight, which he considered injurious, and spent a good deal of time at the bar, which, by happy coincidence, occupied the darkest corner of the dining room. He had been here long enough to realize that the food in the Vajra was even more dangerous than sunlight, and every day he would take a taxi into town to eat at one of the better restaurants. Charles had spent fifteen years editing the Fodor guides to India, and consequently his knowledge of the art and architecture of the sub-continent was extensive and scholarly. 'If anyone asks you a question about a temple which you don't understand,' he used to say, 'just slowly shake your head and tell them, "It's very Tantric."' He talked of Durbar Square, which for visitors is probably the city's greatest attraction, with contempt. 'Most of it's ghastly,' he exclaimed if he heard praise of it. 'It's horrible late-Malla stuff.' His main preoccupation when I arrived was Ascot, to which he intended to go in June. He liked the grand life, and he knew many grand people, including a Saudi prince who had a box at the races.

It was through Charles that I got to know Christoph Giercke, a man who was blessed with gigolo-ish good looks and who spoke a florid and metaphysical English in the way that East Europeans often do. He was by origin East German, but he had spent most of his adult life in New York and France, where he had produced films and managed a punk band, Johnny Thunders and the Heartbreakers. Back in his twenties – he was now forty, although he didn't look it – he had made a film with Andy Warhol called *Cocaine Cowboys*. It was, he explained when I first met him, a very bad film: 'just a beat movie'. On the film posters they had used the Coca Cola typeface and the company had successfully sued him. In 1983 he made *The Rise and Fall of President Marcos*, which showed great prescience on his part, after which he turned his attention to the Buddhist monastery of Tupten Choling. The fruits of his labour in Nepal had been a film about the monks called *Lord of the Dance – Destroyer of Illusion*. He had arrived at the Vajra a few days before I had and was waiting for his girlfriend ('A French countess,' whispered Charles, who thought highly of countesses) before heading into the mountains. He said he intended to put on a private showing of the film when he returned. He hoped I would be back in time to see it.

The founders of the Vajra, and those who ran it, had evidently hoped to attract a Bohemian clientele. Perhaps they did for a while; but most of those who came during the spring and early summer of 1987 were well-shod tourists, middle-aged, frequently overweight, and here just long enough to give their Pentaxes a bit of action and their bowels an unpleasant surprise. Most of the men wore shorts and at least half had beards. The older women favoured cotton dresses with floral designs, while many of the younger ones – particularly the Germans and Americans – wore shorts and *décolleté* T-shirts; in other words, the sort of clothes they would have worn for a trip to a Mediterranean beach. 'Doesn't it make you sick?' asked Sabine one day. 'All these women wandering about the temples with their tits hanging out.'

Indeed, the insensitivity of many European tourists was quite stagger-ing. If you went to Pashupatinath any time between ten o'clock in the morning and four o'clock in the afternoon you would see groups of tourists, many immodestly dressed, standing on the little bridge and clicking away at the funeral pyres; and up at Swayambhunath, fifteen minutes and a short climb west of the Vajra, you would find the Buddhist's holy shrine turned into a circus. I went to Swayambhunath only twice. The *stupa* was a dramatic rather than beautiful structure: it looked like a white breast with a ladder of golden rings for a nipple, from which were draped lines of prayer flags. On my first visit I encountered two guided tours: one German, the other American. The guides, who were Nepalese, were bellowing out the history of the *stupa* and its associated monastery. Some people listened; some bought postcards and souvenirs; others scurried round snapping away at the Buddhists who had come here to visit the monks or to perform their devotions. One Tibetan woman was making a slow perambulation of the *stupa* on her belly, and a tourist (with shorts and beard) followed her round with a cine-camera. COKE IS IT! said the adverts on the houses behind the *stupa*. That seemed an apt summary of the Western attitude to these holy places.

Affection has much to do with familiarity, and the first street I knew well became my favourite. It began where the bridge crossed the Bisnumati below the Vajra, and wound its way up a hill to Chetrapati, a district which, not long ago, defined the western limits of Kathmandu. It was a country road which was gradually being claimed by the city. Early each morning farmers on the way to the vegetable markets descended to the meagre threads of river which twisted between the wide gravel banks below the bridge. Here they washed their carrots and cauliflowers before proceeding up the hill, down which came a constant trickle of Buddhists on their way to Swayambhunath. The women wore long Tibetan dresses which reached down to their ankles and as they walked they spun their prayer wheels and mumbled their mantras. Around seven o'clock the gravel-diggers arrived, and they would spend the day shin-deep in water. Sometimes the gravel was carried away in bamboo *dokos*, conical baskets suspended by a band across the forehead to rest against the porters' backs; sometimes it was taken by lorries or tractors.

No one seemed to take much notice of the herd of pigs which spent the whole day rootling among the riverside debris. A little before sunset the big-titted sows led their piglets up the hill towards the Vajra and into a house which they shared with their owners. On many evenings when I passed this way I would see a girl with black eyes and tumbling black hair leaning against the jamb of an open door, her lips held slightly apart, her feet bare, her small breasts tight against a ragged purple shirt. I used to wonder what she was thinking about as she watched the last of the sun's rays strike the golden roofs of the temple which sparkled across the river with all the brilliance of contraband in a jackdaw's nest. Charles said the temple was Tantric. A lion and a peacock stood on the two pillars outside its entrance. When the dead were being burnt here the rickshaw drivers would go more slowly to take in the beauty of the scene. I used to do the same.

Like so much of Kathmandu, the riverbed was filthy. Into it were thrown rotting vegetables, buffalo skulls, buffalo hocks and rubbish of every description. Once I saw six dead dogs in a pool on the western side of the river. Some may have died natural deaths; some may have been poisoned. By this time I had developed such a hatred for the city's dogs that the sight of these corpses afforded me a degree of satisfaction, if not pleasure.

There was a gang of eight dogs which spent the days sleeping on a tin roof by the bridge and the nights roaming the streets. They were vicious creatures and I lived in constant fear of being bitten by them. You often saw rabid dogs staggering about and slavering, and each year hundreds of Nepalese die of the disease. Westerners are luckier, of course, as those who are bitten can generally afford the anti-rabies vaccine. Poisoning the dogs doesn't seem to do much good; or perhaps they don't poison enough of them. Someone told me that the poisoned dogs are soon replaced by others which drift in from the countryside. All through the night the dogs barked and howled and yapped, and sometimes I used to wake up and think I was in hell – I imagine that's where these dogs go. I noticed, incidentally, that the dogs by the bridge were much more prone to harassing Europeans than Nepalese or Tibetans.

Hugging the banks of the Bisnumati, from this bridge all the way downstream to the confluence with the Bagmati, were the shanties where many of the poorest people lived. Below the Vajra lived a community of sweepers. I never went there, but Panna Lal Khadge, who belonged to another untouchable caste, the butchers, took me round the slums farther south, where butchers and sweepers lived together.

I met Panna through Trailokya Man Singh Shrestha, a high-caste Newar about whom I shall have more to say later, as he accompanied me on a trip into the hills to visit a tribe of hunter-gatherers called the Chepangs. Before we went to see Panna I spent some time in the British Council library, where I skimmed through the few books I could find which mentioned the Newar caste system. The Newars of Kathmandu are divided into sixty-four occupational castes. In his *History of Newar Culture*, U. P. Chattopadhyay gave four different schemata for the untouchable castes, all derived from the writings of Europeans who were here during the last century. The one below is taken from Brian Houghton Hodgson, who was the British Resident in Kathmandu from 1833 to 1843.

Kasai	Butchers
Jugi	Tailors and musicians
Dung	Musicians
Cooloo	Leather-workers
Pooriah	Fish-catchers, executioners and dog-killers
Chamokhullak	Sweepers
Sanger	Washermen

The other three versions were roughly the same, although Francis Buchanan Hamilton, who spent a year in the Kathmandu Valley in 1802–3, placed butchers, who were also 'palanquin bearers for the vulgar', below musicians and above dyers (Chhipri).

Panna was a long-faced, sad-eyed, sallow-skinned man in his early thirties with the most marvellous, though ephemeral, of smiles. I went to see him several times, sometimes with Trailokya, sometimes alone, and we'd either chat in the café beside his house or in his sitting room, which was small, clean and pleasantly furnished with a comfortable sofa and several wooden chairs. There were cotton prints on the wall alongside family snaps, and on a sideboard there was a large photograph of Ganesh Man Singh. Singh was Trailokya's uncle and one of the founders of the now-banned Nepali Congress Party. He spent many years in prison, both under the Ranas, who were overthrown in 1951, and under the royal family, the Shahs. There was a small bookcase beside the sofa with books written in English and Nepali, and on top of the case were two stuffed squirrels. When I came in the evenings one of Panna's sisters used to join us. She always wore European-style summer frocks and talked with the assertive manner one would expect of a student leader. She was extremely proud of her photo album, which consisted mostly of pictures of herself addressing public meetings, many of them from the same platform as Singh and B. P. Koirala, the one-time leader of the Nepali Congress Party and something of a hero among the many opposed to the present partyless system of government.

I was unceasingly surprised by the Nepalese preoccupation with history. Even the illiterate seemed to know more about their country's past than I did about mine; and people would talk of events which happened many centuries ago as though they were personal recollections. 'If you want to understand the caste system,' announced Panna on my first visit, 'you must go back to the fourteenth century, to the time of King Jayasthiti Malla.' Apparently a caste system of sorts already existed among Hindus, but it was under this king's rule that it was refined, and even the Buddhists, who did not adhere to any caste system, were allotted positions within the new hierarchy. King Jayasthiti had been worried about the ascendancy of Tantric Buddhism and he invited some of the Brahmans – the Hindu priests – who had recently fled the Moslem invasion of India to divide the Newar population into occupational castes. Once they had done so he introduced a rigorous series of laws and by-laws to ensure that the caste system functioned successfully. For example, members of a low caste couldn't touch the food of a higher caste, and if a man married a woman from a lower caste he was converted to that caste and ostracized by his own. Butchers had to wear cloaks with long sleeves; sweepers had to go barefoot and bare-headed.

The Brahmans, explained Panna, created four main divisions. First, and unsurprisingly, came the Brahmans, the priestly caste; second came the Chhetris, who were warriors; third, the Baishya, who comprised many of the merchant castes; and finally there were the Shudra, the untouchables. The latter, wrote Hamilton, 'scarcely venture to draw near any other Hindu, but would consider themselves much degraded by eating, drinking or cohabiting with a Musulman or Christian'.

'Where the priests were so clever,' explained Panna, 'was in dividing the untouchables into different castes. We are butchers, the highest of the untouchables, and we won't eat with tailors or sweepers.' This, he believed, went some way towards explaining why the untouchables were still very much at the bottom of the social heap: so long as the sweepers and butchers and tailors continued to behave (by not eating with one another, intermarrying and so forth) as the old caste system ordained they should, then there was little chance of the untouchables uniting to better their lot. King Mahendra passed a law in the year 2020 (Nepalese dates are fifty-six years ahead of our own) which did away with previous legislation discriminating against the untouchables, but throughout most of the country they are treated pretty much as they always have been. 'Maybe things are changing in Kathmandu,' said Panna. 'Most of the young people know how the caste system came about and they no longer observe it so rigidly as their parents did. But two or three miles away from the city you'll find little has changed.'

One afternoon Panna took me on a tour of his neighbourhood, which began a little way down the hill from the temples in Durbar Square and became progressively poorer and shabbier as we approached the river. The people living along his street were Khadge, the butcher caste. Most of the Khadges made a living in the butchery business, but some pedalled rickshaws, drove taxis and ran stores. Panna had a store which sold parts for machines. Compared to most members of his caste he was well-educated, but he was far from rich. He and one other member of his close family supported ten others. They had to live on somewhere between 75 and 100 rupees a day.

While I am on the subject of money, I may as well dwell on it for a short time, because it will crop up again and again. I had never in my life been so aware of money as I was in Nepal. This was not because I was suffering from a lack of it; on the contrary, I had never travelled with so much. Nor was it because the Nepalese were avaricious. It was simply because poor people often talk about money; and also because the sums which were being spent by foreign governments and aid agencies on development projects throughout the country were often enormous – and the source of considerable wonder to those whom these projects were supposed to benefit. To put Panna's 100 rupees (or $5) a day into perspective, the best I can do is mention the price of various goods. A cup of tea: 1–2 Rs. Soft drinks: 3–4 Rs. A short taxi ride: 10 Rs. A kilo of rice: 15 Rs. A packet of Yak cigarettes: 7.50 Rs. A small pack of biscuits: 5 Rs. A small jar of marmalade: 60 Rs. A bottle of imported washing-up liquid: 90 Rs. A metre of good Indian cotton: 30 Rs. A cheap hotel in Kathmandu: 20 Rs a night. A night at the Vajra: 200 Rs. A night at a five-star hotel $65 (1300 Rs). A small Toyota car (the standard taxi): $9,000 (180,000 Rs). One ropani (or one-seventh of an acre) of land on the city outskirts: $2,000 (100,000 Rs).* Western expatriates, almost without exception, I suspect, will scoff at lists such as this. The Nepalese, I often heard it said, didn't need washing-up liquid, marmalade or Toyota cars. Nor did they stay in hotels. And so on.

Panna and I followed an open sewer down to the river, then turned south along its left bank. There were about fifty shacks here. We walked into one of them to find Narayan Khadge sitting on the floor on a filthy rush mat. He was a big man with a shaven head, a wide neck and muscular arms. He had a wife and three daughters, two of whom were with him. One was four years old, the other seven, and both were naked, thin-legged and pot-bellied. The family lived, ate and slept in this one room, which measured about fourteen feet square. They had no toilet, and no tap-water. The walls were made of mud-bricks and the roof of corrugated iron. It was unbearably hot. Flies were everywhere: on the walls, on the floor, on the bed and on the children, who didn't seem to notice them. In one corner there was a kerosene stove on which the family cooked. From

---

* In 1987 the US dollar was worth about 20 rupees. I have largely avoided converting rupees into dollars (and vice versa) except when referring to the prices of goods or services at the time of my visit. Since the 1970s the Nepalese rupee has undergone a series of devaluations. In the late 1970s there were 12.5 rupees to $1; by June 1983 there were 14.30 rupees to $1. I have converted prices to dollars rather than pounds for the simple reason that the Nepalese relate to US currency rather than sterling.

the ceiling hung strips of dried meat of the gristly, not the lean, variety. There was one small shelf, on which stood a frame of family photos and a clock which told the wrong time. Below this was a tin bowl full of bones with small pieces of meat, fat and tendon sticking to them. It must have been a Saturday, because Narayan wasn't working. His job consisted of slaughtering animals and carrying meat, at a wage of 30 rupees a day. He said they ate badly and never enough – sometimes they had rice, but not always, and he knew that the children were suffering. Occasionally he managed to find work in the temples, where he was paid a few rupees for sacrificing animals. We asked him if he sent the children to school. He didn't. He was illiterate and so was his wife. The shack smelt unpleasant, but that wasn't surprising as the river, with its load of raw sewage and rubbish, ran outside the door. The nearest water tap was a fair walk away.

We looked into some of the other shacks, and they differed little from Narayan's. Some were rather more crowded – one sweeper widow had six children – and some had little hovels of pigs attached to them. The pigs looked rather healthier, and certainly better fed, than most of the people.

A little way to the north, in a cobbled courtyard where local farmers held their religious festivals, there was a building which used to be a buffalo shed but which a group of Khadge, one of whose leaders was Panna, had turned into a community centre. The government, which is dominated by the high-caste Hindus, had never done anything for areas like this, and the community centre was an attempt by the *Khadge Sewa Samati* – the Khadge Welfare Committee – to help themselves.

The Committee began life as a talking shop. 'At first,' said Panna, 'we just encouraged people to come along and air their grievances. We tried to get everyone to talk about how they felt about being untouchable. Touchables have always looked down on us. They see us Khadge as a rough, cruel people. This gives us much pain. We looked at our manners, and we realized that they were crude: we swear a lot and we're always quarrelling. We wanted to show that we have humanity; that we're not cruel.' For a while the meetings were well-attended, but people soon tired of so much talk and no action. 'We had to do something which would bring economic benefits to the area,' explained Panna. Through Trailokya, who worked as a volunteer for an organization called Service Civil International, Panna met some representatives from Oxfam, which gave 45,000 rupees towards the conversion of the buffalo shed. For six months sewing classes for Khadge girls were held here. Unfortunately, the girls didn't become skilful enough to get jobs in tailoring shops. Instead they just stayed at home. The sewing courses were abandoned; the Committee ceased functioning; and now the community centre is closed.

Back by the river we walked over a muddy, blood-streaked patch of land where animals were slaughtered. Across the water a herd of thirty buffaloes stood silently chewing the cud, oblivious to the fate which awaited them the following morning. Their bones would be joining a pile which two men in shorts were picking through as we passed. A little farther on we came to Kankeshwari temple and Panna pointed out the cremation sites. One is born into a caste; and in that caste one dies. There were three places for cremations: one for farmers, one for butchers, and another, set slightly apart, for Manandhars. The Manandhars, explained Panna, used to be untouchables, but during the last century the Rana rulers gave them permission to run restaurants, and they became touchable.

The temple had copper roofs, and it was surrounded by mythical beasts and sculptures of Hindu and Buddhist deities. In the days of Jung Bahadur, the man who overthrew the Shahs to establish the Rana dynasty midway through the nineteenth century, the temple witnessed a remarkable event which took place on a certain day each year. The whole town would gather beside the river near the temple and divide into two groups, which then engaged one another in battle. Those captured by the rival group were sacrificed to Kankeshwari.

We made our way up the hill from the temple, passing some substantial houses in which rich Khadges lived. I asked Panna whether the rich helped the poor of his caste. 'No,' he replied simply. A little later we looked into an old building in which three bare-chested Tamangs – the Tamangs are a Tibetan-featured hill tribe – were sweating over a wooden contraption which squeezed oil from mustard seeds. The press was worked by hand, and the men were coated in oil and dust. Small paneless windows allowed shafts of coarse golden light to pierce the interior and play across the muscular backs of the men.

Finally we arrived at the office of the chairman of Ward 19. Shanta Bahadur Shahi is a Khadge, and the only untouchable chairman in Kathmandu's thirty-three wards. There were ten other men in his office, and presumably each was waiting for an audience. Panna and I were invited to sit at the chairman's desk and a boy was sent out to fetch us some refreshments. While we drank, the chairman talked about the problems of his ward, the population of which was somewhere in the region of 12–15,000. There were no health clinics in the area and few people had tap-water or private toilets. I asked him about education among the Khadges and he deflected the question to Panna, who thought that out of the 30,000 Khadges in the country perhaps 100 had received any form of higher education. He knew of only four with university degrees: one had become a doctor and three were engineers.

By the time we left the ward office the sun was hanging low over the hills across the river and the western walls of the buildings were awash with orange. We wandered through a maze of dank alleys, passing more mustard mills on the way, then headed up to Durbar Square, just before which we ran into a crowd of people queuing to enter a small temple. They may have numbered no more than fifty, but such was the raucous exuberance of the occasion that it seemed as though half of Asia were here. Swirling against the crowd, like angry waves licking over a bouldery shore, was an anarchic mélange of hawkers and petty traders selling everything from gaudy plastic toys to bamboo flutes. There were pigs snorting, hens crowing, women laughing and jostling; the temple bell was continually clanging; in the square beyond taxis honked and rickshaws juddered over the cobbles. But perhaps I remember such scenes best not so much through sound but through colour, and especially the colours of the women's clothes: the parrot greens and soft pinks, the burnished reds and dusty oranges – clean, natural colours such as you will see on a fruiterer's stall or in the paintings of El Greco.

Here I left Panna and made my way along Sukra Path, a street which plunged from the comparative modernity of New Road – which was constructed after the earthquake of 1934 – into the bowels of the old city. There were dozens of shops selling silk, cotton and nylon, many of them run by Indians, and above some of them were small tailoring concerns. I had a tailor in one of them. He was small, thin and gaunt. He sat with two others in 'Lucky Tailors', and they spent the days making suits, shirts and trousers on old-fashioned treddle machines. I used to buy material in the bazaar at Indrachowk, at the end of the street, and my tailor would always inspect it carefully, stroking it like a cat, before announcing, regardless of its quality, 'Bootifool mitaariel. Zee very best.'

When I arrived he was putting the finishing touches to a silk shirt I'd ordered, so I sat down and told him how I'd spent the afternoon. His black eyes fixed me critically. 'In your cuntree,' he enquired, 'tailors low caste. No?'

No, I replied, we didn't have a caste system. This answer didn't satisfy him, so I tried to explain our class system, which was a task I found none too easy. Once I'd embarked on my discourse it struck me – and possibly my tailor – that it wasn't all that different from the Hindu caste system, although it was undoubtedly simpler and its existence was reinforced by custom rather than law. For reasons which escape me now, I told him about *Lady Chatterley's Lover*. He thought it was a shocking story.

'So,' he said, 'in your cuntree only working-class work? Middle-class, top-class – not working?'

'No,' I replied, 'most people work, if they can find work.'

'But tailors bottom-class?'

'No,' I said. 'Tailors can be any class.' I explained that some people who made clothes were very well-to-do.

'Well-to-do what?' he asked indignantly, adding before I had time to reply, 'But you can't eat with tailors! You can't marry tailor girl!' It was a statement, not a question, and delivered with such fervour that I thought it best to drop the subject.

To see how the other half – or other hundredth – lives, or lived, where better to start than in one of the old Rana palaces?

Once I'd handed my bag and umbrella to the morose peon at the side entrance to the Ministry of Education and Culture and gone through the stately doors into the main room of the Kaiser Library, I nearly always had the place to myself. It was a room which still looked lived-in, although Kaiser Shamsher Rana had died in 1964, and both the palace and his library had been left by his wife, as he had requested, to the government. On either side of the door there was a magnificent globe. The one on the left was of the constellations; the one on the right of the Earth. Someone – a bored child, I imagine – had scratched out Nepal, leaving a white hole surrounded by sepia. Scattered around the room were some unexceptional bronze statues, a stuffed tiger and a few pieces of heavy wooden furniture, including a table on which had been placed a small photo of Kaiser Shamsher, a bald, sallow-skinned man with rimless spectacles similar to those Gandhi wore. He had the face of a sensitive and cultured man; indeed, he looked more like a Jewish psychiatrist than a Nepalese field-marshal. The books which ran the length of one wall, and which were just a fraction of his collection, most being stacked away in cupboards upstairs, suggested an eclectic taste. Not surprisingly, there were hundreds of books about military history, most of them in English: the *Dispatches* of the Duke of Wellington, Churchill's *History of the Second World War*, works by Nelson and Curzon ... And there were thousands of novels too: leather-bound editions of Dickens, Dumas and Dostoesvsky; paperbacks by Graham Greene, Lawrence Durrell and E. F. Benson.

However, it was the paintings and photographs, rather than the books, which attracted me most to the library. Tucked away beside the staircase which led to the upper floor were three oil paintings. The one on the left was of Captain Knox, the first British Resident in Kathmandu. He arrived in 1801 and departed the following year. He had a wild, handsome face which reminded me of Gustave Courbet's famous self-portrait. Next to him was Professor Joseph Se Tucchi (1894–1984), a russet-haired man in late middle age. He had an intelligent, gaunt look about him and he wore a grey pin-stripe suit, out of whose breast-pocket poked a fountain pen. The last of the three was Professor Sylvain Levi, a man with a good nose and an excellent moustache. The only other Europeans in the room were Lord Kitchener, who visited Kathmandu in 1906 when commander-in-chief of British India, and a pleasant-looking lady with chubby cheeks, a clear complexion and a string of pearls. This, according to the label under the photograph, was Mrs Smith. I imagine she was a governess to Kaiser Shamsher's children. I have no idea who the two professors were or what they were doing here.

There were many more portraits along a corridor upstairs. Most were hung in groups of three, the middle one in each group set a foot or so above the other two. I particularly enjoyed the eccentric juxtapositions. King George V was flanked by William Shakespeare and Leo Tolstoy; William Kaiser by Napoleon Bonaparte and Lenin; and George Washington by Bismarck and Tojoko. Mao Tse-tung and the Queen of China made an unsuitable couple; while Nehru was hung, as he might have wished, next to Gandhi.

The library occupied a small corner of Kaisher Mahal, one of the many great neo-classical palaces which had been built by the Ranas in the latter half of the last century and the first half of this one. The Ranas came to power in 1846, shortly after the Queen of Nepal, who was incensed by the murder of an ally whom she had hoped would help her wrest power from her husband, had called upon a young army general, Jung Bahadur Rana, to wipe out her opponents. This he did. Fifty-five members of the aristocracy were murdered in the armoury at Durbar Square in an event which became known as the Kot Massacre. A few weeks later Jung Bahadur declared himself prime minister, then Maharaja. He gave himself powers greater than those of the monarchy and made his office hereditary. The Ranas ruled the country for a little over a hundred years, during which time they amassed great fortunes, did little to better the lot of the common people and dealt brutally with all opposition. But history, given a little time, can be a benevolent judge: sooner or later most tyrants become figures of fun and future generations remember them for what they left behind and still exists rather than for what they did or didn't do during their lifetimes. And what finer monuments to themselves could the Ranas have erected than Singh Durbar, the former prime minister's residence, which, before it was damaged by fire in 1973, had 1,700 rooms and seventeen courtyards; or Kaisher Mahal and the scores of other palaces dotted around the city?

One wonders what the peasantry of the last century thought as they saw constructed buildings and follies, secular in purpose, grandiose in size and design, whose architectural precedents sprang from a world which existed many thousands of miles away and 2,000 years before, and about which they knew nothing. Even before Jung Bahadur set off to Europe in 1850, from where he returned with his plans to transform Kathmandu, the city's inhabitants had been treated to a taste of what was to come. Bhimsen's Folly, which took its name from the prime minister who commissioned it in the 1820s, still towers above the city's roofs. It looks like a tall thin lighthouse, and it serves no purpose whatsoever. 'It was not raised to commemorate any particular epoch,' wrote Ambrose Oldfield in 1880, 'but apparently merely for the purpose of "astonishing the natives".'

Kaisher Mahal, the field-marshal's residence, was built in 1895. It has neither the grandeur nor the fine proportions of Singh Durbar, nor the eccentric charm of Bahadur Bhawan, whose columned façade is topped by a collection of pagodas which make it look like a cross between a wedding cake and a hat-stand. Kaisher Mahal's classical façade is spoilt by a row of circular windows above the third floor: they give the whole building the appearance of an ocean liner. However, it is infinitely more beautiful than anything constructed during the post-Rana period. Compare it, for example, with the King's Palace along the street, a vast affair not unlike London's King's Cross Station with a few rococo embellishments. That too suffers comparison by its proximity to a fine Victorian edifice, the neighbouring station of St Pancras.

Many of the Rana palaces have – or had – lovely gardens. In the one beside Kaisher Mahal there is a small classical temple, surrounded by trees where egrets nest and bats roost. It wouldn't look at all out of place in a Capability Brown landscape. Set into the façade is a slab of marble on which is engraved a short, unattributed poem. It deserves repetition, not on account of its literary merits (it hasn't any), but because it somehow reflects the romantic spirit in which these buildings were conceived.

> One Moment in Annihilation's Waste
> One Moment of the Well of life to taste –
> The Stars are setting, and the Caravan
> Starts for the Dawn of Nothing – Oh, make haste!
>
> Alas that Spring should vanish with the rose!
> That Youth's sweet-scented Manuscript should close!
> The Nightingale that in the Branches sang
> Ah, whence and whither flown again, who knows!
>
> Ah, love! Could thou and I with Fate conspire
> To grasp this sorry scheme of Things entire.
> Would not we shatter it to bits – and they
> Re-mould it nearer to the Heart's Desire!
>
> Ah, moon of my delight who know'st no wane,
> The moon of Heav'n is rising once again
> How oft hereafter rising shall she look
> Through this same garden after me in vain!

Unfortunately, the temple has been turned into offices (for Unesco and a Norwegian aid agency); the lily-pond is waterless; the flower-beds have been strangled by weeds; and much of the garden has become a building site. The same sort of thing is happening to many of the old palaces and their gardens. Indeed, wherever one looks, beautiful buildings are being left to collapse or are in the process of being destroyed to make way for characterless concrete structures. The Ranas will be remembered for their good taste (in architecture, if not in poetry); the rich and powerful of today for their lack of it.

Had one lived at the time of the Rana building boom one would doubtless have deplored the way in which members of this curious oligarchy lavished vast sums of money upon their own dwellings while ignoring the great poverty which enslaved the rest of the population. However, one views the palaces now as *faits accomplis*, and I found myself excited not only by the aesthetic pleasures they afforded, but by the knowledge that these earliest and most conspicuous signs of European influence were not the result of a Western power imposing its own taste upon a subjugated people. The classical ideal was voluntarily embraced.

Nepal is one of the few countries in Asia which was never colonized. By the beginning of the nineteenth century Tibet had fallen to the Chinese and India to the British. The latter managed to pare away some of the outer-lying territories claimed by Nepal, but no system of colonial government was ever established in Kathmandu. There is little point in speculating upon what might have happened if Nepal had been colonized, although one can surmise that the country's heaving topograpy would have prevented it from benefiting to any extent from Britain's greatest gifts to those who fell under her suzerainty: cricket and the railways. Admittedly, there is a thin strip of flat land, seldom more than twenty-five miles wide, which stretches along the entire length of Nepal's southern border with India; but this boasts precisely thirty-two miles of rail, and such is the poverty of the national diet that there are good practical reasons which render the conversion of rice paddies into cricket pitches improbable. Oddly enough, cricket is a sport in which many Nepalese, particularly among the educated classes of Kathmandu, take a great interest. I was surprised to discover that the back page of *Rising Nepal*, the English-language daily, was devoted to European sport, and I was able to follow the progress of the English county cricket season as well as if I had remained at home.

For a country of seventeen million people, only a quarter of whom can read, Nepal has a remarkable number of newspapers. In 1985 there were 459, of which fifty-eight were dailies. Most of these were one-page affairs, and you'd see people buying them in batches of ten or more. *Rising Nepal*, with eight pages, was altogether more substantial, and a highly entertaining paper it was too, despite the fact that it was a mouthpiece for the government, or rather the royal palace, which is roughly the same thing. The front page was always given over to the affairs of King

Birendra and his family, recounting, in prose of ludicrous sycophancy, how the monarch had just graced such-and-such a factory or ministry with his noble presence. On the inside pages there was the local news, where one read about village elections, cow thievery and crimes of passion; in addition to which there were always three or four large features, at least one syndicated from the press agencies in the West. During my stay in Nepal I learnt about the public transport system in Croydon; about attempts to repeal an Italian law which forbade the city of Florence feeding a contraceptive to its pigeons; and about the consumption of petfood in West Germany (each year seventy-five million pets cost their owners $4 billion in food alone, a sum which exceeded by a factor of six the Nepalese government's budget for 1986/7).

The remaining features and the editorial always gave a good indication of the main concerns of government. A week never passed without there being at least one article lamenting the fuelwood crisis in the Himalaya and another touting hydro-electric power as its solution, and every day, without fail, the paper ran pieces about the country's development programmes. The home news, paradoxically and with rare exceptions, was also foreign news. Virtually every road, bridge, hospital and college had been built, or was about to be, with the help of a grant or loan from one of a score of countries which had set up shop here since Nepal opened its doors to the outside world in 1951.

It would be disingenuous of me to profess surprise at *Rising Nepal's* preoccupation with development and foreign aid. Indeed, it was the presence of foreign interests which attracted me to Nepal in the first place. Almost a year to the day before I arrived in Kathmandu I had attended a conference in a mock-baronial Quaker hotel in the hills some seventy miles north of New York. At the time I was loosely attached to a documentary department of BBC Television, and the organizers of the Mohonk conference – the United Nations University and the International Mountain Society – kindly offered to pay for my trip. The conference had the grand title 'The Himalaya – Crisis or Super-crisis?' It lasted a week and most of the sixty or so participants delivered a paper about some aspect of the Himalaya. Over half those present were scientists, and we were treated to erudite lectures on deforestation, soil erosion, river sedimentation and overgrazing – in short, to the ragbag of subjects which make up the grist without which the environmentalist's mill would be redundant. Most of these scientists came from countries in the Western world, where they were attached to universities or research institutions. Also present were about twenty Nepalese. Most were employed by His Majesty's Government of Nepal (HMG), though some worked for private agencies involved in the development business.

I was one of the few people present who had never been to Nepal, and though this put me at a certain disadvantage, it meant that everything I heard was fresh. I was, so to speak, a blank sheet of paper ready to soak up the ink of whoever wrote most persuasively. Apparently, it had for many years been assumed – by His Majesty's Government, by aid agencies and by scientists – that the greatest threat to the future of Nepal, and indeed to the 350 million people who lived in the Ganges Basin, came from the destruction of forests in the Himalaya. But there were some doubting Toms here, even among those who had been the first to forecast an environmental disaster.

The most persuasive challenge to the old assumptions came from an Englishman who had known the Himalaya through climbing rather than through scientific research. Michael Thompson had scaled Everest with Chris Bonington, and during the less interesting moments of the Mohonk conference he could be seen shinning up the cliffs near the hotel. A small, neat, shy man, he talked slowly and spent most of the time during conversation staring upwards, as though on the lookout for a sudden rockfall.

Scientists thrive on figures, and for several days before Thompson took to his feet we had been barraged with them. 'Perhaps the only number which has any scientific validity at all in the Himalaya is sixty-seven,' began Thompson enigmatically. This, he explained, was the factor by which estimates for the *per capita* consumption of fuelwood varied. Thompson pointed out that countries with such remarkable topographical and cultural diversity as Nepal were notoriously difficult to study, yet this hadn't deterred dozens of scientists from extrapolating their findings from one hillside, or mountain-top or valley, to cover the whole country. Their generalizations were meaningless, yet HMG, the international lending banks and the aid agencies frequently took these figures as the basis for determining policy. Furthermore, they tended to latch on to those figures which best suited them. For example, when the United Nation's Food and Agriculture Organization (FAO) cast its eye over the estimates for fuelwood consumption, it was forced to discount the upper and lower rates. Were the former true it would mean that the Himalaya would be washed down the Ganges next week and there would be nothing anyone could do to stop it; if the latter were correct, then the mountains would shortly be smothered by vegetation, thus precluding any action on the part of FAO and the aid agencies. FAO plumped for a figure with which it was capable of working. Organizations, suggested Thompson, defined problems in such a way as to justify their actions. And their capacity for action depended on how much money they had.

Thompson's arguments are a good deal more sophisticated than the few lines above suggest, and I shall return to them later. Suffice to say here that he was one of the people at Mohonk who pushed the discussion about what was happening to the environment in Nepal away from the prosaic business of measuring rates of soil erosion and fuelwood consumption and into the realm of politics. There were many people at Mohonk who suggested that it was in the interests of Nepal's ruling and middle classes to overstate the environmental crisis. After all, it was argued, it was they who were the main beneficiaries of foreign aid, and the worse the perceived problem, the more certain it was that the money would keep flowing in. And it certainly had been flowing in. The aid programme began in 1951/2 with a grant of 22,000 Rs from the United States government. By 1984/5 the annual flow of aid money into the country was over $130 million. Since 1951 Nepal has received over $500 million of foreign aid from the United States alone.

As one of the purposes of my visit was to look at the ways in which foreign governments were spending their money in Nepal, I spent a fair amount of time during my first week slogging round Kathmandu and introducing myself to the aid agencies whose projects I hoped to visit. The British suggested I go out to the far east of Nepal, to the region north of Dhankuta. The Americans told me whom and what I should see in the area to the west of Annapurna. The Swiss said they would be happy for me to visit their projects in and around Jiri. And the Australians invited me to accompany their field staff to the headquarters of one of their forestry projects in Chautara. However, the principal pleasures of these early days derived not so much from visits to embassies and offices – though most were housed in Rana palaces – as from my casual wanderings round the city and the evenings spent with two friends whom I had first met at Mohonk. Soon after my arrival, Hemanta Mishra rescued me from a touristy hotel in the Thamel area of the city and introduced me to Sabine and the Vajra; and once I had settled in there he invited me to dinner at his house, explaining that there would be some other 'English blokes' there. One was Major Spain, a former officer in the Gurkha army; the other was Lord Montagu of Beaulieu. Both men had been helping to raise money in Britain for the organization which Hemanta ran, the King Mahendra Trust for Nature Conservation. I also passed many hours with a close friend of Hemanta's, Brot Coburn. He met me at the airport, invited me for frequent meals at the house he shared with Didi Thunder, and bombarded me with advice on where I should go in Nepal. He and Didi were about to visit Namche Bazar, a Sherpa town in the Everest region, and he suggested I accompany them, which I did.

2

Namche Bazar

MR HAGAYUKI, THE OWNER of the Hatago Lodge, was sitting in his kitchen when we arrived in mid-afternoon. He looked like an old samurai who'd gone to seed: his hair hanging in long grey strands below a white, or once white, headband; his sharp eyes peering through the smoke which curled above the open fire to settle in undulating drifts below the roof. His face was the colour and texture of knotted teak and he looked frail yet indestructible. 'How's business?' asked Brot, who hadn't been up here for two years.

'Business no good,' replied Mr Hagayuki emphatically. 'No enough money pay my boys.' He roared with laughter. 'Very good boys,' he added, glancing nervously at the five young men engaged in preparing and serving food to the handful of trekkers who sat in the large dining room next to the kitchen. Although the sun was shining brilliantly, the gloom inside was crepuscular. What little light did get through the dirt on the small windows was soaked up by the smoke and the heavy, unhewn timbers which were stacked one upon another to make the walls. It made me think of the log cabin by the Mississippi in which Huckleberry Finn was imprisoned by his drunken father.

Mr Hagayuki had been here, midway between Luckla and Namche Bazar, for many years, but his knowledge of Nepali was limited to counting (even this he did ineptly), and his English was at best highly eccentric. Didi knew a little Japanese, Mr Hagayuki's native language, so she addressed him in that. He greeted whatever it was she said with a blank stare and mumbled gruffly that he was a Sherpa.

'One time I have many book,' he suddenly announced as we waited for our food. 'History of Nepal, history of India, history of Buddha. But six years ago, daytime fire. All gone!' He treated himself to another uproarious bout of laughter. 'Englishman, he send me book by Homer. *Iliad*. I read it. Then I say, "No so good as *Mahabharata*."'

Indeed, Mr Hagayuki had put up a little notice in the dining room which read:

Please Read These Books
I   Dhamma Pada
II   Anatomy of Peace by Emiles Lieres
III Mahabharata. Hindu classic. More interesting book than Homer's ILIAD & ODYSEY.

There was another hand-written notice explaining to guests 'The Habit of Hatago':

In this lodge it is in the habit of counting by yourself of your eating and drinking...

And please pay the bills of the staying-guests, to the master of Hatago, after the dinner. As we regret deeply a few guests who run away without paying their bills, unseen in the early dawn, in spite of advanced nations in Europe and America by birth, coming to this beauty scene with poor – difficult life – surrounding. After dinner we shut the door of restaurant at 7.30 p.m. because our labour must get up early in the morning. Pardon us!

In one corner of the dining room there was a shelf with a dozen books, most of them in Japanese. None of Mr Hagayuki's favourites were there, having left, perhaps, one early dawn. Beside the shelf a large picture frame was tacked to the wall. It was a shrine. Under the words 'In memory of Cynthia Coleman' there was a photo of a slight, pretty girl with olive skin and plaited black hair shaking hands with Mr Hagayuki, who smiled seraphically. Beside it was a letter from the girl's friend telling Mr Hagayuki that Cynthia had been killed in a climbing accident. 'Her body remains here [in Nepal], in her adopted country,' ended the letter, which came with some fruit pips from the United States. Mr Hagayuki had planted them in the garden, which was one of the most beautiful I saw in the Himalaya. In the orchard behind the lodge there were apple, pear and peach trees. It was early spring, so they were leafless still, but the wild cherry was already in flower. I asked him what vegetables he grew and I don't think there were many temperate ones he didn't mention. Quite a few of them went into our salad.

The evening found us only a little way farther up the valley, and we stayed the night in Mondzo, a small village whose wide-eaved, shingle-roofed houses were perched a couple of hundred feet above the Dudh Kosi River and several thousand below the ragged ridges of almost sheer mountains. The water was a cold, opaque green, like the glass slabs on which old-fashioned dentists mix amalgam. Above us the lower slopes of the mountains were a darker pine green; and higher up, where the trees thinned out and disappeared, green gave way to the hard greys of granite and schist. The mountains to the east were topped with snow which caught the sun long after the village had fallen into shadow. Four women were spreading mulch on a ploughed field and the sharp odour of manure mingled with the sweet smell of pine sap. Once the sun had gone it became bitter, and we sat round a wood fire trying to keep warm while we waited for the rice to cook. Brot and Didi drank some *chang*, cloudy grain beer, and when our porter arrived we smoked some of his *bedis* as we'd run out of cigarettes. While Brot and Didi chattered away in Nepali with the young Sherpa couple with whom we were staying, my mind drifted back over my first day away from Kathmandu.

We had flown in that morning on an eighteen-seater, but it seemed like a week ago. My legs ached pleasantly, my lungs were full of fresh air and my skin already felt tight and weathered. There had been mauve primroses on the grass airstrip at Luckla, and primroses lined the path the whole day long. There were rhododendrons, too, though few were in flower; and nearly always we were in sight of at least one magnolia, whose fleshy white flowers stood out against the sombre pines and firs, as did the cotton prayer flags which fluttered untidily on bamboo poles above nearly every house and on lines of twine slung between trees and buildings. Each flag was printed with the Buddhist mantra *Om mani padme hum* – hail to the jewel of the lotus – and the same words were carved on the *mani* stones which were piled in heaps in every village and at frequent intervals along the path.

For much of the way the path was flat and ran only a little way above the river, but from time to time a cliff or landslide pushed it up a few contours and we climbed high enough to see the peaks above Namche Bazar. We stopped four or five times on the way, our first rest being at Phakding, where the woman who owned the lodge, having served us tea, stripped a small child and washed him in a brass bowl. He screamed a lot before she put him back into his trousers, which, like those of all small children here, were split up the seam behind so he wouldn't have to take them down when he did his business. The lodge was a mix of old and new. On the shelves there were rows of tureens and pots made of beaten copper and brass. Beneath were large plastic barrels, all salvaged from climbing expeditions. One had 'Argentinian Himalaya Expedition' stamped on it; another, 'Norwegian Mount Everest Expedition 1985'. They were used for fermenting *chang*. On the wall behind us there was a poster of King Birendra and the queen. The king wore a moustache and tinted spectacles (even his statues were bespectacled), which made him look like a pale-skinned *Tonton macoute*.

On the path there was a constant traffic of people making their way up to Namche or coming down from it. There were many barefoot porters carrying rice, sugar, cigarettes and shoes – indeed anything which wasn't manufactured or didn't grow in the Khumbu region. Some had probably come from the roadhead at Jiri, four or five days' walk to the south-west; others from the Arun Valley to the south-east. The porters' loads weighed anything between thirty-five and seventy kilos and each carried a small T-shaped stick which he or she slipped beneath the loaded *dokos* when resting. Then there were the trains of *zopkioks,* the yak crossbreds which carried the heaviest loads – cement and ironware and climbing gear for the expeditions. Brot didn't know any of the porters from the lower valleys but he knew everyone from Namche or nearby, and our progress was continually halted while he exchanged greetings with old friends and acquaintances.

Brot spoke fluent Nepali and could get by in Sherpa and Tibetan. He knew Nepal as well, if not better, than any of the other Europeans or Americans who lived here, and he had walked throughout most of the country apart from the far west. He had also written one of the best books to come out of Nepal, *Nepali Aama,* a portrait of the old peasant woman with whom he had stayed when he first came. Over the last fifteen years he had spent eight in Nepal, working first with the American Peace Corps in the hills south of Pokhara, then later on various development projects, including one we were going to see at Namche. He was the ideal guide. For one thing, he was a rationalist, not a romantic. (Much of what had been written about the Sherpas and the Khumbu region made it sound like a Shangri-La, which, as I was to discover, it wasn't.) And for another, he was hugely entertaining. He was given to telling very funny stories with the sort of deadpan expression one associates with pall-bearers, and he had a lusty turn of phrase. Sometimes I would ask him what questions I should put to some official I intended to visit. He'd wrinkle his forehead, tug his moustache, then suggest something so undiplomatic as to be unaskable. 'Well,' he'd drawl, 'I guess that would shake the lead out of Mr So-and-so's pants.'

By the time the goat stew was cooked Brot and Didi had drunk a fair amount of *chang*. Both they and the Sherpa couple were most affectionate towards one another, and Brot suggested to them that I would feel less left out if I took up with the old mother. She sat in a dark corner, shrivelled, immobile and silent, like a recently exhumed mummy awaiting archaeological inspection. Once we had eaten we went to bed. We left at six the next day, which was among the most unpleasant of my life.

I lost sight of Brot and Didi soon after we'd passed through the village of Jorsale, and I didn't catch them up till an hour later. By that time I had been up and down a couple of spurs which in Britain would have been classed as decent-sized mountains, but which here were nothing more than wrinkles in the valley bottom. They were waiting for me by the river and once I got my breath back I asked where the path went. Brot pointed over a bridge to a cliff on which I could just make out a thin scar which climbed steeply towards the top. I said I wasn't going. 'What?' asked Brot, under the impression he had misheard me. 'I can't go up there,' I repeated. After some cajoling I agreed to proceed, providing Brot held my hand. We ran up the cliff, and I adopted a low-slung, crab-like posture, keeping my eyes firmly on my feet. About 300 feet up there was an unnecessary arrow painted on the cliff with the word NAMCHE next to it. In places the path was quite wide, but for much of the time it was little more than a yak's breadth. I looked down only once and if Brot hadn't been holding on to me I would have fainted. Brot chuckled most of the way up, and once the path left the bare rock and began zigzagging, still ridiculously steeply, over shrubby grassland, he went speeding on ahead. Some twenty minutes later Didi and I climbed on to a small ridge where there was a tent in which one could buy tea and soft drinks. The Coca Cola cost eight times more than in Kathmandu. Outside the tent was a resting place for porters and a sign which said 'Everest View', which was quite true. Didi left me here and I did my best to recover my nerves and my breath. The air was noticeably thinner than at the bottom of the cliff, even though we were only about 500 feet higher. It didn't seem to matter how much air I took into my lungs, there was never enough of it. It reminded me of drinking skimmed milk.

I was joined here by a thin, scruffy Frenchman with lank hair and broken spectacles. He was waiting for his wife, who had left the cave where they lived above the village of Thami over a week before. She had gone down to Kathmandu to renew her visa. He was so worried about her that for the last three days he had walked down here, several thousand feet below the cave, to stare expectantly down the trail in the hope of seeing her return. 'When there's two of us up there I'm very happy,' he said. 'But when she goes and I'm alone I feel terrible. I just can't tell you what goes on in my head.' He was so deeply in love with her that it pained me to listen to him. He had met his wife when she was a nun and he a monk; they had fallen in love and married. While she continued studying Buddhism under a local *lama*, he cooked and cleaned and fetched food and firewood. He talked enthusiastically and knowledgeably about the wildlife – he could see musk deer and vultures and eagles from his cave, and during the winter there had been a wolf near Thami. He thought it had come over from Tibet and he was angry with the Sherpas because they had poisoned it.

Phobias, as I discovered once I reached Namche, are absolutely obsessional. I don't suppose I ever went more than two or three waking minutes without thinking of the cliff, and at night I slept so fitfully that it didn't even feel like sleeping. Every time I thought of the cliff it was higher, and the path thinner and more treacherous; and there, a terrible distance away, far below the choughs and the eagles, were the waters of the Dudh Kosi, ready to sweep whatever fell into them down to the Ganges. It did me no good to think of the hundreds of people who trotted cheerfully up and down the cliff every day. I simply convinced myself that sooner or later someone had to fall off it, and that I would be the one to do so.

The scenery round Namche did nothing to allay my fears. It was unremitting in its vastness. If you walked up the hill to the army post you could see Everest and Lhotse and half a dozen other peaks looming over the barren valleys. They were a long way away – twenty miles or more – but they felt very close. It looked as though they had been carelessly chucked down from a great height and they made a disorganized and terrifying landscape: they didn't seem to belong to this earth. Looking back, the town appeared insignificant, like a tiny filling on the cusp of a stained and broken tooth. There were sixty or seventy houses arranged in a semi-circle round a dozen small fields. The fields were fallow now, though some had been rowed up for potatoes, and the breeze which blew up from the gorge below brought with it the smell of human manure, which I could see lying in black streaks on the grey-brown earth. While the sun shone brightly it set off avalanches, which cascaded down the cliffs opposite Namche; and then the clouds came, rolling up the valley in waves of spume to swallow the tin-roofed lodges and the older shingle-roofed houses. For a while the ochre-painted monastery, which looked down on the town from a forest of prayer flags, stood facing the wall of cloud; then that disappeared too, and so did the sacred lump of rock a little higher up which was said by the Sherpas to have fallen off Khumbi-yul-lha, the holiest of their mountains. All that remained of Namche were its sounds, muffled by the wet clouds: the barking of dogs, the rhythmical axing of firewood, the clanking of bells round the necks of the yaks and *zopkioks*, cocks crowing and people laughing and shouting. This was how I liked Namche most and how I remember it best.

On our first day in Namche, Brot and I went to see the man who had just been re-elected *pradhan panch,* a post equivalent to that of mayor. Ang Phurba was a well-built, middle-aged man with a lined face, hooded eyes and whispy black hair. His wife had cheeks the colour of russet apples and crimson thread entwined in a black pigtail. She served us small cups of Tibetan tea, for which Brot had developed a taste but whose rancidity almost made me retch. While Brot and the mayor discussed electricity, about which more later, I admired the house. It had a hard, utilitarian beauty. The ground floor was given over to cattle, hay and firewood; the upper floor to the business of eating, sleeping, entertaining and praying. The kitchen was smoky and colossal: for the Sherpas who built these houses – this one dated from the 1830s – a decent kitchen was one large enough for the whole community to dance in.

What impressed me most about Namche's old houses were the private monasteries, which were found on the upper floors beside the kitchens. We didn't see the mayor's, but an old friend of Brot's showed us one in a house along the street. Its walls were covered with exquisite paintings, depicting the life of Gautama Buddha in rich reds and greens, blues and golds. A photograph of the Dalai Lama, the spiritual leader of the Tibetan Buddhists, stared impassively into the room. Though now cold and gloomy, this room was frequently enlivened in past times by the *lamas* and monks enticed into temporary residence by the wealthy owners.

At the opposite end of the social spectrum – the term is ill-chosen, perhaps, as Sherpas are among the more egalitarian of oriental societies – were Kusaang and Peti Tsering, who led a life of stark simplicity in a one-room shack tacked on to the lodge in which we were staying. In fact the Tserings were Tibetans, not Sherpas, and they were among the many thousands who had made their way over the Nangpo La, the high pass to the north-east of Namche, following the unsuccessful uprising against the Chinese in 1959. We sat beside a small charcoal brazier, drinking tea, while the old lady spent her time laughing, possibly at her own private jokes but more probably at the white visitors. She was a wonderful old bird, emaciated and almost blind, yet cheerful and agile. Her husband Kusaang had little plaits of grey hair which ran round his skull like tattered laurels. He sat stiff and straight as he talked about their flight from Tibet, the Dalai Lama and their life here. He scratched a living as a cobbler and supplemented it by looking after the prayer wheel in his back yard. The wheel was barrel-shaped, twelve foot high and meticulously painted with scenes from Buddhist mythology. It spun on a vertical axle and with every revolution a bell was struck. Before we left, the old man grabbed the rope which hung from the wheel and trotted round, repeating the mantra *Om mani padme hum*. We gave him a few rupees, and when we sat down to eat in our lodge five minutes later the bell was still clanging furiously.

More representative of modern Namche than either the mayor's house or the Tserings' shack was the lodge where we and a dozen other tourists were staying. Cattle still occupied the ground floor, but upstairs a dining room and a dormitory were attached to the kitchen. The tourists' material demands were few and simple: a bed, a couple of solid meals a day, and perhaps a shower, which was provided by a device that was admirable in terms of both its simplicity and profitability. Lhakpa Dorje or one of his family heated up a few gallons of water and sloshed it into a barrel in the kitchen, whence it made its journey down a pipe into an outhouse in the yard and drenched, at a cost of 15 rupees, whoever was taking a shower. On some days they made 300 rupees from the sale of showers alone.

The first European to see the Nepalese side of Sagarmatha – Mount Everest – was George Leigh Mallory, when he looked down from the Tibetan border in 1921. However, it wasn't until the 1950s, when the present king's grandfather opened the country's doors to outsiders, that climbers could approach Everest through Nepal, since when there have been over fifty expeditions, about half of which have put men (and occasionally women) on the summit. Nearly all of those who came to the Khumbu in the 1950s were mountaineers, but soon others bent on less strenuous pleasures followed, and they came in increasing numbers, attracted by the remoteness of the region, its dramatic landscape and even the yeti legend. In 1970 about 650 tourists visited Namche Bazar and the surrounding areas of the Khumbu. Ten times that number now make their way here each year, and Namche has developed to accommodate them. Today there are some thirty lodges in town, and families which a generation ago made a meagre living as traders and peasant farmers now have business interests both here and in Kathmandu.

Sir Edmund Hillary, the first man to reach the summit of Everest, described the Khumbu as 'the most surveyed, examined, blood-taken, anthropologically dissected area in the world'. It is also one of the most written about, which should encourage brevity on my part. Before leaving England I had read several books and numerous articles on Nepal. Apart from the dozens of books about climbing expeditions and their feats in the Himalaya, which didn't interest me and which I ignored, well over half of those in print, and to be found in London's best bookshops, concerned the Khumbu. I learnt about the arrival of the Sherpas from Tibet in the sixteenth century; about the arrival of the potato in the nineteenth; about the arrival of the Tibetan refugees in the 1960s; and, of course, about the arrival of the Westerners. There will be many more scholarly books and papers appearing on subjects such as these shortly, and quite possibly some will be written by the four soil scientists, two ecologists and one anthropologist whom I met during my short stay. I have neither the competence nor the inclination to compete with them; though in passing I must remark that I was both surprised and entertained by the anthropologists who had spent time in Namche. Their books and articles were generally better written than those of the scientists and invariably more memorable. They were great peeping Toms, and they asked all the questions I had never dared but always wanted to ask in strange places. Most of all I enjoyed Christoph von Fürer-Haimendorf, the grand old man of Sherpa anthropology, who informed me, among other things, about the sex lives of Sherpas. Pre-marital love affairs were evidently common:

Girls are free to receive at night the visits of young men and, as all the members of a Sherpa family sleep in the one large living room, parents obviously turn a blind eye to their daughters' amorous adventures. A young man will find out the place where the girl usually sleeps and having silently entered the house creep up to her without attracting any attention. Before doing this he will have made sure that his advances will be well received.

A rapport with the girl is established, explains von Fürer-Haimendorf, by indulging in a 'peculiar kind of rough horseplay', involving wrestling and rolling around in the grass. The few Western men I met who had had affairs with Sherpa women recalled their experiences with shocked admiration. Foreplay was apparently a vigorous and often bruising ordeal.

For 400 years the Sherpas lived in a state of quiet seclusion. Admittedly, they had always controlled the great trading route which linked the Tibetan plateau to the Middle Hills of eastern Nepal, but they experienced no cultural trauma of any note – the introduction of the potato in the 1830s being one of the most significant events in their history – until the early 1950s. Since then their lives have been transformed by tourists and the continual interference of central government and foreign aid agencies. Whether the changes which have occurred over the last thirty years have been for better or worse is, to some extent, a matter of opinion.

That the Sherpas are collectively wealthier, healthier and better educated than they were a generation ago is beyond dispute, although not all have gained in a material sense. A bartering economy has given way to one based on money, and inflation, fuelled partly by the high prices which Westerners are prepared to pay for goods and services, has impoverished those who haven't climbed on the tourist bandwagon or the aid gravy-train. The presence of tourists and aid workers has also had its effects on the family lives of the Sherpas. Women have increasingly found themselves marooned at home as their menfolk spend more and more time away with trekking groups; and one hears many stories about Sherpas becoming amorously entangled with Western girls, for some of whom, according to von Fürer-Haimendorf, a Himalayan trek is not complete without an *affaire* with one of the guides.

Inevitably, there is considerable resentment among Sherpas at the way in which outsiders have come to dominate – and determine – development issues in the Khumbu. Administrative posts have been filled by Hindus from outside the region rather than by Buddhists from within, and the newcomers are both resentful, viewing the Khumbu much as a Muscovite does Siberia, and resented. A national park was established in 1977, not on the initiative of the Sherpas, who still view it with suspicion, but because Sir Edmund Hillary and the government of New Zealand wanted one. And over the years New Zealanders, Japanese, Austrians, Americans and many others have come here to build dams, schools, bridges, hotels and all manner of other things whose purpose, purportedly, has been to improve the quality of life of the Sherpas.

With rare exceptions, it has been a story of outsiders telling Sherpas what is good for them, and one shouldn't perhaps be surprised that they have become adept at making a fast buck whenever the opportunity arises. One disillusioned American aid worker wrote:

Perhaps no other rural, mountainous region in the world has experienced the levels of free commodity, monetary, service and technical gifts as the Khumbu, with the result that these items have become more or less expected and perceived as a fact of life by the corresponding generation of Sherpa villagers. Trekkers provide down coats, sleeping bags and scholarships; climbing expeditions do not climb without the guaranteed provision of an average $3,000 of technical climbing gear and related goods to the *sirdar* [expedition leader] and climbing Sherpas; schools and hospitals are simply built and often staffed by foreigners; and the installation of major hydro-electric projects is provided with no required investment.

This brings me to the subject of the Khumbu's hydro-electric schemes. Hydro-electric projects have been seen for many years – not just in the Khumbu, but throughout the mountainous regions of Nepal – as one of the keys to solving the problem of forest destruction. The logic which links the two is simple and seductive, as is the logic which purports to explain 'the environmental crisis'. Simply stated, it is this. Since the introduction of health care in the 1950s, the population of Nepal has doubled, thus leading to ever-increasing demands for fuelwood, building timber, livestock fodder and food. The peasants have ravaged the forests and brought into cultivation marginal lands. The result has been deforestation and massive erosion, evidence of which you will see throughout the hills. The monsoons wash away the topsoil, destroying once-fertile farmland and causing floods which threaten crops, livestock and people lower down the valleys and in the Ganges Basin. The argument, if taken to its logical conclusion, foresees, in the not so distant future, an environmental catastrophe whose consequences will be just as devastating as those of the African droughts of the 1970s and 1980s: millions will die of starvation; tens of thousands will drown in floods. This crisis (or 'super-crisis') will be averted only if something is done to save the forests. And what better way to save them than to tap the Himalaya's vast water resources and turn them into electricity, which would at least reduce the demand for fuelwood? Hydro-electric power (HEP), it is claimed, will not only supply the peasantry with power but also the government with a 'cash crop' which it can export to India, which desperately needs more electricity.

The stream which surfaced beside the main street in Namche was nothing much to look at. It dashed down the hill, spun half a dozen prayer wheels, then disappeared over the lip of the gorge to power a small flour mill, on whose roof sat a couple of serene old men who waved cheerfully at us when we passed. Brot and I followed the stream down a steep drop of 200 feet and came to the power station, a modest hut with three rooms, one housing a turbine, one in which equipment was stored, and another where the three men who ran the plant ate and slept. A photo of the king and queen looked down on the turbine, and on the shelf beside them was an empty bottle of champagne, signed by Brot and others when the power was turned on in 1983. Everything was clean and tidy, and apparently all had run more or less smoothly since Brot was last here two years ago. The original idea to build the plant had been Brot's, but no other foreigners had been involved and most of the work had been carried out by Sherpas. The project had taken two years to complete. The bill for construction and installation was $78,000, most of which had come in the form of a grant from Unesco, which had previously designated the Sagarmatha National Park as one of its 'world heritage sites'. Most of the houses and lodges in Namche now had electric lights and four of the lodges had electric stoves on which some of their cooking was done.

Before the arrival of electricity in 1983 the people of Namche relied for lighting on kerosene, using it either in traditional *tuki* lamps or in the larger and more powerful petro-max lamps. When we were there kerosene cost 27 rupees a litre, and a litre lasted four hours, in other words one evening. Four hours' worth of light from one electric bulb cost half a rupee, so lighting costs with electricity were roughly one-fiftieth those with kerosene. The Sherpas were understandably happy with the scheme, although ecologists had less cause for celebration as those lodges which did have electric stoves still relied mostly on wood for cooking: the plant had done little to reduce the region's rate of fuelwood consumption.

If this had been the only foreign-aided power project in the Khumbu, I probably wouldn't have given it much thought. Its cost was minute when compared to other 'development' projects in Nepal; it had been swiftly built; and it seemed to be working well. Not much of a story, perhaps. However, its significance becomes clear once one compares it with a much more ambitious plan for another HEP plant near Thami, a few hours' walk to the west of Namche. But first a few words about the region's most famous hotel.

Hotel Everest View was the brain-child of a Japanese entrepreneur who believed there was money to be made from building a classy hotel with bathrooms, heated bedrooms and a fine view of the great mountain. Rather than expecting guests to make their way on foot from Luckla, they would be flown in to a small landing strip by four-seater Pilatus Porter planes. The hotel would appeal to tourists with plenty of money and little time. Funds were raised, and the hotel and landing strip were built near Khumjung.

For a while the tourists came, but a number of factors conspired to spoil the fun. Not least of the hotel's problems was the altitude. At 14,000 feet there are real dangers of mountain sickness, a disease which begins with nausea and a headache and ends, not infrequently, with death. Walking up gradually to that height lessens the chances of falling sick; leaving Kathmandu and landing at that height is madness. Tourists were met at the airstrip by yaks and oxygen cylinders, and there were cylinders in the bedrooms too. Unfortunately many people became ill and one woman expired on the doorstep. The weather here was also a problem: it was often too windy and overcast for planes to land, so the time-obsessed guests used to get stuck, which meant that they missed connections back to their boardrooms and boudoirs in Tokyo and New York. Apart from the lack of oxygen, there were other amenities missing from the hotel, such as electricity and tap-water. The latter had to be carried up to the hotel from over an hour's distance away. This upset the villagers of Khumjung, whose own water supplies were inadequate, and who had already had to suffer, for the sake of the hotel, the loss of local forests: the area felled to supply timber for the hotel's construction had exceeded that which had disappeared round Khumjung during the last three decades. Inevitably, the hotel went bankrupt. Nobody was going to pay $200 a night once they heard about conditions there. The hotel was still open in 1987, but in a state of dereliction – $100,000 was needed, it was said, to repair the roof, and beds were on offer at only $7 a night, although few bothered staying there. The only thing the hotel could boast was a fine view. Namche, Tengboche, Khumjung and Kunde offered that and much else besides.

The hotel's demand for electricity helped spawn the HEP project at Thami, whose troubled history is as ludicrous as that of the hotel. The Bhote Kosi River at Thami was identified as a possible site for a power plant in 1975. In 1976 HMG invited the Austrian government to provide money and technical assistance to construct the dam, install turbines and plug Hotel Everest View and the principal villages in the area (including Namche) into the mains. The Austrian government agreed to put up the bulk of the estimated $4 million required to carry out the work. The first excavations began in 1978 and completion was planned for 1982. Work proceeded fitfully and the completion date was gradually pushed back. In 1982 there wasn't much to see, but by 1985 the main dam had been built along with some of the other installations. By then Hotel Everest View, one of the Thami scheme's *raisons d'être,* had folded, and one or two geologists had pointed out that the dam had been sited in an area of great instability. In geological terms the Himalayan region is very young. The mountains are continually shifting and landslides are a perennial and unstoppable hazard. On 4 August 1985 a glacial lake burst its banks and sent a wall of mud and water some thirty feet high rushing down the Bhote Kosi. The dam was washed away together with twenty bridges downstream of Thami, thirty houses, many cows and several people. Nine years' work on the dam, at a cost of $2 million, had been wasted.

Neither the Nepalese government nor the Austrian contractors had given much thought to either the economic or the environmental factors which should have determined the shape of the project. Had the flood not occurred then, it would have come later. However, the project has not been abandoned, and work was scheduled to begin again in the summer of 1987. Like many expensive aid projects, Thami has gained a momentum of its own: apparently nothing is going to deter the Austrians and HMG from pursuing it. Many questions remain unanswered. Nobody knows what impact the new installations (which will still be near Thami) will have on the environment, for the simple reason that no proper surveys have been carried out. Indeed, when an official in the national parks department suggested that Brot Coburn should do one, the idea was strongly resisted. Instead the task is being left to a small government department, the Environmental Impact Study Group, which, judging from its study of the HEP scheme at Jomsom, exists simply to give credibility to the discreditable. Nor have HMG or the Austrian consultants made any attempt to assess the demand for electricity in the area. No efforts have been made to enlist the support of the local population, and Namche's *pradhan panch* had not even been approached when we were there in March.

Nepal's previous experience with small hydro schemes in the hills suggests that Thami will be money down the drain. The most economic plant in the country is at Dhankuta, yet after fifteen years, sales of electricity there recoup only half of the operation and maintenance costs. On average, the revenues from Nepal's small hydro schemes amount to less than one-sixth of the running costs, and according to the Water and Energy Commission Secretariat (WECS), whose task force has studied them all, the government subsidy for every consumer comes to 2,750 rupees a year (or $135, which is about three-quarters of the annual *per capita* income). There are ten HMG-run plants already in operation and a further sixteen are planned. In subsidies alone these will cost HMG $1 million a year. WECS studied the latest proposals for the Thami project and advised against it. Its advice has been ignored. Ironically, Nepal's small hydro schemes may even contribute to deforestation, as people who have electricity go to bed much later than those without and keep their fires burning longer. The only small hydro schemes which pay their way (or make a profit) are the one below Namche and those run by private individuals who use water to perform such tasks as milling corn and sawing timber as well as to generate electricity. Had the Namche plant been run by one of the big government departments, then it, like the others, would have had a staff of eighteen, which is the HMG minimum. The losers in the Thami affair will not be the people of Khumbu, although they may not gain anything either. They will be HMG and the Austrian tax-payer. And there will be winners too, among them the consulting firm and a fair number of people who will siphon money out of the project budget and into their pockets long before it gets to Khumbu.

As one of the principal justifications for constructing hydro-electric plants in the hills rests on the supposition that they can help reduce fuelwood consumption, a few words are in order here about deforestation in the Khumbu. It has been widely assumed that the environment in the Khumbu has suffered considerable damage, particularly since the 1950s. Blame for deforestation is levelled both at local Sherpas and at foreign visitors. After the overthrow of the Ranas, the government nationalized all forests, a consequence of which was the abolition of the traditional system of management whereby local communities safeguarded their own patches of forest. Once the state had intervened, the Sherpas began to plunder the forests as never before. The demand for fuelwood created by trekkers and mountaineering expeditions simply made matters worse. This explanation seems to be accepted by everyone who has looked at the matter, but there is considerable disagreement about the extent to which the Khumbu's forests have been damaged. Forests have certainly disappeared in the immediate vicinity of many villages, but vast tracts some distance away from the centres of population and the main trekking routes still remain intact.

I needed four Lomotil, two Sherpas and a rope to get me down the cliff on Thursday morning. I was up at six o'clock, hoping to leave immediately and get the whole thing over and done with, but my two companions viewed the trip with perverse languidity. Ang Nima,. the eighteen-year-old son of the lodge owner, wanted breakfast first and the other, a *sirdar* called Phurba Tharkey, didn't turn up till 8.30. Meanwhile, Ang's nine-year-old brother trotted off to school at Khumjung, a couple of thousand feet up from Namche, and Ang entertained himself by showing me his exercise books, which included his answers to some recent exam questions. They seemed horribly portentous.

Q. Why did the bus driver jam on the brakes?
A. The bus driver jammed on his brakes as the front wheels were hanging over the cliff top before he knew anything was wrong.

Q. Why did the girl jump back from the edge of the cliff?
A. The girl jumped back from the edge of the cliff because the path was crumbling away.

He asked me if I knew the answer to another question which went, 'What was the joke which Mark Twain played on his friend?' I didn't know, and nor could I answer the questions on *Aesop's Fables*, which was Ang's favourite book.

Didi had already left to visit the monastery at Tengboche and Brot was spending another day in Namche. 'I'll probably be running around like a fart in a bottle,' he announced when he joined us by the fire for a tea. He then told me that I was ten times more likely to be killed in a bus accident than on the way down the cliff. He had lost three friends this way, and not long ago thirteen Sherpas had died when their bus driver failed to jam on his brakes. In any case, said Brot, death always came when you least expected it. He had a sad story about a climber who, having just scaled one of the most difficult peaks near Everest, tripped over his stick when walking along a flat path on the way back to Namche. He broke his neck and died. 'So you see, you'll get down the cliff; but you'll probably do something stupid afterwards.' By the time we left I had smoked half a packet of Yak cigarettes. 'See you tomorrow if you make it,' grinned Brot.

I was in favour of making a rapid descent once we reached the tented café at the top of the cliff, but Phurba insisted on stopping for a drink. When I had hired him the day before he had assumed I wanted to abseil down the cliff. Once he realized it was simply a matter of sticking me on the end of a rope like a dog on a lead, he treated the whole affair with the levity it probably deserved. I suppose it took us about three-quarters of an hour to get down to the river. I had a stick in one hand and gripped Ang Nima with the other, while Phurba Tharkey followed behind with the rope. I kept my eyes firmly on the ground, although such was the steepness of the slope that there were times when I couldn't avoid seeing the river far below. We would have got down the first stretch much quicker had we not passed several groups of Sherpas coming up, all of whom demanded an explanation, which, once delivered, elicited reactions of bemusement. But they couldn't have been more sympathetic and one even admitted that his knees shook when he crossed bridges. By bridges, I think he meant the rope affairs which are sometimes slung between cliffs many hundreds of feet above the ground. We passed only one Westerner, an American listening to music on a Sony Walkman. I knew he was American because he said 'Jeez!' a couple of times while he stared disdainfully at me and the rope. I wished him plenty of bad luck and a generous dose of altitude sickness.

My knees trembled a good deal, but I was never in any danger of fainting, which is what I had most feared. I did a tremendous amount of praying and promised God all sorts of things if He'd just get me down safely. I tried saying the Lord's Prayer several times, but I couldn't remember the last bit. However, I needed to recite something to keep my mind off the descent – it was just a matter of getting my eyes and feet to act independently of my imagination – so I tried 'Remember also thy Creator in the days of thy youth' and 'The lips of a strange woman drop honey', but after five or six lines I got stuck on these as well. I'd managed the first verse of 'Ode to a Nightingale' and I was in a tangle with the second, trying to work backwards from 'With beaded bubbles winking at the brim', when all of a sudden, and for no apparent reason, fear deserted me and I suggested we stop for a cigarette. We were about two-thirds of the way down and low enough now to hear the river as well as see it. I even enjoyed the view. A flock of snow pigeons tumbled down the cliff and far above a lammergeyer floated in a depthless blue sky.

Ang returned to Namche once we reached the Dudh Kosi, while Phurba and I walked on together to the Hatago Lodge. We ate lunch there, then he continued alone to Luckla.

I had a glorious afternoon. The sun went, the clouds came and I walked in thick drizzle to a village a mile or so south of the lodge. Flocks of goldcrest were fooling around in the fir trees and redstarts flicked their tails on the grey boulders by the river. There were willows in the village which from a distance looked like dollops of Colman's mustard, and lily-of-the-valley bushes lined the path. There were women in the fields and goats browsing, and men on horseback and porters and *zopkioks* on the path, and everywhere the smell of wood smoke, wet wood smoke, and cowdung and wet earth and sappy smells from the trees and the smell of the rain itself. It was very good to be alive, and I thanked God and promised to keep my promises, and smoked a lot of cigarettes that tasted particularly good. When I got back to the lodge it was still raining and nearly dark and Mr Hagayuki told me Homer was quite good but not that good. There were many people staying that night – Japanese and Israelis and Americans, and a Spanish TV crew and a French couple – and some were drinking Mr Hagayuki's peach brandy and getting drunk and noisy, but I hardly noticed them, and once I had eaten I went to bed and put on my Walkman and fell asleep listening to Mozart's *Requiem*.

I took the whole of next day getting to Luckla and while I waited in the evening for Brot and Didi to appear I thumbed through an old copy of *Society*, an Indian magazine which had been left in Buddha Lodge. There was a profile of Sir Edmund Hillary, which ended with a quote of his that impressed me.

I think the main conquest is between man and himself. The fact that he is overcoming a technical problem in the Himalaya, Antarctica or a river is incidental to the fact that the man is trying to overcome his own fears. He is trying to overcome his own inadequacies and use whatever skill or experience he has to reach his objective. The greatest challenge is within.

This was better than Homer.

3

Shooting Tigers

Nowadays most foreign travellers either come into Kathmandu by bus from one of the towns on the Indian border or they fly in, as I did. Neither journey has much to recommend it. Certainly, the scenery as one drives up from Birgunj is lovely, as I discovered later, but the journey passes quickly, the road is poor and the bus crowded. As for the flight from Delhi, there is scarcely time to eat the meal, and though there are views of the Himalaya when the weather is clear, they don't compare with the ones you get from the small planes which fly up to hill towns such as Luckla and Jomson, when the proximity of what the guidebooks call the 'snowy mountain fastness' makes you feel like a bubble fizzing among the ice cubes in a gin and tonic. But not so long ago the journey to Kathmandu was the stuff of adventure, and its recollection enabled writers and journalists to impress readers with their bravery and editors with their dedication. I wish I had come then.

Penelope Chetwode, dispatched to Nepal by the *National Geographic* in the 1930s, had hardly climbed on to the train at the Indian border town of Raxaul before she was getting off again in the 'tiger- and rhino-haunted jungles'. And then it was on to an elephant:

. . . and before I quite realized what was happening a huge bristling mass of black and yellow was hurtling towards us. It is a wonderful thing, the charge of an angry tiger – the break from cover in a crash of thunder, the mighty bounds towards the foe, the gleaming teeth, the flaming eyes, and roars of savage hate.

Having witnessed the death of the tiger, Miss Chetwode progressed to Kathmandu, with the help of many an exclamation mark and much hyperbole, by a combination of motor car, Tibetan pony and coolie-carried *dandi*.

There were still a few old-timers among the European community in Nepal who had arrived this way. One of them was Major Dudley Spain, to whom I had been introduced by Hemanta Mishra. When I returned from Namche I paid him a visit at his home in the countryside beyond Patan. He and his delightful wife, a handsome, immaculately dressed lady with a fine complexion and a wonderful head of silver hair, were sitting on their terrace having breakfast when I arrived. The scene struck me as being thoroughly Edwardian. Before leaving for the hairdresser's in Kathmandu, Mrs Spain showed me round the garden which they had created here. Little songbirds tweetered among the branches of the fruit trees, and from the colourful flower-beds came the sultry buzz of bees and the squeaking of less sonorous insects. It was a perfect spring morning, and all, it seemed, was well with the world.

Major Spain first came to Nepal as a guest of the British ambassador in 1945. He stayed for three weeks. Twelve years later he returned to serve with the Gurkhas, since when he had spent much of his time in the country. In 1945 he took the narrow-gauge train, whose first-class carriages had lace antimacassars and fresh roses, from Raxaul to the foot of the Siwaliks, from where he made the journey over the Mahabharat Lekh range on horseback, escorted, at times, by a band of dancing minstrels. The ambassador's car – it had been carried over the hills some years before (he thought it was probably a Daimler) – met Major Spain at the edge of the Kathmandu Valley and conveyed him on the country's only tarmac road to the British Residency.

At that time the country was virtually untouched by the industrial revolution, and there were few places in the world so lacking in hospitals, schools, roads and dams – indeed in virtually any of the trappings which are considered a *sine qua non* of development in the twentieth century. To men like Major Spain, or for that matter to any Nepali born forty years or more ago, the changes which had occurred over recent years appeared enormous; and in the light of what then existed, or didn't exist, they were. By 1984 there were 2,645 miles of tarmacked road, whereas in 1945 there was next to none; electricity had spread beyond the Kathmandu Valley, across the whole Terai and into parts of the hills; schools had been built in nearly every town and village; and some form of Western-style health care, albeit of the most basic kind, was available to the majority of the population, which had risen from a little over eight million in 1951 to seventeen million today.

The area which had experienced the greatest changes over the past forty years was the Terai, and had it not been for the isolated remnants of forest in areas such as Chitwan, upon which Hemanta, his wife Sushma and I descended on a day which was pleasant in Kathmandu and steamy there, I could never have imagined how it once was.

Whether there will be any forests – or tigers or rhinos – left in the Royal

Chitwan National Park at the end of this century is a matter for conjecture. To suggest there may not be is no slur on those who run the park. It is simply to acknowledge the realities of life in Nepal. As Hemanta said on the way down, 'When people are poor and hungry, you cannot expect them not to cut down trees and clear land; you cannot expect them to love rhinos when rhinos raid their land.' Most people in Nepal are poor and hungry, and over half exist in a state which the World Bank describes as 'absolute poverty'. Over four-fifths of Nepal is mountainous and the peasants have cultivated as much of the hills as it is possible to cultivate (and rather too much, from the point of view of environmental stability, in some areas). The high country is now 'full up', and indeed has been for some time: the ratio of people to cultivated land is as high in parts of the Middle Hills as it is in India's much more fertile deltas. For the last half-century the main export from the Himalaya and its foothills has been people, who have flooded down to the plains of the Terai in search of land and a living. There is nothing unusual about this phenomenon. Many of the great population movements in medieval and, to some extent, contemporary Europe were simply a consequence of the mountains shedding their human surplus, whether from Albania, the Pyrenees or the Alps.

Some of the Terai forest was cleared for farming during the last century. Indeed, the Rana government derived much of its revenue from the export of rice and mustard oil, which were grown in the Kathmandu Valley and in small pockets of cleared land in the Terai. The forests themselves also provided an important source of income, and it was the timber sales to India which financed the building of many Rana palaces. However, when Major Spain first came here a band of forest, in places more than twenty miles wide, still stretched along the Terai from one end of the country to the other. The disappearance of much of it was rapid and inevitable. With the introduction of vaccination programmes against diseases such as cholera and smallpox, the population of the hills rose sharply and so did the numbers living in the plains and leaving for them. At the same time, large amounts of foreign money were channelled into the development of the Terai. The American aid mission, USAID, financed a malarial eradication programme, which, over the twenty years up to 1972, reduced the number of malaria cases from over two million a year to a couple of thousand. The Rapti Valley, which previously malaria had made almost uninhabitable, was opened up for settlement. Roads were built, villages like Hetauda were turned into industrial towns and much of the forest was cleared to make way for crops. The same sort of thing happened throughout the Terai.

We drove through Hetauda in mid-afternoon, stopped to eat some grilled fish at a roadside shack, then turned off the East-West Highway an hour later. The mud track headed south through a flat, almost treeless landscape to the village of Sauhara. Hemanta's camp – he had a wooden bungalow in a complex which housed five elephants, the men who looked after them and two researchers from Washington's Smithsonian Institute – was situated a little way beyond Sauhara on the edge of a strip of forest beside the River Rapti. As soon as we arrived I went down to the river, which was muddy and sluggish and very lovely in the failing light of evening. Rose-breasted parakeets skimmed over the thick crowns of the sal and silk-cotton trees, a pond heron flapped lazily over the long grass and a pair of waterhens moved unobtrusively among the undergrowth on the far bank. The remains of a village dog had been left hanging from the branch of a tree by a leopard. There were Indian cuckoos calling and I could hear elephants snorting and trumpeting back at the camp. The air was hot and soupy and the mountains seemed far away.

After dark Hemanta and I made our way to Gaida Wildlife Camp, where he had arranged to meet an American film crew who were here to make a programme for a series called *Wild Kingdom*. They were paying a large sum of money to the King Mahendra Trust providing that Hemanta, who ran the trust, could find and dart a tiger. We found the Americans watching some Tharu dancers, and on the conclusion of the entertainment we went to the bar, where the film crew proved themselves to be as exotic as anything one could wish to find in the jungle.

There were three of them. Jim Fowler, the 'TV personality', was built like John Wayne and made the rest of us feel Lilliputian: even elephants seemed to shrink in his presence. He wore a fawn safari suit and spoke in a deep Georgian drawl. Like most big men, he had a mild temperament, which was the last thing that could be said of Pete Drown, the director. During the day Pete wore a floppy hat, sunglasses, camouflage clothing and a large knife. His movements were clumsy and his temper volatile. He looked caricaturish in the way white men often do when they dress up for the jungle. After sunset he underwent a spectacular metamorphosis. In place of his drab daytime clothes he wore a snappy-coloured shirt and a *lungi* – a length of cloth – instead of trousers, and around his neck and on his wrists and fingers he sported a dazzling collection of trinkets, bracelets and rings, which between them accounted for most of the precious metals and stones known to man. He looked magnificent, and with his jutting jaw and slicked-back hair he might easily have been mistaken for Jack Nicholson. I liked him best once a few brandies had set his eyes rolling and loosened his tongue. The third member of the crew was a cameraman called Rod. It said so on his belt-buckle. Rod was older than the other two and I haven't a clue what he thought of our stay in Chitwan for the simple reason that he never told us. During periods of real stress the most he ever said was, 'Oh, boy! Oh, boy!'; and for him that was being garrulous.

'There was this one time in the Amazon,' recalled Jim Fowler, as soon as we reached the bar, 'when I was struggling with this anaconda, and he was real big. Yes suh! He was one helluva big anaconda! Well, he had a hold of my arm and he began swallowing it, so the next thing I knew I had his jaws right up by my shoulder and my arm down his throat. Now, I don't know whether you people have ever wrestled with an anaconda . . .' Much to my astonishment, some six months later, I watched Jim repeat this anecdote on BBC's *Nine O'clock News*. That he found himself figuring so prominently on our screens was entirely due to Sarah Ferguson, the Duchess of York, who had reacted to the sight of one of his snakes with the sort of irrational terror I had experienced on the cliff at Namche.

'Now that reminds me of the time I was in New Guinea,' chipped in Pete Drown. 'Yeah, it was coming on night and there we were in this swamp. Oh, man, if you could've seen . . .'

'I got so I could sleep jus' bout any place,' said Jim. 'That was when I was in the Kalahari with the Bushmen. I was down there four months and by the time I finished I could sleep in trees, no different from them . . .'

'Now, you take the Central African Republic,' suggested Pete. 'Wow! That's a real inerestin' place. They got bongo down there . . .'

And so the evening continued. By the time we finished we had grappled with reptiles in Central America, been stalked by lions on the plains of East Africa and witnessed all sorts of remarkable occurrences in south-east Asia. We hadn't done much in Nepal yet, but then there was plenty of time for that. When Hemanta and I returned to our camp there was a paraffin lamp burning outside the guest house where I was sleeping. Hemanta suggested that if I wanted to pee during the night I should do it from the balcony, as rhinos often grazed on the lawn in front. I followed his advice, and I think one must have come as there was some vigorous snorting around three o'clock.

The next morning was overcast and it began with a sacrifice to Ban Devi, the goddess of the forests. A black goat, a cockerel and three pigeons were taken into the forest by the elephant drivers. They cleared away saplings and laid out banana and sal leaves, on which they put little piles of rice and votive powder. The men spoke in whispers or were silent, while the goat behaved as though it was a Sunday picnic, munching away at the herbage. 'It's a quick death, isn't it?' I asked Hemanta nervously when the knives appeared. 'No,' he replied. 'No, it's a bit slow. But it's okay,' he added, 'we whisper into their ears that they'll go to heaven.' I wanted to watch but I didn't have the stomach for it and I retreated. Judging from the noises which came through the forest the least the goat deserved was a place in heaven.

After the sacrifice the men came out of the forest with *tika* on their foreheads and bougainvillaea petals in their hair. Sixteen elephants lumbered round to the front of Hemanta's bungalow, two men on each, and Hemanta prepared the tranquillizers, which he kept in an old Tampax box. As soon as he was ready, Pete Drown rolled up in a jeep and announced, to everyone's chagrin, that the light was too poor for filming. The elephants dispersed, the drugs were replaced in their box, and before lunch we went for a stroll round Sauhara. I read Jane Austen for a couple of hours in the afternoon, then set off with three men, an elephant and four buffalo calves around five o'clock. I sat on the elephant with the driver, while the other two urged the calves on. We rode south of the camp, waded across the Rapti, then continued for a couple of miles through the tall grass at the edge of the forest before staking out the buffaloes. These animals are said to be more intelligent than cows, which I can well believe, but ours had poor memories. Each had spent the previous night as live bait for the tigers, though none seemed to remember this until they had been staked and left, whereupon they bleated pathetically as their possible fate dawned on them. The two men who had led the buffaloes now climbed on to the elephant, which ambled slowly back towards Sauhara. We were rocked into a pleasant trance, much as a child in the womb must be by the swaying of its mother. We saw some rhinos and hog deer, then the sun sank, the sky turned aqueous yellow and we smoked all the way home. There is something tremendously satisfying about smoking a cigarette on an elephant. I have no idea why. It simply seems the natural thing to do. A stiff gin would probably improve matters further.

One of the Smithsonian ecologists – I forget his name but I remember his cavernous cheeks, amused eyes and toothbrush moustache (he, like Brot, was from Seattle) – was leaving Chitwan the next day and he invited us to a party that evening. There were about fifty people there, most of whom were men who drove the elephants or looked after them (elephants are very labour-intensive, and each employs three men). The party was held in a forest clearing near the river and there was plenty of food and *rakshi*, a harsh local brandy. Once we had eaten, there was dancing and singing. The elephant drivers were wonderful dancers. Some of them were Tharus, dark-skinned, delicate-featured lowlanders; others had the lighter, wider, Mongoloid features of the hill tribes. They never took their wives out on evenings like this, but some of them made up for the absence of women by dancing licentiously and wiggling their behinds and bellies in a show of eroticism which came close to being shocking. 'Nepalese men do not like dancing with their wives,' explained Hemanta later. 'They like dancing with other men's wives. In fact, it is a traditional Nepali pastime.' Some of them sang ballads, making up the words as they went along, and there was a lot of laughter and fooling around and they made us dance as well, but our movements were clumsy compared to theirs.

I enjoyed myself and so did Pete Drown, who tried to tell me, after a few drinks, what he thought about life. 'Now, you see, the way I look at it, Charlie, is this ... People are just beginning to realize you can go up to a shirt-maker and have a shirt made for you. They'll say to the shirt-maker: "Jeez! You can make a shirt jus' specially for me?" And the shirt-maker, he'll say "yeah".' Pete took another swig of *rakshi*, shook his head and grinned. 'Well, shit!' he exclaimed, 'that's what shirt-makers are for! But people are only just realizing it! It's what you might call a renaissance of seventeenth-century arts – personal shirt-making! Now one day all this'll be gone,' he continued, encompassing the dancers and the forest with a great sweep of an arm. 'Makes you kinda honoured to be here. Now ain't that something?'

That night a tiger took one of the buffaloes and by the time I woke at seven o'clock the elephants were waiting to leave. They were quiet, as though apprehensive about the day's task, and they would have been quieter still had it not been for their stomachs, which rumbled like thunder and expelled loud, sweet-smelling farts. The elephant drivers, the *pandits*, looked dashing in their khaki uniforms and orange and crimson waist sashes. They lolled across the broad-backed elephants and smoked while they waited. We left at eight o'clock, by which time the sun was well up. Nobody talked, except occasionally in whispers, and once over the river we followed a track through the forest to a small clearing. Most of us stayed here, but four elephants went off to lay out two long lines of cotton cloth in the shape of a letter V. One line went into the forest, the other into the grassland; the tiger was somewhere between the two. When they returned we all moved, as soundlessly as it was possible for sixteen elephants and forty-odd people to move, towards the hunting area. Before we reached there I was deposited in a tree. The film crew wanted only one white man on camera and they reasonably rejected Hemanta's suggestion that I blacken my face and wear a *topi*, a piece of Nepalese headgear like a floppy Egyptian *fez*. I climbed into the crown of the tree. Two rhinos came past and I watched a golden oriole bring food to its nest. It was quiet apart from the calling of cuckoos and the screeching of a peacock. After half an hour Hemanta and Sushma came back and waited till the drive began. Sushma had come for two reasons: for the fun of it and to make sure Hemanta didn't do the darting of the tiger. She thought the excitement might be too much for his heart, which had undergone by-pass surgery the year before.

I know what happened next as we had to reconstruct the hunt for the cameras the following day. The silence was suddenly broken by a fearsome din as the *pandits* drove the elephants at a canter towards the neck of the V. The men hollered and shouted; the elephants trumpeted and screamed. The tiger zigzagged back and forth between the cotton walls and within a matter of minutes it had been funnelled towards a tree in which the man with the dart gun was perched. Although tigers will sometimes turn on the elephants – some had scratches on their heads to prove it – they never jump over the cloth. I heard the plop of the gun, but no roars of savage hate. An elephant retrieved me from the tree and by the time I arrived Hemanta had put a cloth over the tiger's face to protect its eyes from the sun. The elephants stood round it in a circle, and everyone seemed relieved, including the elephants, which were pissing copiously. Much to the annoyance of Hemanta – he was unsure about the efficacy of the drugs – filming was delayed for ten minutes while we waited for Pete Drown to descend from the tree in which he had taken refuge. Apparently he suffered from vertigo, which shouldn't have amused me but did, and he had a dreadful time getting down.

Jim Fowler helped Hemanta to measure the tiger and take blood samples. He even put his ear to the animal's flank to listen to its heart, which struck me as eccentric, though it may have impressed American viewers. Pete made a lot of noise, shouting and cursing and tripping over bushes and demanding re-takes. 'If we do that,' said Hemanta after one of Pete's odder stage directions, 'it's going to look like an Indian movie.' Once they'd finished filming we all had our photos taken with the tiger. 'You mustn't think it's always like this,' said Hemanta. 'Normally it's all done very quickly and quietly.' Hemanta then injected the tiger with an antidote and we waited for it to wake up, which it did after a few minutes. It staggered around and slowly stumbled away from us. Pete was still talking excitedly. 'You talk too much,' shouted Hemanta. 'You should be filming.'

I don't know what King George V would have made of all this. I imagine he would have thought the whole affair both modest and bizarre. According to one of his biographers, J. Wentworth Day, the ten days he spent in Chitwan in December 1911 were among the most exciting of his life. The king was received at the terminus of the Bengal and North-West Railway by the British Resident and the prime minister of Nepal, Major-General His Excellency Maharaja Sir Chandra Shumsher Jang Bahadur Rana. On crossing the Nepalese border his car was showered with rice and red powder and 101 guns saluted from the hills. He and his staff of eighteen were put up in a bungalow whose drawing room had an electric light, while the rest of his entourage – the doctors, clergy, taxidermists, launderers and so forth – were billeted in tents. The Maharaja had pitched his camp a little farther down the River Rapti, and in the forest behind there was 'a veritable city of tents and huts in which were encamped 12,000 of the Maharaja's followers and retainers, in addition to over 600 elephants, who had 2,000 attendants and mahouts'.

The shooting began on the afternoon of 18 December, the day of the king's arrival, and over the next week he and his retinue had a fine time killing tigers. 'On the morning of Boxing Day,' wrote Day, 'news came in that out of sixty baits put out the previous evening only one had been touched by the tigers. Evidently the bags of the previous days had begun to thin out the stock of dangerous game.' Altogether the king and his party shot thirty-nine tigers, twelve rhinoceroses and four bears, the king bagging most of them. Day's account is full of descriptions of the kills themselves. They do not make interesting reading – I don't believe that the king was in as great a danger as Day made out – but I enjoyed the conclusion to the trip. Back in India, 'A great crowd of many thousand natives cheered the King-Emperor as the train gathered speed, and many of them ran, shouting wildly, along the metals in its wake. At every station through which the Royal train passed the people congregated in their thousands, shouting, "Victory to the King".' Over whom, I wonder?

By the time Queen Elizabeth and Prince Philip visited Chitwan in 1961 much of the Terai had been cleared of forest. To his credit, Prince Philip turned up with a bandage on his trigger finger and declined to join the morning shoot, which sounded rather a comic affair, with Lord Home, the former British prime minister, missing a tiger three times and leaving the job to a rear admiral. Michel Peissel, in his biography of Boris Lissanevitch, *Tiger for Breakfast*, described the lunch-time banquet which Boris laid on for the queen. She was offered the choice of twenty-two varieties of game, 'including the rare florican crane'. She chose peacock pilau, which she evidently enjoyed. 'The afternoon,' according to Peissel, 'was reserved for shooting a rhinoceros, unfortunately one of the last few of the once-numerous one-horned rhinos of Nepal.' It was bad luck on the rhino that the rear admiral was again present to help Lord Home, who missed it.

I was told an amusing anecdote by several Nepalis. A tented camp had been created for the queen next to the village of Meghauli, and it was claimed that although she had a room with a toilet and shower, the workmen had forgotten to provide running water. A man was installed on the roof with a spyhole and he would watch to see whether the queen turned on the cold tap or the hot one. Depending on which one she chose, he then poured a bucket of either cold or hot water, or a mix of the two, down a spout. The queen thus had a satisfactory shower and the Nepali had the distinction of being the only person in the world apart from Prince Philip to see her in the nude. In fact, as Peissel points out, this is what happened to King George V and Queen Mary when they stayed with a Maharaja. The queen's camp was, as they say out here, very pucka.

Hemanta and I made the great mistake of allowing alcohol to pass our lips that evening. Both of us, for different reasons, had been teetotal for over a year, and when Sushma left to pay a visit to a Hindu temple we went to a bar in Sauraha with no intention of drinking anything more dangerous than Coca Cola. Once there we decided to split a bottle of beer in celebration of the day's events. The Americans had got their tiger and the trust its money.

Masahiro Iijima, a Japanese friend of Hemanta's and one of the best wildlife photographers in Asia, was sitting in the bar when we arrived. 'Success?' he asked. Hemanta nodded. 'Ah!' said Masahiro, 'daytime coming buffalo.' Yes, agreed Hemanta, the tiger had taken the bait. The waiter handed me a book of Masahiro's photographs, many of which had been taken in Chitwan. 'Nine people eating tiger,' explained Masahiro, pointing to a picture of a tiger which had accounted for nine people. He was off to photograph snow leopards in China soon. 'No necessary success,' he added enigmatically. I soon got the hang of his English, which was remarkable for its dependency on the present participle. As we rose to leave he said, 'Teaching your address?' I wrote it down. 'Possible using?' he asked, pointing to my pen. By this time even Hemanta, whose English was fluent, colloquial and racy, had resorted to pidgin. 'Going now,' he announced, and we made our way to Gaida, where we drank too much. Pete Drown was in fine form, and he and Hemanta told some excellent stories, none of which I remember. At midnight Hemanta's driver, whom he referred to as 'the flying saucer', eventually managed to winkle us out of the bar and shovel us into the car. Approaching the camp we could see a lamp burning. It appeared to be floating through the air on its own, which amused us until we realized it was being propelled by Sushma in a dressing-gown. She accused Hemanta of being drunk, which he vigorously denied, but we spoilt everything by leaning against each other and roaring with laughter. Before we went to bed we woke up the cook and ate a large plate of *daal bhat* – rice and lentils. The next day we both felt terrible.

We tend to look back on the past with a curious mixture of nostalgia and disdain. We envy our forebears for having lived during times which, from a contemporary perspective, seem less troubled and taxing than our own – listening, as it were, to the Romantic poets rather than to those who catalogued the miseries and injustices of the day. But there is a part of us which knows that deception is the mother of nostalgia, and as though to compensate for it, we judge the activities of some of our ancestors with a harshness which is not always deserved. Scrutinizing the mores and morals of past generations is indeed one of life's singular pleasures, and I doubt whether there has ever been a time when the dead have failed to provide the living with examples of philosophies to mock and actions to deplore.

The killing for fun of animals (and people) has always aroused controversy, and each generation has been able to look back through history with the knowledge that its sports were less barbarous than at least some of those of earlier times. No doubt the men who enjoyed bear-baiting and pig-sticking in medieval England found repugnant, if they cared to think about them, the human sacrifices which had taken place a millennia before in the amphitheatres of Rome; and presumably King George and his subjects held in contempt these same bear-baiters and pig-stickers, whose activities the law had long since sanctioned. It is now our turn to be sanctimonious, and one is tempted to view the king's hunting trip to Nepal as a disgraceful display of bloodthirstiness. Perhaps it was; but it should be pointed out that when he came to the Terai big game existed in plenty, and the thirty-nine tigers which he and his party killed probably represented no more than the annual natural increase in the population. Tigers became increasingly rare as the century progressed, not because they were hunted but because their forest habitat was cleared for human settlement. In any case, had anyone confronted the king on the issue he could have retorted that there were more important things to worry about, such as the immolation of Hindu widows on their husbands' pyres, which was still being practised in some parts of the sub-continent, though not in Nepal, and slavery, which the Ranas had yet to abolish.

One of the many differences between a developed country such as Britain and a developing one such as Nepal is that the former modified or destroyed most of its wildlife habitats long ago while the latter is still in the process of doing so. The conservation ethic did not begin to emerge in Britain – at least, as we think of it today – until long after the bear, the wolf, the lynx and the beaver had been driven to extinction, by which time nine-tenths of the country's original forest cover had disappeared. The situation in Nepal is quite different, for the notion of conservation, though it took root much later than in Europe, was introduced at a time when a fair proportion of the country was still in a natural state. There was more to save; and thus more to lose. This may go some way towards explaining why Western conservationists often spend more time telling people of other countries how to look after their wildlife than they do worrying about their own.

Responsibility for managing the country's national parks, the most important in the Terai being at Chitwan and Bardia, rests with the Department of National Parks and Wildlife Conservation. Life for the department has been far from easy. It is under-funded (but then so are most government departments), and it comes under the auspices of the Ministry of Forests, whose activities in the Terai have had more to do with felling trees than planting them. When the park was first established at Chitwan in 1973, and for some time afterwards, the department employed about sixty guards, most of whom came from the local villages. They successfully suppressed poaching and controlled wood-cutting and the grazing of cattle inside the park boundaries. In recent years, however, the protection of national parks has been entrusted to the army, and there is now an entire battalion of some 1,400 soldiers stationed permanently in Chitwan. There are, presumably, strategic reasons for having them there – the Indian border is just down the road; but there is certainly nothing else to warrant their presence. Rhino poachers in the early 1970s were given long prison sentences, upward of fifteen years, and this acted as an adequate deterrent to intending miscreants. Until recently, when two rhinos were taken, there had been no cases of poaching since 1973. This had nothing to do with the army, whose presence has done little to convince the local populace of the desirability of having a protected area on their doorstep. I heard of nothing in particular against the soldiers in Chitwan, but from Bardia have come rumours of rape, pillage and extortion.

The parks department has periodically alienated people by appropriating their land. The most notorious case occurred in Jumla district in the west of Nepal, when two villages near Lake Rara, which was to be encompassed by a national park, were evacuated and destroyed. The Thakuris, who were used to the harsh climate of the mountains, were moved to the Terai, where many succumbed to malaria. This was a disastrous mistake, and the government now recognizes that national parks cannot be imposed willy-nilly on people who already find it hard enough to make a living.

In many parts of the developing world the success or failure of a national park is measured solely in terms of whether its wildlife flourishes or declines, and little or no thought is given to the fate of the people displaced by the parks or living next to them. This is (or, at any rate, was) particularly true of the countries of East Africa, whose game parks were set up by Europeans shortly before or after the granting of independence. It was assumed that successful wildlife conservation hinged on the exclusion of those who grazed their cattle and hunted within the parks, and consequently they were shifted out of them, often on to poorer land. Parks such as these are viewed with resentment rather than respect (except by the tourists who visit them), and as populations – and therefore the pressures on land – increase, it becomes ever harder for conservationists to justify the parks' existence.

Conservationists have rationalized their activities on all sorts of grounds, and those who have put their ideas on paper – myself included – have generally got into a fine old mess. Some have invoked moral arguments: animals have a 'right' to exist. Some have contended that if we reduce the diversity of wildlife, then sooner or later the gross national product will come plummeting down. Others have claimed that our spiritual existence is enhanced by the knowledge that all sorts of wonderful creatures still survive, even though most of us never see them. One could quibble with all these arguments; but there is another which few ever bother to challenge, and that is that we should conserve nature not just for ourselves but for our grandchildren and our grandchildren's grandchildren. This is all very well, but you cannot expect the farmers near Sauhara, some of whom lose four-fifths of their crops to wild animals, to be impressed by such an argument. 'The problem of park management,' said Hemanta, 'is not so much in the parks as outside. The people need animal fodder, and they need fuelwood and water. They are poor and what they are worried about is the next meal, not whether their grandchildren see a tiger.'

If one looks at Chitwan only in terms of its wildlife, then the park has been a resounding success. Since 1973 the population of the great Indian one-horned rhino, of which there are only 1,200 in the world, has risen from about 250 to 350. The Bengal tiger has also become more numerous: in and around the park there are about a hundred animals, thirty of which are breeding females. But in the long term Chitwan's survival will be assured only if those who live round it receive some tangible compensation – for the loss of life occasionally caused by man-eating tigers; the loss of crops resulting from the marauding of rhino, deer and other wild animals; and the loss of forest land which, were it not for the park, they could fell and farm.

One form of compensation comes in the form of tourism. Each year 15,000 people visit the park. Some stay at Tiger Tops and Gaida Wildlife Camp, for which pleasure they pay $145 and $100 a day respectively, while a much larger number – known as 'budget tourists' – stay in the small lodges at Sauhara, where they spend anything up to 100 rupees ($5) a day. For the local people it is the latter, paradoxically, who constitute the more important source of revenue. Tiger Tops and Gaida may employ local labour, but they are owned by individuals or consortia in Kathmandu or outside the country, and the vast majority of those who stay there will have paid in advance. Their money, apart from what little they spend on souvenirs, stays well clear of the area. In contrast, every rupee spent by the budget tourists goes into local pockets. A few years ago there were only three lodges in Sauhara; now there are over thirty, mostly simple affairs converted from existing houses or built out of cane and mud. People who not long ago had trouble subsisting are now prosperous.

More interesting in many ways, and certainly more revealing of the attitudes of those who run the park, is the annual grass harvest. Since 1979 the villagers of Chitwan Valley have been allowed to come into the park for two weeks at the end of every January. They pay one rupee for a permit and they can take out as much cane and thatch-grass as they can carry on their backs. The value of this cane and grass, were it to be bought on the open market, is enormous. One estimate I heard was 10 million rupees ($500,000). Some people use the grass for their own homes; others sell it to neighbours. It was said that a few make 300 rupees a day by selling it to a nearby paper mill. Needless to say, the grass harvest has gone down well with local people, who not only profit from it but realize that the park is the only place left in the Chitwan Valley where such grass and cane can still be found in any significant quantity. This has gone some way towards showing them that conservation is not simply a government ruse to attract Pentax-garlanded tourists and their foreign currency into the country.

For turning erstwhile enemies into allies the credit must be shared by the Department of National Parks and the King Mahendra Trust. While the former concentrates on conserving wildlife within the parks, the latter, which was set up in 1982, concerns itself with land both within and outside the parks. On paper the trust is a non-governmental organization, but as King Birendra is its patron and his brother, Prince Gyanendra, its chairman, it has considerable influence, possibly more than the government department, one of whose officers admitted that its power had waned since Hemanta had been seconded to the trust. I am instinctively wary of praising the work which Hemanta has done, both as deputy-director of the government department, a post he still holds, and as secretary of the trust, for no better reason than that he is a friend. All the same, most people admit that he has done as much as, if not more than, anyone else to conserve Nepal's wildlife, and it is no coincidence that he believes national parks to be worthless, and in the long run doomed, if they conserve tigers and other creatures at the expense of the poor.

A few weeks later, when I was in the hills to the north, I went to a village where there was a serious shortage of cultivable land (and food). The peasants talked of leaving for the Terai, and when I asked them whereabouts they would go they all gave the same answer: Chitwan. They'd heard that there were still some forests which hadn't been cleared. That land, they said, would suit them nicely. The population of the Chitwan Valley is already well over double what it was in 1970, and once these last unprotected forests go, as they almost undoubtedly will, the pressures on the park will increase further as the next generation finds itself suffering from precisely the same scarcity of land which forced their parents out of the hills.

My last two days at Chitwan passed pleasantly enough. A hangover dampened my enthusiasm for a rhino hunt, but I went nevertheless, and had the pleasure of witnessing a ritual which should ensure that Pete Drown is remembered here for as long as there are tigers and rhinos to hunt and film crews to film them. There has always been a tradition among elephant drivers that they clap when their quarry wakes up. The applause is not so much for the creature – I imagine it traumatizes rather than soothes it – but for themselves and, more particularly, for the marksman, who has judged things to a nicety by immobilizing the tiger or rhino without killing it. After our rhino had been anaesthetized, measured and woken up, Pete Drown was still unsatisfied with the film and insisted on doing several simulated re-takes. None of this went down well with the elephant men, who wanted lunch, but they complied with his wishes. When it was all over Pete turned round and clapped them. They replied by clapping back, which only excited him further and induced him to whoop and shout and clap with even greater vigour. A further wave of applause, which would have been the envy of any diva, was then directed towards him, and so it was that every subsequent piece of shooting was followed by a ritual which delighted everyone and momentarily silenced all the other occupants of the jungle.

My final day was spent on the far side of the park, where Masahiro Iijima was photographing two types of crocodile. The gharials had thin snouts like herons' bills and they were in every sense pleasanter than the marsh muggers, the hooligans of the river world, which looked much as their name would lead one to expect: stupid, stout and vicious. The men who were helping Masahiro were fascinated with his underwater camera. 'Body no very expensive,' he explained. 'Only five hundred dollars.' He stood with his feet in the water and aimed his camera in the general direction of the gharials. 'No necessary success,' he announced after he'd taken six reels of film.

The most dangerous moment of the day had nothing to do with crocodiles. Hemanta's driver, the 'flying saucer', decided to ford the river at a particularly treacherous place where the water ran deep and fast. We had picked up two soldiers who had no particular desire to go to the other side but who seemed to think the journey itself would be interesting, which it was. Half-way across, the water came over the bonnet and we had to wind up our windows to stop it coming into the jeep. We drifted downstream for a while before hitting solid ground and continuing to the far side. We were all badly shaken.

That night there was yet another party, at which we ate goat stew. To Pete Drown this was very plain fare, and he told us how to cook grizzly bear should we ever come across one. Apparently you fry them in a beer sauce. After the meal he began a round of toasts, prefacing each with phrases such as, 'Like the men of Paraguay say ...', and 'Here's an Irish toast for you people ...' and 'Have you heard this one from the Dominican Republic ...?'

Hemanta said that he wanted to write a book about all the people he'd taken round Chitwan, and indeed he was an excellent source of information about many world leaders. He had shown Prince Philip and Prince Bernhard of the Netherlands round the park, and among those who had been entrusted to his care were President Carter, Henry Kissinger and Zbigniew Brzezinski, the former US defence secretary. I was delighted to hear that Kissinger had such bad vertigo that he couldn't even climb on to an elephant. Brzezinski, in contrast, was brave enough to accompany Hemanta on a hunt for a man-eating tiger, which, had things gone wrong, might have done more to influence American foreign policy out here than any number of books or speeches decrying it.

4

Along the Kali Gandaki

AFTER A WHILE YOU GROW to hate the buses in Nepal. The seats are made for the Nepalese, who by European standards are diminutive, and if you are anywhere near six foot tall you spend the time with your knees jack-knifed up to your chin. Occasionally the seats have padding; more often than not they don't, and after five or six hours your backside becomes bruised and sore. Most buses have seats for sixty-odd passengers but frequently everyone who wants to get on does, so it's not unusual for a hundred or more people to cram inside. If you climb down for a tea at one of the many stops the chances are you'll have lost your seat when you get back, or at least you'll be required to share it with whoever pinched it in your absence.

When I think of the journeys I made through the Terai I remember heavy musks and perfumes; in the hills, stale sweat and dirty clothes. Many of the Nepalese are poor travellers, and I once had four people within a few feet of me throwing up at the same time, one of whom, a slim Indian women with kohled eyes and warm breasts, lay across my lap while she projected her breakfast out of the window. There are times when the discomfort and overcrowding get to you and you spend every minute willing your destination closer. But there are times too when none of that matters; when you enjoy the antics of the boys who man the doors; when you realize – as you should – that you are among people of astonishing tolerance and friendliness; when you remember that to be blasé here is almost a crime, for wherever you look there are things to see of extraordinary beauty. However, you should do everything in your power to avoid travelling inside the buses: the roof is the place to be.

It was a glorious journey from Chitwan back to Kathmandu. I lay in the roof-rack on sacks of courgettes which were so comfortable that I could sleep whenever I felt like it. Otherwise I stared dreamily at the landscape and watched it change as we climbed out of the plains and headed north along the Marsyandi River to Mugling. Sometimes the road ran along the riverside; sometimes it wiggled at a great height on a track which had been blasted out of the cliffs. There were women dressed in lush greens and crimsons planting rice in the paddies by the river, and men with *topis* and tapered trousers walking bent-kneed, like old retainers, behind buffaloes and single-furrow ploughs on the tiny terraces higher up. The beige thatched roofs and ochre walls of the houses blended with the red earth and grey rock of the hillsides, and in every village there was a piple tree under which men sat smoking and drinking, while their women washed clothes and children played in the dust or chased metal hoops along the road. During the eight-hour trip we were twice flagged down by police, who ordered the three of us on the roof to get inside, but once we had rounded the next corner the driver stopped to let us climb up again. We had lunch at Mugling, a sprawling, tin-roofed town mid-way between Kathmandu and Pokhara, whose wealth derived almost entirely from its kitchens, which manufactured enormous quantities of *daal bhat* to sustain the travellers going to and coming from the Terai and Pokhara. I ate well here – better than I ever did at the Vajra – and after lunch we continued along an increasingly bumpy and pot-holed road, taking five hours to cover the last seventy miles to Kathmandu.

I spent just long enough in Kathmandu to hear the latest rumour and visit the United States aid mission. I enjoyed both.

The 'powdered milk scandal' had all the elements of a really good story: the misuse of foreign aid, corruption, a government cover-up, detention without trial and the threat of radioactive poisoning. If I've got the story wrong then the blame lies entirely with the government, which subjects the press to the harshest censorship imaginable. Criticizing the royal family is tantamount to treason, and attacks on government policy are simply not tolerated. There is no such thing as 'freedom of speech', and consequently one relies on neither newspapers nor the radio to find out what is going on, but on gossip and rumour. Much of the gossip one hears concerns the goings-on in the royal family, and indeed some of the rumours are so widely known, and accepted, that they have assumed the status of established truths. I don't intend to repeat them here. If you go to Nepal you will hear them all within twenty-four hours of your arrival. If you haven't, just ask the taxi-drivers. As far as I know, the milk scandal didn't involve any wheeler-dealing in the palace.

In Kathmandu the milk was a mixture of three components: cow's milk, buffalo milk and imported milk powder. The latter either came into the country as part of a foreign aid package, or it was bought by merchants on the world market. The aid milk was supposed to be distributed by the government to the people who needed it most: the very poor and those living in areas where there were food shortages. In the countryside I often saw piles of hessian bags with the words 'A gift from the people of the United States of America – Not to be sold' written on them. Sadly, this milk frequently ended up in the areas where it was least needed.

In April 1987 word went round that samples of milk in Kathmandu had been found to contain high levels of radioactivity, whose origin was milk powder imported from Bangladesh, which had in turn imported it from Poland, whose cows had been grazing land which had been heavily dosed with fall-out from the nuclear-reactor explosion at Chernobyl. The milk powder was unfit for human consumption and the authorities of Bangladesh had condemned it. Somehow it had made its way up to Nepal, and it was alleged that a prominent businessman or politician had bought it at a knock-down price and sold it in Kathmandu. Many people believed that whoever was responsible probably made a habit of requisitioning the US aid milk. He had run out and needed to find another source of powder to tide him over until some more of the free stuff was available.

This was the rumour circulating when I got back from Chitwan, and it may have been true, although its credibility was spoilt by some of the embellishments. For example, some said the government was trying to poison them; others that it was a Russian scheme to destabilize the country; and some even claimed that stores of the 'Chernobyl powder' were emitting radiation in the towns. All this was obviously nonsense. Once news was out that the milk was unsafe to drink, people took to the streets to broadcast warnings and give their own version of events. The police arrested some of them and when I left in late June twenty-five to thirty people were said still to be in prison. There were numerous denials from the government that anything was amiss. Nothing of consequence was ever printed in *Rising Nepal*, but I was told by those who followed events in the Nepali press that the government pronouncements were contradictory and did nothing to allay people's fears. Most stopped drinking milk altogether.

I was glad to see, as I waited for Burt Levenson to arrive at the US aid mission, that the jar of Coffee-mate on his desk came from America. The Americans in Kathmandu had a supermarket in which they could buy turkey and cranberry sauce and everything else you cared to think of, all imported from the States. Why they couldn't use the shops in town like everyone else I have no idea, but then Nepal is classed by the US as 'a hardship posting', and the supermarket went some way towards compensating the American officials for the inconvenience of being here. While I waited I read a glossy brochure which had been published by the United States Agency for International Development (USAID) to mark 'Thirty-five Years of American Assistance to Nepal'. USAID, it explained, was here 'to promote economic growth and education, combat hunger and disease and control unmanageable population pressures'. Since 1951, USAID had channelled over $500 million into Nepal: 'The United States is proud to have participated in these efforts [to develop the country], and is prepared to extend the resources, the time, and above all, the commitment necessary for the future.' I had come to talk about the $32 million Resource Conservation and Utilization Project, or RCUP for short, which operated in an area where I was about to spend a couple of weeks.

As I was saying, I arrived early, which gave me time to admire the classical portico of the old Rana palace – an orange creeper was strangling the white-washed columns – before passing through the security gates. Levenson had a small and pleasant office which looked over a courtyard. The walls were hung with photographs: five were black-and-white aerial photos of the hills, three were of the Himalaya in colour (blue-and-white, in other words) and one was an aerial photo of Detroit. Beneath them were two smaller pictures, one of crabs being landed from a fishing boat, and another in which two white clapperboard houses stood beyond a plaque stating 'Edwziepfel, 2940''. There were some family snaps as well. On his table was an unopened bottle of rum and a well-thumbed copy of *Don't Let the Goats Eat the Loquat Trees* by Thomas Hale. I had never heard of Edwziepfel or Thomas Hale; loquat trees are oriental members of the rose family. Levenson greeted me with great courtesy and offered me a coffee, which I accepted. He was in his late thirties and stocky, with black hair, a wide and heavy jaw, a thick moustache, large spectacles and dark brown eyes. He had been here for two and a half years and was now in charge of the RCUP, whose operation had begun in 1980. This meant that he couldn't be held responsible for its failures, about which I had already heard much, and he had the unenviable task of defending it, which he did with great verve. He admitted that things had gone wrong, but he said that plenty of good had come out of it.

That evening Pat Harris, a friend from London, arrived in Kathmandu. Together we set off to the valley of the Kali Gandaki for a long walk and a look at the RCUP.

We took off from Pokhara just after dawn, skimmed over hills whose jowls were powdered with pink rhododendrons, skirted round Annapurna and Nilgiri, landed on the small airstrip at Jomsom, left my umbrella on the plane, shivered against the cold, ate a hearty breakfast, hired Mék Bahadur, found the man who'd hijacked my umbrella (the bank manager), began walking, passed half a dozen stringy *sadhus*, or holy men, who'd walked all the way from southern India, ate lunch at the one-house village of Eklebhatti, and finally arrived at Kagbeni in mid-afternoon, by which time the sun was hanging above Dhaulagiri and the wind had risen to gale force. The landscape was otherworldly, like the moon yet infinitely more lovely: the riverbed shingled, bouldery and immense; the barren hills on either side pale brown and grey, the summits beyond wreathed with snow and wispy clouds. The only green in the landscape came from a row of pollarded willows and some terraces of buckwheat on the way in to Kagbeni. We walked under the village *chorten*, an arched entrance whose roof was painted with peeling Buddhist frescos, and followed a path which forded two small canals and then disappeared into a maze of constricted alleys. These ran like veins in a leaf between the walls of the houses, from the lower floors of which came the sweet, silagey smell of cow-breath and the gentle snorting of pack horses. It was impossible to tell where one dwelling ended and another began, and the stone staircases which linked the flagged streets with their upper floors lay in curious diagonals which warped perspective and made Kagbeni feel like an illusionist's invention. The whole place reminded me of an unsophisticated mesozoan – a sponge, perhaps – whose cells divide and split and multiply, always haphazardly but without ever destroying the overall form of the creature. A room and a window had been added here; a staircase and a door there.

We dumped our stuff in a lodge, left Mek to sleep on the roof and spent what remained of the afternoon walking round. The burnt-sienna *gompa*, the monastery, commanded views both down the valley towards Jomsom and up it towards the old Kingdom of Mustang, an area into which few Europeans have penetrated and which remains out of bounds to tourists. There were no monks here now, although one could imagine them in past times watching through the small windows, with a sense of anticipation and fear, as they waited for distant figures to reveal whether they were traders and porters bringing much-needed provisions, or Khampas, the bandits who used to ride down from Tibet and Mustang to make a nuisance of themselves. Outside the monastery two men had just slaughtered a goat. They laid its head on a wall while they cleaned out its entrails, and its eyes still glistened in the manic way that goats' eyes do. Farther down the village, on a wooden gate which led into an apple orchard, someone had been practising their English with a piece of chalk: 'What is your nem?'; 'You will give a Ans?'; 'Who do you live?' The children in the village simply chanted 'One rupees! One rupees!' wherever we went. We passed a row of prayer wheels, some beaten out of mustard-oil tins, embedded into a schist wall, then came across a small paddock in which a women in Tibetan dress was weaving long strands of colourful cotton while her husband rocked a red-haired baby. Down by a little stream ten youths were practising their archery; every now and then one of the arrows hit the wooden target, but most sailed into the orchard beyond.

We ate soon after dark and brushed our teeth on the roof, which overlooked a yard in which mules and ponies snuffled under the full moon, which had risen magnificently above a triangular, snow-capped mountain to the north-east. Then we went to bed: a delicious sleep full of fresh-air dreams, disturbed only by a rat, which clambered over our sleeping bags before waking up the French couple next door.

It took us most of the next day to get to Jharkot. It wasn't far, but we had to climb from about 9,100 feet to a little over 11,300. In any case, there was no reason to hurry and such was the scenery that it was impossible to go more than a few hundred yards without stopping to admire it. It was barren, gentle, austere, massive, terrifying, pagan, lifeless, soulful, heavenly. There were no trees to give it scale, nor any houses; just occasionally a man on horseback, or a trekker, or some porters would appear in the distance like specks of dust and take what seemed an infinity of time to reach us, then disappear. Once we heard a lark and saw some choughs; and there were stretches along the hillsides where small stunted rose bushes grew, but they were so parched and dry that their colour was little different from the grey-brown rock. Around midday we arrived in Khingar, a small village with two tea shops, a few leafless poplars and a monastery. Some monks were blowing horns which sent a deep resonance through the thin, chilly air. While we drank tea Mek told us, not for the first time, that we had just delivered him from hell. He'd spent ten days in Jomsom, the first few drinking the wages he'd received for leading some people there from Pokhara, the last seven washing up in return for two plates of *daal bhat* a day. He'd cut his hand quite badly and the ball of his right thumb had turned septic.

Before we left Khingar three porters came stumbling along the track. They were in a bad way and we asked Mek to stop them. One man had fingers so bloated that his hands looked like those of a corpse pulled from a river; they were the size of courgettes and their tips had turned blue. His toes were also frostbitten. He was wearing a light jacket, a T-shirt and a pair of shorts. His two companions also wore clothes more suitable for a summer stroll than an alpine trek. Both had frostbite and one was snow-blind. These men had been hired as porters for a trekking expedition which was doing the 'Annapurna circuit', a three-week walk round the great massif which includes the Annapurnas, Nilgiri and Macchapuchhare. The day before they had been caught in a heavy snowstorm as they came over the 17,500-foot Thurong La Pass. Before they left they said we'd see much worse on our way up. We did.

In fact three expeditions had come over the pass that day, and we came across band after band of weary porters, many of them snow-blind and most suffering from frostbite. Some seemed so weak it was difficult to see how they would get down to Jomsom before evening. We met the European tourists too. All of them seemed very well indeed. They wore climbing boots, padded gloves, parkas, ski-glasses, the lot. We suggested to an English couple (they were with Exodus Expeditions) that it was shocking to see them looking so well when their porters, who were carrying all manner of things – tents, chairs, stoves, tables, kerosene lamps – were in such a state of distress. 'It's easy for you to say that,' replied the man curtly. 'You can't imagine how bad it was up there.' He said the porters had all been provided with the proper clothes when the trek began in the lowlands. They'd sold them on the way up. It was, he implied, their own fault. However, he was shocked by the behaviour of the Frenchman who was leading one of the other expeditions. Apparently, he had confiscated the shoes of two porters and made them walk for four hours through snow in bare feet. The porters had jettisoned their loads – they were exhausted – and this was their punishment. The French expedition had even left a French girl behind in the snow and the English, who were following, had picked her up and helped her down. A little later we talked to some more porters. They described how they had hugged one of their friends in a blanket as they thought he was dying of hypothermia.

None of the tourists had bothered to share their clothes with the porters; and none was helping to carry the gear now, even though many of the porters could barely walk. In fact, no one was helping at all, except for two young women who brought up the rear. They were leading four mules which carried two men and two girls too weak to walk. Seeing these two women actually doing something useful did little to lessen the shame I felt at being European – but I could have kissed them all the same. Mek didn't seem at all surprised by what we'd seen; he said this sort of thing happened quite often. One Nepali friend told me later that he'd once found four dead porters on the way down from the Thurong La – they had frozen to death during the night, outside the tents in which the tourists who'd hired them slept.

Most of the porters we saw would have been paid between 30 and 50 rupees a day (less than $3). By selling the clothes they'd been provided with they would have made a bit extra. Those who had suffered from frostbite were faced with the prospect of weeks without work and money (and possibly a life without fingers). There is no porters' trade union in Nepal. Some of the bigger trekking companies are said to treat their employees well (although their wages are pitiful); others – like those which came across the Thurong La on 13 April 1987 – don't give a damn. Nor, evidently, do many of the tourists who come with them.

The climb to Jharkot was gentle and pleasant. There was a thin veneer of grass on the black earth and we walked through fields of sprouting corn. Here and there small springs gushed out of the ground and sent rivulets down the path, beside which were yellow clumps of coltsfoot and silverweed. There were also a few primroses, but they were stunted affairs compared to those lower down the valley. We found a small lodge on the edge of Jharkot and drank tea in the courtyard, sitting on a mattress whose hessian covering had FOOD AID BY JAPAN printed on it. There were three posters tacked on to the white-washed wall: one of the pop group A-ha, one of the Argentinian footballer Diego Maradona, and another of a Pakistani squash player. They had all been taken from *The Sun*, an Indian newspaper whose centre pages have had a profound effect on the decor of houses in the Himalaya. Once we were here whatever thoughts we'd had about making it up to Muktinath, the Hindu pilgrimage site a little way to east, soon disappeared. We were tired, and we were glad to be somewhere where there were few other trekkers.

Two teachers came by and we talked to them. They were good-looking men, dispirited by their isolation up here – they were Hindus from the Middle Hills – and glad to have some outsiders to talk to. They explained the eccentric system of fines whose intention was to stop children playing truant. In class one the parents were fined 1 rupee for each day missed; in class two 2 rupees; and so on up to class seven. If a child in class seven (there was only one child) missed a month the fine was 40 rupees, which meant that if he was going to miss six days he might as well miss the whole month. There was much truancy, as parents often preferred their children to work in the fields. The more voluble of the two teachers had been here eight years. He said the pay was terrible. After they left we were joined by Jharkot's *pradhan panch*, a swarthy character called Churruk Gurung. Mek asked him about the RCUP, but he didn't want to talk about it. Instead he told us about the forestry programmes which the *panchayat*, or village council, had undertaken without any foreign or government aid. They had planted hundreds of apple and apricot trees, and he thought that his recent re-election for another term of five years was a reflection of the orchards' success.

I believe that there are a few memories which we carry with us beyond death and from which we shall never be free. They sustain us now, and they will sustain us always, beckoning like beacons of hope which no misfortune or misery can extinguish. Perhaps it is just a smile or a strand of hair or the smell of warm breath, caught in a chink of light and time and frozen like a fly in amber. But sometimes there is more than that, a whole world with movement and sound and changing colour.

I remember the next ten days with that rare clarity which is normally reserved for brief moments of intense love. I will remember for all time the soft, clammy silences in the sacred forest at Baglung and the louder, windy silences among the stunted juniper near Tukuche; the porters' stompy legs laced with veins and the thin legs of young girls with long necks and torn dresses; the wrinkled faces of the old women and the tight brown stomachs of the girls-turned-women near Beni whose breasts were held in velvetine *blousiers*; the slate-grey hide of the buffaloes and their slack udders with fat teats, and the tin roofs of the houses which glittered in the sun; the wheat and apple blossom at Marpha and the bananas and caged boar and rice paddies below Karkineta; the goats and the mule trains and the bells around the necks of the mules; the temples with the dried blood of sacrificed animals and the Indian *sadhus*, pink-robed and arrogant, begging for a few rupees on the path or cooking in a field, and their legs were long and slim and strong. All of these things I shall remember, and much more besides, and whatever I write now will be nothing compared to the memory of them.

It was seven o'clock in the morning when we left Jharkot. Mek wanted us to get to Jomsom as quickly as possible to avoid the gales which blew up the valley every afternoon, but Pat was suddenly struck by a violent sickness, and when we arrived at Khingar she lay on a mat outside a house and clutched her stomach. I suggested we spend the next night there, but she insisted on carrying on, and for her the rest of the day was hell. She took some antibiotics and somehow managed to keep walking. By the time we reached Eklebhatti, Pat had a fever and a furious wind was scouring the hills. It took us four hours to walk what on a breezeless morning would have taken two, and at times the gusts were so strong we had to stop and shelter behind a rock or in the lee of a cliff. Nobody with any sense was walking now, and the only others we met were two young Hindu couples. The men were dressed in Western clothes, while their wives wore saris which fluttered in the wind like coloured streamers. When we reached Jomsom we had our trekking permits checked by the police, who were playing karem board, then found Mek, who had gone on ahead of us, in the Moon Light Lodge. Pat took some more antibiotics, went to bed and slept right through till the next morning, by which time she was as good as new.

When we left the next day there were soldiers jogging through the town and people had already gathered to watch for the arrival of the daily plane. It took us about two hours to reach Marpha, which was tucked into an alcove in the cliffs on the west bank of the river. We followed seven pack mules into the village and marvelled at its cleanliness. It was the cleanest – and neatest – place I saw in Nepal. The stone-flagged streets were spotless and the water which ran in the culverts sparkled like Perrier. Marpha exhibited a Cubist purity of contour and colour which was in sharp contrast to the more anarchic villages from which we had come. The white-washed houses had flat roofs on which piles of firewood were neatly stacked, and their walls were punctuated by wooden windows which looked like roughly carved misericords. We had tea in the village and lunch on the trail south, after which we dropped in at the National Temperate Horticultural Research Station, otherwise known as Marpha Farm.

I wanted to meet Passam Sherpa, who had established the farm over twenty years ago and still ran it. He was a famous man whom everyone in Kathmandu seemed to know, but unfortunately he was away. However, it didn't really matter as we were shown round by a charming man called Devendra Gauchan. It was a lovely time to be there. The apple, peach and apricot trees were all covered with white blossom, bees buzzed, the sun shone and the air smelt sweet. Before Passam Sherpa came here the only apples and apricots growing round Marpha had been small wild ones, and the farmers had devoted their fields to barley, buckwheat and potatoes. They knew little about apples and at first were highly suspicious about growing them. However they gradually took to them, and now they grow so little grain that they have to import food from farther down the valley. They are happy with their apples, which they sell to tourists, porters and pilgrims, who eat them, and to the distillers, who turn them into alcohol. The distillery at the farm was the most primitive-looking affair, but the brandy and cider produced here were excellent; so good, in fact, that the farm supplied the palace and the army. From an ecological point of view the distillery left a lot to be desired. The farm was supposed to burn only dead wood in the furnace, but such was the state of the local forests that live trees were obviously used too. Each distillation, which yielded eighty litres of brandy, required 170 kilos of wood.

There were quite a few new buildings here, including two coolage stores, one paid for by the United Nations Development Programme (UNDP) and the other built by USAID as part of its Resource Conservation Utilization Project. Levenson had told me to look out for both the RCUP's coolage store at Marpha Farm and for its greenhouse, of which he seemed rather proud. He had complained that people trekking in the Kali Gandaki often underestimated the achievements of the RCUP, partly because some of its creations could not be seen from the trail. This greenhouse, a large steel and glass structure, was one of them. It was used for raising seedlings of cold-sensitive species such as capsicum and tomato, a task which could equally well have been done, at a fraction of the cost, under polythene or glass frames.

There were about fifty people working at the farm. Most of the trained agronomists came from the Kathmandu Valley or the Terai. One man from Birgunj said he enjoyed the work, but it wasn't much of a life for him as he couldn't bring his wife and children here. You heard this complaint all the time in the hills. Schools where a decent education was to be had were confined to the Kathmandu Valley and the larger towns of the Terai. Indeed, those who could afford it often sent their children to India for schooling. Consequently, one was always coming across well-educated married men living like bachelors in the hills, and this meant that an air of sadness shrouded even the pleasantest of places.

Had we arrived a week earlier we would have witnessed an event of considerable interest. Once a year the Nepalese government invites all the foreign ambassadors in Kathmandu on a short trip to see part of the country. Hemanta had invited them down to Chitwan one year. This year nineteen of them had come to the Upper Kali Gandaki. They were flown in to Jomsom, conducted on horseback up to Muktinath, then brought down and shown round Marpha Farm. Apparently they were very impressed by the brandy and cider.

These trips gave the ambassadors the opportunity to see some of the country's problems and observe the progress of foreign aid projects. The evening meals must have been fascinating. Nepal is very serious about its policy of non-alignment and, much to its credit, it will not countenance diplomatic squabbles on its own soil. I was told that on one occasion a representative of an Arab country rebuffed an Israeli official and was promptly ordered to leave Nepal. 'The foreign ministry is very clever on these ambassadorial trips,' said one observer. 'They put people next to each other whose countries are at loggerheads and they are effectively forced to talk together in a civilized way.' For the ambassadors these trips must make a pleasant break from the endless rounds of cocktail parties and dinners on Kathmandu's diplomatic circuit.

During my time in Nepal I developed a great affection for Stan Armington's book, *Trekking in the Nepal Himalaya*. This was one of half a dozen books – the best being Stephen Bezruschka's rather-too-bulky-to-carry *A Guide to Trekking in Nepal* – which described the most popular routes in the country. Why walking should be referred to as 'trekking' I have no idea. Perhaps it is to make it sound more daunting. My dictionary defines to trek as 'to journey by ox-wagon: to migrate: to tramp and camp, dragging one's equipment', so I suppose the third of these comes closest to describing what one does in Nepal, although it was Mek who was doing the 'dragging' and I never camped. All of which is by the way. I read Armington's book with the frequency and devotion to detail I normally reserve for the King James Bible and Rabelais, often re-reading the same passage describing a particular day's walk four or five times. I did this for two reasons. For one thing I found it impossible, unlike Pat, to read novels in the evenings; for another, I was searching for warnings of any particularly nasty cliffs which the next day might hold in store.

The problem with Armington's book was that while it had much to say about rabies, dysentery, malaria, typhoid, cholera, meningitis and lesser afflications like sore feet and pulled muscles, it was absolutely silent on the subject of vertigo. I had already learnt from my Namche experiences that what he described simply as 'a steep climb' was for me an almost unscaleable cliff. Nevertheless, I did my best to read between the lines as we made our way down the Kali Gandaki, and though I was never given the warnings of danger to which I felt I was entitled, I came across odd bits of information which stuck in my mind. Thus it was that Tukuche became the place where I would find at the the north end of town the Yak Hotel, which 'advertises a "real yak on display inside" – it's worth a look'. I suppose it was, but we took Mek's advice, which was always excellent, and stayed in a lodge which had a stuffed duck pinned to the wall in an attitude of awkward flight.

In 1950 Maurice Herzog led an expedition of French climbers up the Kali Gandaki to Tukuche, which he described as 'the Chamonix of Nepal'. Judging by what he found, the only similarity between the two towns was their proximity to high mountains. 'There were ... far fewer people than we expected,' he recalled in *Annapurna*, which they successfully scaled.

Numbers of dirty children surrounded us, observing our every move with curiosity, and playing about in the water conduit in the middle of the village in which the women washed their pots and got their water for their tea. The old men remained on their doorsteps, suspicious and mistrustful of these white men who were here with such obscure intentions.

Fourteen years later Michel Peissel came up the valley on his way north to Lo Mantang. His book *Mustang: A Lost Tibetan Kingdom* provides a highly readable and informative account of life in the Kali Gandaki Valley before the trekking boom:

The main street of Tukutcha was most impressive, with its enormous houses, homes of the Serchans and other merchant kings. They lined the trade route, down which all day and much of the night bells tinkled and the hooves of ponies, mules and donkeys clattered. Tukutcha is a true caravan town, an important terminus and junction in the vast network of tracks that cover the Himalayas.

The town looked deserted, and so it was, for most of its wealthy inhabitants had gone down to live in Pokhara and Kathmandu, leaving their ancestral homes to caretakers, who now paced about the empty galleries and through the vast storerooms which had once been bustling with the trade in wool and salt from Tibet. Times had changed for Tukutcha, and in its decline we saw one of the first effects of the Chinese invasion of Tibet.

Since Peissel's visit, Tukuche's population has dropped further, from around 500 in 1962 to a little over 200 by 1976. The inhabitants of Tukuche, like those of Marpha, were Thakalis, the great trading people who now run many of the lodges along the Kali Gandaki, in Pokhara and in the towns on the road to Kathmandu. The main street was still imposing, though off the side streets there were many buildings which were locked up and gradually falling to bits. If it hadn't been for the tourists – over 25,000 visit the Annapurna region every year – it would have been in a much sadder state. Although the old route to Tibet was now to all intents and purposes defunct, we could still watch from the handsome balcony of our bedroom the trains of mules and porters carrying rice and other goods up towards Jomsom. As it happened, our stay was unenjoyable, which was entirely due to the presence of four Israelis in the room next to us. They behaved boorishly and talked long and loud into the middle of the night. Such was the thinness of the walls that you could have heard a mouse sneezing next door.

Tukuche was built on a wedge of land between the Kali Gandaki and a tributary which carried the waters from the peaks to the west. The main riverbed was over half a mile wide in places, although the river itself was no more than a series of interwoven streams, and it was here, when we left Tukuche the next morning, that we looked at one of the RCUP's forestry schemes. It consisted of a post-and-wire enclosure in which had been planted many thousands of young trees, of which scarcely one remained. This wasn't at all surprising because during the summer months the riverbed did what one would expect it to do – carried melt-water, by force of gravity, from the mountains down to the plains. Trees do not grow on pebbles in riverbeds, and whoever was responsible for this scheme knew remarkably little about forestry. Some of the villagers pointed out one of the more obvious ironies: large numbers of trees had been felled from what little remained of the forests on the valley sides in order to make the fence posts to protect the saplings. Much of the planting had been done by contract labourers who had no interest in the success of the plantation, and many of the saplings had been planted in the plastic bags in which they had come from the nursery.

We walked along the riverbed for a couple of miles, stopping at a bamboo-and-thatch shack for tea, and again to watch a long train of mules, the leading members of which had large crimson-and-white plumes on their heads. A shepherd stood alone with a few sheep way out in the middle of the riverbed. He was playing a flute, an instrument which Mek also carried, but from which, when he blew it, came sounds far inferior to those we listened to now. And then it was into a small cypress forest, across another stretch of gravel, and through a rich deciduous woodland whose floor was dotted with white violets, wild strawberries and blue gentians. From here south the landscape lost its ruggedness and nature became more profuse and generous. As we dropped down towards a grove of walnut trees, whose leaves lingered uncertainly between green and bronze, we saw shrikes, wagtails, stonechats, redstarts and warblers. There were butterflies along the path – yellow brimstones, fritillaries and meadow browns; and in the lodge at Kalopani, where we stopped for lunch, there was a vase of ladies' smock and purple iris on our table. The barley was almost ripe; the police were playing karem board in the sun.

The drop down to Lete Pool was steep without being too daunting, though my heart sank when Mek pointed to where the path ran over a scree beyond the large suspension bridge which straddled the river. There had been a landslide and those going along the path did so slowly and with great caution, for in places it was barely two feet wide. I announced, not for the first time, that I couldn't possibly continue. Much to my relief, Mek, who was comfortingly solicitous whenever we came to anything approaching a steep cliff, announced that we could drop right down to the river and climb up the bank farther down, which we did in due course, but not before we had an encounter with a very drunk *sadhu*, who was making his way south having visited Muktinath. He had a mop of long grey hair and fine brown eyes with which he fixed Pat in the most unholy of stares. He grabbed her by the arms and pulled her to the ground, had a good feel around, then grabbed me as well when I suggested to Pat that she should disentangle herself as quickly as possible. For such a skinny man he was remarkably strong and his grip hurt. Anyway, he blessed us, kissed our heads and insisted on showing us his collection of ammonites, black fossils found in the Upper Kali Gandaki which Hindus recognize as symbols of Vishnu, the deity whose present incarnation is believed by Nepalis to be King Birendra. Pat gave him 20 rupees for one of his ammonites, so presumably that enabled him to stay in high spirits for a few more hours. We met his friend, a younger man, once we'd crossed the river and rejoined the path. He apologized for the other's drunkenness. The local villagers frequently complained about these pilgrims from India, claiming that they begged aggressively and expected people to feed them on their journey. I thought they were admirable.

The Kali Gandaki is the deepest gorge in the world and we began to feel it once we reached Ghasa, a small village whose houses tumbled down a steep hill like grey pebbles in a waterfall of golden barley. Ghasa was 6,500 feet above sea-level, 2,000 feet below Tukuche, and 20,000 feet below and between Annapurna and Dhaulagiri. The barley was ripe and there were men and women in the fields cutting off the ears with small sickles and throwing them over their backs into cane *dokos*. We were back in buffalo country and attached to every house was a simple bamboo lean-to in which these excellent creatures stood or sat impassively, some with calves, others in the company of fine cockerels whose rich plumage was little different from that of their jungle-fowl ancestors. There were many goats and pigs as well, and the stone flags on the trail were spattered with dung and straw. The houses were quite different from those at Tukuche and Marpha. The flat mud roofs had gone and in their place was sloping thatch, under whose eaves were hung hollowed logs which served as bee-hives. Mud walls had replaced dressed stone, and the houses had an altogether gentler and more organic look about them.

We stayed in a lodge at the lower end of the village, which suited both

Mek, who disliked the proprietors of the one farther up, and us, as the other lodge was where the Israelis were staying. Behind our lodge there was an orchard whose floor was carpeted with trekkers' rubbish: old toothpaste tubes, cigarette packets, empty medicine bottles and toilet paper. But I ignored this and watched a pair of rosy finches hopping about in the apple blossom. A flycatcher with streaks of azure on its wings appeared briefly, then tumbled out of sight as it chased something too small for my eyes to see. Before supper we went for a walk and put a dressing on Mek's wound. 'Hand still a bit dodgy,' he announced once we'd done the job, but it seemed to be improving.

For the first time since we'd landed in Jomsom we were warm in the evening, having walked in four days through three seasons: late winter in Jharkot, spring in Marpha and summer here. We sat in shirt sleeves till long after dark chatting to Mek. We even tried practising Nepali with two charming children who served our dinner. I'm ashamed to say that my Nepali was almost as poor when I left Nepal as when I came. It isn't a difficult language to learn, but I was nearly always with people who spoke it, so my efforts to get beyond counting to ten and learning a few words and greetings were few and unmemorable. My phrase book remained a source of entertainment rather than enlightenment. I particularly liked its translation of the word *hunuhunna*, which was 'not alive (does not exist) – this is used for respective person if someone is no more or not existing'. It also, as befitted a country with so much disease, devoted a lengthy section to medical matters.

If you are walking in the hills of Nepal for ten days you will probably spend two days constipated, another two or three evacuating like a canary and the rest more or less as you would wish. As there are few doctors in the hills it is up to you to work out whether you are suffering simply from a change of diet, from the altitude (the higher you go the more windy you become) or from something more serious, such as dysentery or giardia, either of which could ruin your trek if left untreated. All this leads you to inspect whatever you deposit with great interest, and it is remarkable how candid strangers become. Quite often the first thing someone will tell you when they meet you on the trail is how their insides are bearing up. My phrase book tackled the practical aspects of emptying one's bowels with an admirable lack of reserve:

In Nepalese toilet, generally toilet paper is not available, so to use it, you have to take water in a container and to sit comfortably you have to slip off your pants or under wears to your knees. In village many people go out in the fields or to the banks of river or streams. Use your left hand to clean after defecating.

Most trekkers took with them a supply of toilet paper, but few bothered to bury it, which meant that in places the trail looked like an open sewer.

I commend to anyone travelling in Nepal the section on health in Armington's book. It was written by David Shlim, an American doctor who ran the International Clinic in Kathmandu and whom I met at Didi's one night. Shlim was said to know as much about tropical medicine as anybody in this part of the world, though it was as a musician, rather than as a doctor, that I shall remember him. Soon after I returned from the Kali Gandaki I went to a party held in a marquee in the grounds of the British Embassy. It was a good old-fashioned stomp, with plenty of drinking, and music provided by Kathmandu's only rock band, Fear of Heights, for whom Shlim played lead guitar and sang, both of which he did with enormous vigour. The drummer, incidentally, was the tutor to the king's eldest son and the bass player was George McBean, a laconic and delightful Scotsman who worked for Unicef. There can be few rock bands in the world with such a respectable pedigree.

Our routine was the same every day. We would wake up early, around six o'clock, have something to eat, then start down the trail. After two hours we'd stop for a tea and Mek would have a couple of plates of *daal bhat*; another two hours walking before lunch, followed by three or four hours after, then an early supper and bed. It takes four or five days to establish a good walking rhythm, then your legs go on auto-pilot and you go up hills and down without having to apply much thought to the problem of physical propulsion. Some of the time you admire the landscape, but when it is so uniformly beautiful there is a limit to how much time you can devote to that. Mostly I found myself day-dreaming, and I spent the hours on the trail with my head full of all sorts of delightful nonsense. In and among the idle reveries might come, very occasionally, a thought of some consequence. I had one of these on the way from Ghasa to Tatopani. It suddenly struck me that we had been walking, day after day, in a world without machines. This needs a little qualification. There were numerous water-wheels which milled corn and rice; and there was a hydro-electric plant south of Jomsom. But the mills had been here long before the invention of the internal combustion engine, and we never saw the power station (which was built, incidentally, with Saudi Arabian aid). Never in my life had I gone so long without hearing and seeing cars, buses, motorbikes, food-mixers, pneumatic drills, and all the other bits and pieces which contribute to the background noise of most places in the world. It was the crickets in the woods below Ghasa that made me think of machines. They were very noisy and the sound of their legs rubbing together reminded me of the old wooden rattles people used to take to football matches when I was a child.

Shortly after leaving Ghasa we crossed the river, then walked for an hour through a dense wood on the east bank before crossing back to the other side and climbing to a huddle of houses at Rupse Chhahara, a hamlet which nestled at the foot of a magnificent waterfall. A woman sat in a mill dropping maize, grain by grain, on to a grindstone; a black redstart flicked its russet tail on the boulders in the stream. A little farther on bananas, apricots and lemon trees were interspersed among terraces of maize and sugar cane, and on the stone walls which surrounded the gardens of the fine houses in Dana were spiky thickets of spurge with small red flowers the shape of cloven hooves. There were poinsettia bushes in the gardens, cannabis growing in the ditches and an enormous pumpkin on the roof of the post office.

Tatopani must have been lovely once, for its situation was idyllic. Now it was something of a tourist slum, and there were lodges here which had been specially constructed for the trekkers. These and the older establishments catered for people going up towards Jomsom, or coming down from there, as well as for others who came from Pokhara to Tatopani, stayed a few days, then returned. The main street was crowded with Westerners and the place reminded me of Aviemore, a town in the Scottish Highlands which shares the same deity, Mammon. In our lodge there was even a video, which was showing *Sophie's Choice* and *The Big Chill*. Among the town's attractions were the hot springs – *tato pani* – which spurted out of the rocks along the riverbank. There were substantial springs some way to the south to which most people went, but we found a small one – not much more than a trickle – which was deserted. The water was too hot to touch, so we mixed it in an aluminium bowl with the icy water of the river, stripped, and washed ourselves thoroughly for the first time in six days. The near-boiling water also served the useful purpose of cooking the lice which had taken up residence in the seams of my shirt.

We sat by the river for a long time, listening to the mesmeric sound of the water and observing the small dramas of river life. A lizard with a crimson dewlap sunned himself on the rocks beside his drab mate, like an old gent whose children had long since left him with nothing but memories and a wife; a swallowtail butterfly landed on the spring water, fluttered momentarily, and died; leaves and insects fell into the river from trees on the far bank, then disappeared swiftly. Nature, if you care to sit silently for a little while, never fails to display the impermanance of things: procreation and fruition, decay and death; a world of order, certainly, but one from which chance – armed sometimes with a scythe, sometimes with Venus's bow – is never absent. Little wonder that men turn to God.

There were two ways to Pokhara from Tatopani. Most people took the route which climbed high up the hills to the east to Ghorepani, and indeed this was the only one mentioned in Armington's book. But there was another way, quite a bit longer, which involved fewer steep climbs, attracted few trekkers, and followed the river for another two days down to Kushma. Mek called it the *daal bhat* route, as that was all you could get to eat, and we left the main trail early next morning. We had met thirty or forty trekkers each day on the way down to Tatopani; now there were days when we saw only half a dozen. For the first few miles south of Tatopani the trail clung to steep cliffs, at the foot of which the river rushed and foamed with noisy vigour. By the time we stopped for lunch the cliffs had moved back to recline against the hills and the landscape gradually became more gentle and populous. We ate in a shack which overlooked a field of harvested barley, and once we'd finished a man appeared and asked us to treat his hand. He'd slashed the ball of his thumb with a knife and the wound was dirty and full of pus. We washed it for him and suggested he go to Tatopani, where there was a French medical mission. Just before we arrived in Beni we came to a sizeable village with a diesel-powered rice mill, near which was a small temple to which Mek insisted we pay a visit.

By now Mek had become as much a friend as a porter and guide. Every day he would thank us for taking him on, and we, in turn, would thank him for coming with us. He was always good company, impeccably honest and consistently charming. We saw countless sights we would never have come across had we been on our own, and as he spoke adequate English he was also able to translate for us. He was thirty-three years old and apart from a short spell in the Nepalese army and a year or so as a janitor in an embassy in Kathmandu, he had spent his adult life working as a guide. He obviously enjoyed the job, though outside the two main tourist seasons – spring and autumn – he had difficulty keeping body and soul together. He was a *bon viveur*, and no sooner did he get money than he spent it, frequently on drink, for which he had a great weakness. He also had various debts to settle on the way down the valley, and the daily advance on which we had first decided, 40 rupees, gradually climbed towards the hundred mark, his full pay, in order to satisfy such exigencies. Mek had frequently told us about his parents and his family, whose home he hadn't visited for ten years. He'd said he was going to go there that summer, and for some reason we had assumed it must be a long way from this region. When we announced that we wanted to go by Baglung and Kushma, he became very reflective: yes, he knew the route well; in fact his home lay between the two towns. 'But you haven't been that way for ten years?' I queried. 'Yes, sir,' he replied, 'I've seen my home recently, but from the other side of the river.' We suggested we visit his parents and the idea delighted him. 'Thank you, sir,' he said. We had by now given up telling Mek to call us by our Christian names, and when addressed directly we were always 'sir' or 'sahib' and 'madame' or 'mem'sahb'.

The closer we got to Mek's home the more apprehensive he became. In Tatopani he'd had a pair of purple trousers made up and he'd washed his hair, and our visit to the temple was another part of the preparations for his homecoming. The temple was very small and perched on a knoll of land overlooking the river. Mek gathered some bougainvillaea flowers, then circled the temple and gave each of the bells a hearty ring as he muttered, 'Ah, Shiva! Shiva!' – the goddess to whom the temple was dedicated. When we reached the two iron cows at the entrance, an old man came out and offered us some small chunks of unleavened bread before applying *tika* to our foreheads and putting flowers in our hair. Inside the temple two women and a clutch of small children squatted among a chaotic mess of old bottles, lighted candles and piles of powder and dried rice. It looked like a medieval apothecary's shop. Mek was offhand and cheerful and showed none of the piety I had expected.

We reached Beni a little before dark, by which time the sky had turned the colour of iodine and thunder rumbled down from the north, bringing with it jags of lightning and torrential rain, which swelled the river and sent some ponies rushing for the stables opposite our lodge.

Beni was a substantial town, the largest we had passed through so far, and a very pleasant one too. We were now well south of the Buddhist regions and among Magars and Brahmans. There were well-stocked chemists here and stores selling everything from clothes and fruit to psychedelic *bindis* (which are a substitute for the rice and powder *tika*). When we left in the morning we passed a school whose pupils were all smartly dressed in blue uniforms. Tacked on to the wall of the school was a board on which were displayed marks for four 'houses' under the headings of 'discipline', 'study', 'attendance', 'turn-out' and 'art and culture'. The 'Thought For The Day' was KNOWLEDGE IS POWER. We stopped for lunch at a little village called Belbot and washed our hair under a tap beside a grove of bamboo before climbing up a steep hill to Baglung, a large mud-brick town on a plateau several hundred feet above the Kali Gandaki. The main street was lined by handsome two-storey buildings with fine wooden balconies. I imagine Kathmandu must have been rather like this – although Baglung had no temples of any note and it was relatively clean – in the days before the arrival of the motor car. William Morris and Kropotkin would have appreciated the way in which agriculture, small industry and commerce had blended to create a town which, superficially at least, appeared both peaceful and prosperous.

Along the main street there was a remarkable number of tailors' shops, from which drifted the tremulous whinings of Indian music. You could buy everything here, from *topis* to Wrangler jeans, saris to combat jackets. Mek led us to a grocer's shop, above which hung the familiar sign 'WAIWAI 4-in-1 Noodles', and we bought some provisions from a young man in a Michael Jackson T-shirt. We wanted to get Mek's mother the

Nepalese equivalent of a box of chocolates or a bottle of duty-free perfume, the sort of thing one presents to the mother of a girlfriend on first being taken home. We bought, on Mek's advice, three cups, two glasses, two packets of tea, a kilo of sugar, five packets of 'glucose' biscuits and three packets of cheap cigarettes. Before leaving Baglung we stopped near a family planning clinic and drank some 7–Up, which, curiously, tasted extremely good. The street in which we rested was home to a promiscuous gathering of goats, pigs, hens and dogs, none of which took the slightest notice of an athletic and muscular young man in boxing gloves and a flashy blue track suit who charged past and delivered a series of impressive punches at imaginary targets on his way to a small recreation ground.

I was so used to walking through open countryside, or in woods whose trees were stunted by lopping for firewood and whose undergrowth was grazed out by goats, that I had great difficulty imagining the valley carpeted by thick forest, as it once was. Only when we reached the sacred forest below Baglung did I get some inkling of the earlier landscape. The pine and sal trees were about ninety feet high and the canopy so dense that only the occasional ray of sunshine penetrated to the forest floor. Its sanctity had been its saving, and nobody was allowed to cut wood in the forest, in the middle of which was a large brick temple with pagoda roofs. It was dedicated to *nou dirga* – nine goddesses – whose images surrounded it. Mek rang two large bells with great zest and a marvellous old lady, small and wiry like a stick insect, came out and offered us strands of cotton to tie round our necks and some flowers for our hair. She wished us good luck and a long life, and we wished her the same before making the steep descent to the river. If we'd walked at a normal pace we would have reached Mek's home in ten minutes, but he insisted on stopping for a tea within sight of a field where his mother was working. 'No hurry, sir,' explained the prodigal son, whose anxiety had become painful to witness.

Mek's father, a stringy fifty-year-old in *topi* and shorts with an expression which suggested both sharp intelligence and boundless good humour, waited outside his house as we climbed up the hill to meet him. Mek dropped to his knees and kissed his feet; we greeted him in traditional Nepalese fashion, bowing our heads slightly and holding our hands together as though in prayer. Two of Mek's sisters then came forward. The last time he had seen them they were seven years old; now they were seventeen and both were close to tears. They were wide-boned, of womanly build and unusually beautiful: they reminded me of Gauguin's Tahitian models. Mek's mother must have seen us arriving from the fields by the river, and soon she appeared – a lithe, lank woman, strong and supple, with eyes like capers and a fine hooked nose which supported two ornate and substantial rings. Her imperious features were those of an aristocrat; her feet and hands belonged to a peasant. She stuck a sickle in the thatch roof, which overhung the mud balcony on which we sat, let Mek kiss her feet, then delivered, in a quiet though firm voice, a long monologue. The substance of this, Mek told us once she'd disappeared to make tea, was that it was high time he returned to his family and his home. By the time tea came others had appeared from the scattering of small houses on the neighbouring hillside. Most were related to Mek and the occasion was one of profound joy.

Mek gradually relaxed, though he protested when I suggested we leave him alone with his family. We drank a lot of tea; we smoked many cigarettes. An aunt came and delivered another speech, which, judging from the reactions of her audience, was both acerbic and witty. Mek smiled uneasily; his sisters ecstatically. He explained that the one who laughed a lot was married to a Gurkha soldier in the Indian army; he would be returning at the end of the month. The one who didn't talk had been struck deaf and dumb when she was a small child. She was enchanting and obviously adored by everyone. A cousin in his teens appeared, and then came a small boy. 'This one, sir,' explained Mek, 'before – his penis no good; now very good.' Apparently, he hadn't been able to pee properly, but his mother – one of Mek's aunts, I think – had taken him to the hospital in Pokhara and now all was well. 'Operation very good,' concluded Mek.

A girl chased four cows through the fields by the river. Mynah birds chattered boisterously on some corn sheaves. One of the sisters swept the pile of threshed wheat in front of us on to a cloth mat. A child climbed a tree and ate some small berries. A chicken was caught, killed and decapitated; another small boy played with its head. The sun fell. We remained outside in the warm darkness and Mek's father produced an old radio which he obligingly tuned into the English-language news. It was read in a dreary monotone, like Radio Moscow. Most of it was about the king and queen. Finally, an hour or so after dark, we were summoned into the house, which consisted of a single room on the lower floor, in whose centre was a simple hearth, and a loft, in which the whole family slept. Mek's mother looked on, squatting, as we sat cross-legged eating *daal bhat* and chicken in the light of a candle: she was an excellent cook, and this meal was obviously a considerable extravagance.

Mek had been wary about bringing us to his home, and on the journey from Tatopani, and even once we were there, he kept telling us, 'My family very poor people.' If one assesses wealth, or the lack of it, solely in terms of the availability of such things as tap-water, electricity, drains, good clothing and medical facilities, then yes, they were poor. But it does not follow that material poverty is inevitably the harbinger of misery. In cases of extreme want it obviously is, but Mek's family, like millions of others in Nepal, owned a house, a little land and a few animals. Their diet was drab, but sufficient. I often met people in the countryside who said something along the lines of 'We're poor, but we're happy.' If asked to expand on this, the answer was always the same: if a family has a house and a little fertile land there is always hope and, to some degree, security, as the land supplies them with their needs for at least part of the year. To own land also implies freedom, without which the spirit is quickly crushed: poverty is a state of mind as well as a state of being. Some will say that this is sheer sophistry, calculated to absolve the rich of any guilt they may feel about the existence of the poor (that the rich do experience such guilt has always struck me as wishful thinking). However, to measure poverty solely in terms of material want is one of the surest ways of encouraging action which may make the materially poor *feel* even poorer.

We had no common language, but had Pat and I been able to talk to Mek's father or mother I doubt whether we would have been any better placed to judge whether or not they were happy with their lot. Language, as a means of communication, is greatly over-rated. The opposite is true of physiognomy. The former may help one gauge the precise level of a person's aspirations; but the latter is sufficient to tell one whether their aspirations are being met. To judge by Mek's parents' expressions, by their way of moving, touching, greeting and eating, they lived in a state of harmony – with themselves, with their relatives and with their land. Their unhappiness, if indeed it could be called that, was directed towards Mek, whom they wished would return home.

The trail which ran below Mek's home and beside the river had already been widened by Chinese engineers; eventually it will be paved, and Baglung will be linked to Pokhara, which is four days' walk away. Cars and buses will come and so too will electricity, traders, new ideas, aid-financed irrigation projects, government officials and much else besides. Mek's family will lose some of their land, for which they shall receive no compensation, but even if that wasn't to happen, would they be the richer for the new developments? Time, no doubt, will tell.

As for Mek, he had tasted the fruits of life beyond his home. He had obviously missed his family, but the longer he had stayed away the more difficult it had become for him to return. He had seen both his mother and father during the past year in Pokhara, and his mother, in particular, had put pressure on him to come back. After we left he said he intended to return for the summer. Perhaps he did; but he had friends in Pokhara, and he enjoyed the stimulation of trekking, which introduced him to all sorts of people and to a way of life which simply does not exist for the peasant in the field.

After supper we all slept. Mek joined Pat and me outside, for there was no room in the house, and we woke at sunrise and breakfasted on chapatis and boiled eggs. The women spent the morning harvesting wheat on a small terrace near the house; Mek's father spread manure in a field by the river; Mek went for a drink in a shack on the trail; and Pat and I sat by a small tributary of the Kali Gandaki with our feet in the water, watching kingfishers and dragonflies. At midday we returned for *daal bhat*, and after some long goodbyes we continued down the trail. It was extremely hot and we made heavy weather of the steep climb up towards Kushma, which led us away from the Kali Gandaki and eastward to a rolling landscape whose forests had been severely plundered for fuelwood and animal fodder.

Kushma was unmemorable, and so was the Friendly Hotel, which had few of the attractions which were advertised on the elaborately painted bill-boards whose purpose was to lure us past the town's other lodge, the Parbat: 'Hot and cold showers ... Boiled and filtered drinking water ... Weekly world news magazines ... Apple pies and pumpkin pies'. There were no pies, no hot water and no magazines. Bed-bugs and lice, however, were here in profusion, and the hotel was run by an obnoxious and garrulous little man in a stars-and-stripes T-shirt. We left as early as we could the next day, and soon came across an advertisement for a hotel in Karkineta, a village we planned to reach that afternoon. The Annapurna Hotel, it was claimed, offered 'Calm and quiet with friendly atmosphere ... we serve food of your tist ... clea toilet and bathroom with showera'. The trail was busy and we must have passed several hundred people that day, including some children who sold us handfuls of *owchelu* berries, which looked like orange brambles and tasted refreshingly bitter. We arrived at Karkineta at two o'clock and checked in at the Hotel Lucky, which hadn't proclaimed its virtues on the trail but for which I shall write an advertisement: 'Small lodge, very clean, hot water for washing served in bowl, simple menu, run by a delightful young couple who share cooking, cleaning and looking after their two small children. Fabulous view.'

Karkineta sat on the apex of a sharp ridge and consisted of little more than a single street with a score of houses on each side. At the northern end there was a pond, full of algal slime, beyond which was a grinding mill. This advertised its presence by making a continuous popping sound that could be heard from a great distance, similar to the noise a child makes by plucking a finger against the inside of its cheek. The effect was achieved at the mill by a device of great simplicity, a clay pot attached to the top of the exhaust flue. This primitive musical instrument served no practical purpose whatever, but it was much favoured in those parts of the countryside where petrol or diesel engines were few: 'Look,' it seemed to say, 'we've got a machine!'

Throughout the afternoon the heat rose and the long views were foreshortened by a shimmering haze, presaging a thunderstorm which broke while we ate supper. 'Very bad for centipedes,' commented Mek with satisfaction. He explained that the goddess Indra had a son who was killed by a centipede; with lightning she takes retribution on the species. We woke the following morning to clear blue skies and a fresh breeze and as we left the main street we were greeted by the proprietor of ISHOR MEDICAL SERVICES, a stocky, round-faced man who introduced himself as Dunparsad Gurung. He had served in the Signals Corps with the British Gurkhas, and had been stationed for a while at Warminster, in Wiltshire. He also knew Beaconsfield well, as he'd done a language course there. He had retired seven years ago – he must have been in his late thirties now – and had taken a short course on basic health care before setting up this small privately run pharmacy at Karkineta. Villagers came to him for medicines – he could treat scabies, vomiting and diarrhoea, the main scourges of childhood – but for more serious diseases such as TB and cholera he referred people to Pokhara. 'Anything helps here,' he said.

It took us an hour to descend a steep terraced hillside to the valley below, and on the way down we passed half a dozen porters struggling up the hill with loads of corrugated tin. The younger among them – some were in their mid-teens – were in considerable pain, and they panted and groaned pitifully. Each carried eight sheets of tin which measured eight foot by three, and even the mildest puff of wind retarded their progress. Ours, in contrast, was brisk, and we had covered a good distance by the time we stopped for a drink in a village surrounded by rice paddies. Here we quickly attracted the attention of passing school children, who stopped to practise their English and show us their exercise books. We were also joined by a slight, bearded man who invited us to visit the government health post in the next village, Chilaune Bas. As we made our way through the rice paddies Mr Resham, the assistant health worker, chatted about the problems of health care. I asked him what infections and diseases he came across, and he reeled off a long list which included measles, bronchitis, diarrhoea, whooping cough, polio and TB. Among porters sprains and fractures were common. He also dispensed contraceptive pills to women and sheaths to men.

The health centre was an attractive stone building with a slate roof. The flower-beds in front of the surgery door were full of Madagascan periwinkle, which was decorative here but whose medical significance is considerable: an extract from the plant is used in the treatment of leukaemia. We sat around for a while waiting for a peon to come with the key. A dozen children – some unaccompanied, others with a parent – came and joined us. The surgery was small, clean and almost bare. Mr Resham sat at a desk with a floral-patterned vinyl cover. There were two posters on the wall, one on how to identify smallpox, the other on chicken-pox. Mr Resham was armed with a stethoscope and nothing else. The first patient was a five-year-old girl who lifted her dress and bent down to show her bottom. 'Scabies,' announced Mr Resham, who wrote down in a large ledger the girl's name and age and details of the disease. He had already given her an injection of penicillin, which he thought was working, and he asked her if she had been washing thoroughly. Yes, she said. The next patient, another young girl, had whooping cough, and she was followed by a young boy who was covered with scabies sores. Mr Resham delivered a homily on the importance of washing frequently and berated the boy for not doing so. 'Many of the parents are uneducated,' he said turning to us, 'and they work too hard to bother keeping their children clean.'

It is impossible to understate the importance of cleanliness in a country such as Nepal: the biggest killers, especially of children, are diseases which result from eating and drinking dirty food and water. One in five children dies before his or her fifth birthday, over one-fifth as a result of enteritis and other diarrhoeal diseases, all of which can easily be treated. Many of the rest are killed by illnesses which are curable or can be prevented through vaccination. The worst affected are of course the poor. The rate of infant deaths per 1,000 is 111 for the rich, 195 for the poor and 250 for the very poor. After their first year, mortality among children in the countryside is twice as great as for those in towns, a reflection of the lower family incomes, poorer health care facilities and less efficient immunization programmes in rural areas; the situation is particularly chronic in the hills and mountains. Nutritional standards are obviously worse among the poor than the rich, and the value of the food eaten is lessened by the widespread presence of internal parasites. One survey found that 72 per cent of children were infested by worms, mostly roundworm; another carried out in villages in the Kathmandu Valley discovered that four out of five people had roundworm and everyone had hookworm and whipworm. If you need any proof of the poor state of the nation's stomachs you need do no more than observe the communal latrines in the fields around the villages: most people suffer from a permanent looseness of the bowels.

Health care is about many things: dispensing medicines and setting up immunization programmes are obviously important, but the provision of clean water and the dissemination of messages stressing the significance of hygiene are also crucial. All this costs money, of which there is an acute shortage. The entire expenditure on health for 1986–7 was in the region of $26 million, which is rather less than the cost of the RCUP, about which more in a moment. Some of the most important units in the health set-up are the 800 health posts. 'The ratio between health posts and population is 1 to 21,280,' according to the National Planning Commission, which goes on to state:

Viewed from the angle of the services to be delivered, their number is piteously low, not to say negligible. There is a great need for multiplying their number with all speed so the people can derive benefit from whatever curative and preventative measures they are competent and equipped to provide. In addition, it is also greatly required that the quality of services made available through the health posts be improved appreciably.

In Mr Resham the health post at Chilaune Bas had a man of sensitivity and dedication; but he, like others in his position, was constrained by a lack of medicines and skilled assistance.

We left him to his patients after a cup of tea and followed a train of a hundred mules to a village where fourteen *sadhus* were encamped in a field. 'One or two *sadhus* is okay,' announced Mek. 'Many *sadhus* is no good. *Sadhu* is lazy; he not work.' Our progress during the afternoon was slow. A grey drizzle turned our clothes soggy and we frequently slithered off the trail into rice paddies. The closer we came to the main road, the more the villages resembled shanties. Thatched roofs gave way to tin and the trail widened into a gravelled road. The rain ran in muddy gullies outside the houses and the villages had the unkempt and forlorn appearance of waterlogged dogs. Bits of old machinery and other junk lay rusting beside the road and wild boar, captured from the forests as piglets, shivered miserably in wooden cages. We reached the road in mid-afternoon and took the first bus to Pokhara. We parted with Mek that evening with considerable sadness and caught a bus the following morning to Kathmandu. From Kathmandu Pat caught a flight to Varanesi, whence she made her way to Delhi and London.

It would be imprudent to attempt anything other than the haziest of predictions about the future of the Kali Gandaki. That life for the people of the valley will change more rapidly over the next decade than it has over the last thirty years seems inevitable. The government plans to build a 1,000-kilowatt hydro-electric scheme at Tatopani, and sooner or later a road will link Pokhara with Baglung, and eventually with the towns of the Upper Kali Gandaki. These projects alone will transform the valley. There is ample evidence to show that roads in the Himalaya can lead to environmental devastation and social disruption on a massive scale. Paved roads are invariably expensive to build – in 1978 the estimated cost of building a road from Beni to Lo Mantang, which lies four days' walk north of Jomsom, was 852 million rupees ($70 million) – and they are invariably expensive to maintain.

At present the RCUP stands as a salutary monument to the pitfalls of development. That the project ran into so many difficulties is especially sad, as the Americans embarked on it with the best of intentions. It was conceived in the mid-1970s at a time when most scientists and aid agencies had latched on to the notion that the Himalaya was in the grip of a terrible environmental crisis: the RCUP's aim was to 'halt the rapid degradation of Nepal's environment'. This was also a period of soul-searching for the aid agencies, when many of the problems of the past were being attributed – quite rightly – to the prevalent 'top-down' approach to development. Decisions about what was needed, and where, were made in the remote bureaucracies of Kathmandu (or in the capitals of the donor countries), and dams, roads, irrigation schemes and so forth were imposed willy-nilly on the intended beneficiaries, who were seldom consulted about their needs and hardly ever involved in the planning of the projects. The RCUP was going to be different: it was to be 'bottom-up', with a limited reliance on infrastructure and a strong emphasis on 'people's participation'.

'Right from the start,' said Burt Levenson, 'the project was very complex. We tried to solve all the resource problems in an integrated fashion and, to be honest, the RCUP was over-ambitious.' There were four main components to the project. First, there was a large training programme, which led to over fifty Nepalese receiving masters degrees in the States, the Philippines and Indonesia in such subjects as agronomy, soil science and civil engineering. Most are now working in Nepal. Second, the RCUP gave financial support to the Institute of Forestry at Hetauda, a result of which had been a doubling in the number of qualified foresters working in the Ministry of Forests. According to Levenson, these training schemes were highly successful, and it was the last two components of the RCUP which had attracted most criticism: the construction of over 180 buildings in the areas in which the RCUP operated (Mustang, Gorkha and Myagdi), and the field activities which had been carried out in conjunction with the relevant government departments.

I lost count of the number of RCUP buildings we passed between Jharkot and Beni, and my efforts to meet RCUP personnel working in them were largely unsuccessful. Indeed, many of the buildings were locked up. We seldom had to ask where they were; most stood out like sore thumbs. At Jharkot the compound lay about a mile to the south of the village and consisted of six single-storey buildings with substantial stone walls and flat roofs. The forestry building was closed, as was the RCUP office. The only sign of life was a peon, who was sitting in the 'Animal Hospital'. He told us that we would find the project officer in Jomsom. Unfortunately he had left for Jharkot when we arrived. We passed more RCUP buildings at Ghasa, Marpha and Kalopani – always substantial in size and notable for their lack of beauty. At Tatopani, however, we came across a building of greater architectural merit. It looked like an enormous prehistoric butterfly whose slate wings had been tipped up at unusual angles. I had already heard much about this building. One British aid worker had told me that when he first saw it he thought it must be a holiday residence for the king, and indeed many referred to it as Tatopani palace. 'It's a fine building,' suggested Levenson. Had it been in the United States or Europe I would have agreed, and it would no doubt have been lauded for its adventurous design. Here it looked very out of place.

These buildings had been built to provide homes and offices for HMG staff working on the RCUP. 'It's difficult to get someone with a masters degree from South Carolina to work in remote villages,' said Levenson. 'The only rooms to rent are ones which no one else wants and if they live in them they lose face.' This was undoubtedly true, but the scale of the buildings went far beyond what was called for, thus creating much resentment among the villagers. Even the chief district officers lived in buildings far 'inferior' to those which had been built for the RCUP officials (who, with few exceptions, were to be well-educated, high-caste Hindus from the Kathmandu Valley). USAID decided early on in the project that the buildings should be built by local contractors with local labour and materials, which was praiseworthy. 'It would have been much easier to put it out to worldwide contract,' said Levenson. 'The South Koreans could have done in three months what we did in three years.' Levenson's denial that there had been any corruption or pay-offs was questioned by others I spoke to who had had dealings with the RCUP. Indeed, many thought that the only people really to have benefited from the construction projects had been the contractors, many of whom had made small fortunes. At Tatopani the villagers complained that an entire forest had been felled to supply building timber for the RCUP office. Admittedly, it was not the forest from which the locals gathered their fuelwood; but it was a forest all the same and one of the RCUP's principal objectives was to establish more forests, not denude those already in existence.

The nicknames given to the RCUP were revealing. Some called it the 'helicopter project'. In the early days – the project's planning phase began in 1977 – villagers became used to seeing helicopters. They would land near a village and a few white people would step out, scan the horizon, then climb in again and fly off. This led to the belief that the RCUP was a scheme for training pilots. Other names given to it were 'RC-rupee', with its connotations of free handouts, and the 'Second Arab', the 'First Arab' referring to the Saudi HEP project which was said to entail massive wastage of money.

The RCUP was neither carefully planned nor 'bottom-up'. Expatriate

1 (RIGHT) *Kathmandu: a temple beside the Bisnumati River*

2 (BELOW) *A sweeper family in the slums beside the Bisnumati, Kathmandu*

3 (ABOVE) *Religion on the streets: children playing at the foot of the chariot of the Seco Machchhindranath in Kathmandu*

5 (OPPOSITE LEFT) *Looking down on Namche Bazar*

6 (OPPOSITE RIGHT) *Tibetan refugees, Kusaang and Peti Tsering, at Namche Bazar*

7 (OPPOSITE BELOW) *Brot Coburn with Sherpa porters, Luckla airstrip*

4 (RIGHT) *Swayambhunath Temple, to the west of Kathmandu*

8 (ABOVE) *Chitwan – a tranquillized tiger and* (CENTRE) *Hemanta and Sushma Mishra and Jim Fowler*

9 (LEFT) *A mule train heading up the Kali Gandaki, south of Jomsom*

10 (BELOW) *Mek drinking tea in the Kali Gandaki*

11 (LEFT) *Mek's family, near Baglung*

12 (BELOW) *A wall of prayer wheels, Kagbeni*

13 (ABOVE) *Pakhribas's seed distribution centre, in the* panchayat *of Phalate*

14 (RIGHT) *A market at Jiri Bazaar*

15 (ABOVE) *The main street at Those*

16 (RIGHT) *Luti Maya Chepang and grandchildren, Shimthali*

17 (LEFT) *Chepangs carrying maize*

18 (BELOW) *Nepal Australia Forestry Project – a school nursery near Chautara. Andrew Carter stands at the far end, beyond Don Gilmour*

research teams carried out nearly all the preliminary survey work. Some had never previously worked in Nepal and they spent as little as two weeks in the project areas, during which time they were supposed to identify all the problems and make recommendations for their resolution. It was one of these short-term experts who chose the eleven main components of the field activities, which came under such headings as forestry, drinking water provision, livestock husbandry, fisheries, watershed management and so on. Each was to be implemented by the relevant government department, and this in itself meant that field operations – ultimately, the RCUP's *raisons d'être* – floundered in a mire of bureaucracy. HMG was in many ways as much to blame for the project's failure as USAID.

The project began work in 1980, and apart from the buildings there was little to show for it now along the Kali Gandaki. A few tree nurseries were operating successfully, and Marpha had benefited from an irrigation scheme. There was nothing, however, to justify the amount of money and time which had been expended on the project. 'If they had just done something simple like piping decent water to Tatopani,' suggested one Nepali official, 'then the Americans would have been friends of the villagers for life.' As it was, the story had been one of promises unfulfilled and ensuing resentment. By 1985 the failure of the RCUP was recognized by USAID itself, and funding for the project was greatly reduced. It now operates in only three small areas, where I gather it is having some success. The many empty buildings will no doubt be put to use before long, especially if the road and other development projects go ahead as planned. Their occupants will be government officials. Levenson was keen to stress that their construction had helped to create a skilled force of local artisans who will be much in demand once the road comes and a building boom follows. 'These buildings were built to very high specifications,' he said. 'What we've done is set a new standard for building construction in Nepal.' The idea that Americans, or anyone else for that matter, can teach Nepalis how to build is a novel one. Suffice it to say that there are temples in Nepal which have stood for almost 1,000 years, and in every village along the Kali Gandaki there are houses – of mud and thatch, stone and slate – which display a standard of craftsmanship which would not be improved by techniques imported from Washington or Edwziepfel.

5

Return to
Kathmandu

We were now into May and on most days the weather was sultry and oppressive: Kathmandu sweated like a neglected hunk of cheese and smelt like one too. While the city's inhabitants simmered below a pall of pre-monsoon haze, nature indulged in clammy celebration: the plants in the ditches round the Vajra seemed to grow before one's eyes, not prettily as young girls do, but grotesquely, like sumo wrestlers or force-fed geese. The elderberry was still in fleshy flower, but it was being strangled now by wiry tendrils of lilac convolvulus, and the cannabis had grown, over the short period of three weeks, from seedlings into waist-high plants. The population of dogs along the riverside appeared somewhat diminished – by poisoning, apparently – but the pigs were thriving. I was especially pleased to see that one of the sows I knew had recently farrowed. She spent the days lying in a scrape beneath a piple tree with nine piglets protruding from her glabrous undercarriage like a row of pink bombs.

On my return from Pokhara I booked a ticket for a flight to Biratnagar, which left me with a week to spend in and around Kathmandu. I was happy to be back. Christoph and his countess had returned from their wanderings; Charles was still at the Vajra; and Sabine and her friends were putting on nightly performances of the play, which meant that many strange faces appeared in the hotel each evening. So far I had seen little of the valley beyond Kathmandu and Patan. Now I ventured farther afield, by bus, cycle and foot, into a Brueghelesque world of reapers and gleaners. The countryside was looking mellow, generous, almost autumnal. The wheat harvest had begun and the peasants laid sheaves across the roads for the buses and lorries to thresh. Some of the fields would be ploughed soon, then sown with another crop. Others were being put to a more curious use, and indeed nowhere else in the world have I come across a system of crop rotation which involves the harvesting of the soil as well as what grows upon it: once the corn had been cut, brick-makers moved on to the stubble fields, set up kilns and dug for clay.

I twice took the tram out to Bhaktapur, the most perfectly preserved of the valley's cities, and on another day I took the bus to the botanic gardens at Godaveri, which spread across a gentle hillside some fifteen miles to the south-west of Patan. On my ramble round the gardens I was accompanied by a mangy cur, which I failed to drive away with my umbrella, and an elderly Brahman couple from Biratnagar. The man was small, bespectacled and plump; his wife, tall, heavy-boned and flat-footed. He and I walked together, discussing his wife's medical problems and cricket (he was a great admirer of Ian Botham), while his wife clopped along behind us like an old horse. 'I come here for wife to see doctor,' he confided in a whisper. 'She having her nose done. Very big thing.' He said there was something else wrong with her too, but I waited in vain for the details. Maybe it was her feet.

My affection for Kathmandu increased daily, although the more I heard about how it used to be, the more I envied those who had known it ten years earlier. Kathmandu the intimate village had become Kathmandu the cosmopolitan city: it was larger, more crowded, noisier and dirtier than before. Of all the stories I heard about the changes, the one which struck me as most poignant came from Hemanta. When he was a young man – twenty-odd years ago – he used to walk from his home in Patan to New Road, where he would buy fifteen or twenty newspapers. 'I was for ever stopping to chat to people I knew,' he recalled, 'and a fifteen-minute walk used to take me anything up to an hour. Now I could go all the way there without meeting anyone I knew.'

In those days there were few cars in Kathmandu and the streets belonged to people and animals. Today the traffic is acutely congested, the air reeks of car fumes, and walking in the narrow streets of the old city has become a hazardous occupation. The recently built Chinese ring-road, whose purpose was to take pressure off the city centre, has done little to improve matters. Drivers still take the shortest route from A to B, even if it takes them longer, timewise, than travelling round the outskirts.

I was fascinated by the Nepalese attitude to crime. One was for ever being warned to watch out for thieves, even in the remotest parts of the countryside. Mek, for example, was worried – ludicrously, I'm sure – about us sleeping outdoors when we stayed with his parents; and I was constantly reminded about the two tourists who were murdered in the Annapurna Sanctuary a year or so ago. In Kathmandu I met many people who claimed that street-crime had increased over recent years, though seldom did anyone proffer evidence for this. Blame was generally directed at the city's junkies. According to *The Police Gazette*, an old copy of which I'd found in Beni, the number of heroin addicts in the Kathmandu Valley had risen from 500 in 1980 to over 10,000 by 1987. That people were worried by this trend was quite understandable: to put the figure of 10,000 into perspective one should remember that the population of the valley's three main conurbations – Kathmandu, Patan and Bhaktapur – was less than half a million. However, I have no idea what evidence there is, if any, for a rising crime rate, and unfortunately my edition of Nepal's *Statistical Pocket Book* doesn't give comparative figures for different years. What it does provide is some clue as to the relative occurrence of different crimes. Here are a few of the statistics for 1984–5 collated by 'Police Headquater' (*sic*):

Dacoity with murder	28
Murder	311
Suicide	559
Cow slaughter	35
Rape	46
Street robbery	48
Theft	677
Stealing animals	81
Political crime	23
Dealing in persons	91
Polygamy	137
'Some public offenses'	576
Traffic accidents – injuries	137
Traffic accidents – persons killed	362
Violence of trafficoules	61

One's confidence in the accuracy of these figures is somewhat diminished by the table which precedes it for the 'Total number of legal cases filed in courts'. The figures given for assault, murder and theft are 4,270, 3,902 and 4,090 respectively: the Supreme Court appears to have come across many more crimes than Police Headquarters. Whichever figures you choose to believe, it seems clear that crime against strangers – I have always been comforted by the knowledge that the vast majority of murders are committed among friends and family – is still a rare phenomenon in Nepal. I felt infinitely safer walking round Kathmandu in the middle of the night than I ever have done in an English town.

It was the lack of taxis, rather than the presence of thieves, which aggravated me most after dark. Kathmandu may have become a city, but its inhabitants have retained the peasant habit of getting up and going to bed early. By nine o'clock in the evening the streets were almost deserted and finding a taxi after ten o'clock was impossible. At the best of times, taxi-drivers were loath to make the journey from the centre of the city to the Vajra, and those who were prepared to do so often demanded twice what they would charge for a trip of similar distance in other directions. Had it not been for the dogs by the river the nocturnal lack of taxis would never have bothered me. Indeed, I enjoyed the emptiness of the streets at night.

I remember one late outing in particular. During the early days of my stay, Brot, Didi and I went for dinner in Patan at the home of George McBean and his wife Sarah Cameron. We left around midnight, Brot and Didi on their motorbike, I on a pushbike. My friends kindly chugged along at a pace with which I could keep up, and together we made our way back across the Bagmati and up towards Thamel. Most of the streets were ill-lit or unlit, the latter being the case for the main road which skirted round Tundikhel, the great expanse of mown grass to the south-east of the city where during the day crowds would gather beneath the jacaranda trees to observe soldiers on parade, and sometimes peasants herding ducks or goats. We passed neither cars nor people, and nothing besides tarmac, pot-holes and broken paving appeared in the cone of light which pierced the darkness in front of the motorbike. Then just as we came to the point where New Road met Tundikhel the headlamp illuminated two enormous bulls. Both were reared up on their hindlegs and their heavy heads were locked in a menacing embrace. As we passed they hardly moved; it was as though we'd had flashed before us, in the flickering light of an old magic lantern, a photograph of a bronze sculpture.

I read voraciously during my week in Kathmandu, particularly on the afternoons when it rained. I finished *Huckleberry Finn*, which I had started weeks earlier, then raced through Hemingway's *A Farewell to Arms* and novels by Norman Lewis and Graham Greene. This meant frequent visits to Kathmandu's second-hand bookshops, most of which were to be found in Thamel alongside the cheap hotels, tourist agencies and shops hiring bicycles and trekking gear. In my favourite shop the books were arranged alphabetically by author, and if you were looking for a romantic novel or a pulp thriller you had to wade past the classics and vice versa. There was Cartland next to Camus, Bagley beside Baudelaire, Robbins beside Rimbaud. Having chosen a book, I'd either eat at one of the restaurants in Thamel or retire to the library in the British Council, which squatted across the road from the magnificent Bahadur Bhawan. This building used to be the famous Royal Hotel – it now houses the Elections Commission – and it was here that foreign travellers met the equally famous Boris Lissanevitch, the subject of *Tiger for Breakfast* and by all accounts as quixotic as the dishes he used to serve to visiting royalty and others fortunate enough to dine at his table. I couldn't help feeling, as I sat in the library reading the reports on Nepal written by early

British visitors, that most of them seemed drab when compared to Boris.

The first British visitor to Nepal was Colonel Kirkpatrick, who was sent on a mission by the Bengal government in 1793 at the request of the Nepali rulers, who feared that the capital was about to be overrun by the Chinese. By the time Kirkpatrick arrived, the 'belligerents' had settled their dispute, which gave him time to observe daily life in Kathmandu, Patan and Bhaktapur. He was much impressed by the Nepalis' ability to work hard and by their 'great corporal strength', but disgusted, like many of those who followed him, by the squalor of Kathmandu. 'The streets are excessively narrow,' he wrote, 'and nearly as filthy as those of Benares.' Kirkpatrick was scornful about the vegetables, especially the cabbages and peas, 'both of which were of the worst kind'.

A more thorough observer of the agricultural scene was Francis Buchanan Hamilton, a doctor who came to Kathmandu in 1801 with the first British Resident, Captain Knox, whose portrait I'd seen in the Kaiser Library. He thought highly of the cucumbers, garlic and radishes grown on the outskirts of the city, although he found the fields of wheat strangled by cannabis. He declared that the inhabitants of Kathmandu were much given to drinking spirituous liquors, to intoxicating themselves with cannabis and to behaving in a most dissolute fashion. 'I have seen no country where the venereal disease is so common as in Nepal,' he wrote.

The coming to power of the Ranas led to a building boom but no improvement in public sanitation. Daniel Wright, a surgeon attached to the British Residency in the 1870s, reported:

The streets of Kathmandu are very narrow, mere lanes in fact; and the whole town is very dirty ... to clean the drains would now be impossible without knocking down the entire city, as the whole ground is saturated with filth. In short, from a sanitary point of view, Kathmandu may be said to be built on a dunghill in the middle of latrines.

Plus ça change, plus c'est la même chose. Wright had previously been a surgeon-major in the Indian Medical Service and he brought to this independent kingdom the superior attitudes of the Raj official. He had a dreadful time, and he found the ruling classes arrogant, conceited and ill-mannered, their lengthy leisure hours given up to 'gossiping, gambling and debauchery of all sorts'. He was particularly appalled by their children:

Attempts have been made at various times by their tutors to get the young men to play at cricket and other games, but such amusements are thought degrading. Even to walk is beneath their dignity, and when moving about in their own houses and grounds, they are generally carried pick-a-back by a slave or attendant.

'The subject of schools and colleges in Nepal,' wrote Wright, 'may be treated as briefly as that of snakes in Ireland. There are none.' Needless to say, much progress has been made in the field of education since Wright's day. By the time the Ranas were ousted from power there were only 321 primary schools in Nepal. There are now about 12,000, and much of the credit for this should go to USAID, which helped the government to set up a national education system. Although many of the rich send their children to schools in India, there are some excellent ones in the Kathmandu Valley, including one run by Jesuit priests at Godaveri, and another, which is supported by the British government, at Budhanilkantha. The male members of the royal family go to the latter before proceeding to Eton, where, presumably, they are prevailed upon to play cricket.

Wright's sketch of Nepal is entertaining but superficial, and one is left with the impression that he was simply serving time before being shifted to some other corner of the globe, where he would have to deal with another batch of idolatrous natives bent on pursuing their own ends rather than serving those of the Empire. Of much greater interest is Brian Houghton Hodgson, who spent twenty-three years in the country and contributed more than anyone else to the outside world's knowledge of Nepal. He was born in England in 1800 and came to Kathmandu in 1820. He was made Assistant Resident in 1825 and Resident in 1833, a post which he held for ten years.

Hodgson's letters to his sister Fan showed him to be a man of charm and sensitivity, fascinated by the strangeness of the country, frustrated by the duplicity of the Nepalese rulers, and constantly beset by loneliness, to which he frequently referred: 'So long as I lived in the world I was, by all men's voice, a "lady's man", and truly I feel not that I am altered, albeit I have not seen the fringe of a petticoat for eight years, and therefore dare not speak positively. But then I am, I must be, a bookworm! Books I love!' A little later, in 1833, he told Fan: 'I am thirty-three – the last thirteen years passed in the wilderness without wife, children, or the presence of a female ... My society is unchanging and limited to my suite – a secretary, commander of the escort, and surgeon, all very pleasant in their various ways.' His companions used to join him after dinner to play billiards and backgammon, but mostly we find Hodgson alone, shooting woodcock and riding in the valley during the afternoons, or studying, after the others had gone to bed, the latest work to reach him from his bookseller in Cornhill.

Hodgson's letters referred occasionally to the interests which occupied most of his time. 'Zoology in the branch of birds and quadrupeds amuses me much,' he wrote, in a tone which belied the seriousness with which he pursued his studies, and he went on:

I have three natives always employed in drawing from nature. I possess a live tiger, a wild sheep, a wild goat, four bears, three civets, and three score of our beautiful pheasants. A rare menagerie! And my drawings now amount to two thousand. The antiquities, too, of the land afford me much entertainment. I pore over the pictorial, scriptural, and architectural monuments of Buddhism by the light of the ancient books of the sect; and the learned Thebans of your isle appear to gather up my gleanings with eagerness. But the past chiefly interests me as it can be made to illustrate the present – the origin, genius, character, and attainments of the people.

The tone of the letters was gentle and wry, and had it not been for the stream of learned papers which made their way back to Europe, Hodgson's family might have thought him the typical Victorian gentleman, eclectic in his interests and dabbling in whatever caught his fancy. Hodgson published four volumes on Nepal and some 170 papers. He described the physical geography of the Himalaya; wrote papers on the caste system and Hindu law; discussed the origins and habits of many hill tribes; and discovered and described various animals and plants then unknown to the scientists of the West, some of which, such as the rhododendron *Hodgsonia heteroclita*, were named after him.

Hodgson's influence on affairs beyond the borders of Nepal was also considerable. He experimented with tea bushes in the garden of the Residency, and he urged the colonial government in India to grow tea commercially in Darjeeling, which it did before long. He even joined in the great controversy during the 1830s about the future of state education in India. Five members of the ominously named Committee for Public Instruction, including Lord Macaulay, argued that the Indians should be taught in English; the remaining five championed Sanskrit, which, to most Indians, was also a foreign language. Hodgson resolved the dispute by sensibly suggesting that they should be taught in their mother tongues. His views on education remain of interest today, if only because they constituted a negation of the belief – widely held then, and judging from some of the foreign aid projects I saw, by no means uncommon now – that Western culture is in some way inherently superior to that of the East. Having said that, I must admit to feeling some pleasure in meeting Nepalese children who knew rather more about Aesop, Twain and Dickens than most of their peers in the West. Hodgson, incidentally, lived to a great age and experienced two happy marriages, which, one hopes, went some way towards compensating for the isolation he endured in Nepal.

Most of the accounts by foreigners about life in Nepal during the last century make dull reading. They are descriptive, rather than analytic, and I always found myself frustrated by the authors' reluctance to give vent to their inner feelings. The exception was Hodgson, and from his letters I got a keen idea of how the outsider coped with life in Nepal. What really endeared me to him was the business about the petticoat – but I wanted to know more. Did he desire the girls in the street? And if he didn't take on lovers, which the letters to Fan seem to confirm, did his abstinence flow from moral choice, or because local mores forbade such inter-racial communion? One often learns as much about a country through writers who gossip and resort to reverie than by reading orthodox histories. The modern traveller to countries well-trod by the literary figures of the past is fortunate in this respect. Look, for example, at Africa: you have Flaubert, Forster and Durrell on Egypt; de Monfried and Waugh on Ethiopia; Greene on Liberia; Pepys on Morocco; and so on. No comparable writers came to Nepal during the last century or the first half of this one.

Prior to 1951, Nepal's history was predominantly one of isolation. Until then the only foreign country with a diplomatic presence in Kathmandu was Britain. From time to time special envoys were dispatched to the Nepalese court and once a year officials were sent to inspect the British Resident's escort, but few others were permitted to cross the border with India: between 1881 and 1924 only sixty-four Europeans made the journey to Kathmandu. When the Ranas were overthrown in 1951 King Tribhuvan became monarch in the true sense of the word, and immediately established diplomatic relations with dozens of countries, many of which were keen to help Nepal 'develop'. The foreigners – whether diplomats, development experts or contractors – were enticed into the country not because the Nepalese rulers wanted them to enjoy the scenery, but because their presence was seen as an essential prerequisite of development, which, in its simplest sense, was – and remains – a matter of creating wealth and alleviating poverty. Foreigners were welcomed, and Kathmandu changed rapidly to accommodate them.

Over the years the expatriate community has expanded, both numerically – there are now some 2,000 Westerners living in the Kathmandu Valley – and in terms of its stratification. Besides those working in the diplomatic service and the aid business (a heterogeneous bunch in themselves), there are many others pursuing their own interests and professions. A considerable number work in the tourist industry. They run trekking agencies, lead groups round the country and provide all the services which short-term visitors – there were a quarter of a million in 1986 – require. Others have set up businesses dealing in carpets, antiques and clothes. Some have come to Nepal to study Buddhism under Tibetan *lamas*; others, to write books or to paint.

Nepal has also attracted hordes of academics, some of whom have spent long periods in the country, working on theses for Western universities and conducting studies for aid agencies, governments or posterity.

Prominent among them have been the anthropologists, and it would be instructive if one day they left the Sherpas, Tamangs, Thakalis and other 'ethnic groups' alone and put the expatriate community under the microscope. Rather than asking such questions as: 'How many of your children died last year?'; 'How old were you when you married'; 'How many buffaloes do you have?', they could ask the expatriates: 'Do you have a video?'; 'How much did you pay for your computer?'; 'Do you deserve the amount of money you earn?' Perhaps this is rather unfair (generalizations always are), as there are many expatriates who live quite modestly, and there are still small communities in Kathmandu and Pokhara whose members live a hand-to-mouth existence much as the hippies did in the 1960s and early 1970s. But the fact remains that many expatriates working in Nepal are paid colossal salaries. One good friend, an American, told me he needed $25,000 a year just to live comfortably. This struck me as outrageous, though it was modest compared to the annual salaries of many expatriates who worked in the aid business, for whom $75,000 a year was nothing exceptional. 'I've worked with both Canadians and Japanese,' one Nepalese engineer told me, 'and for doing the same kind of work as my Western counterparts I was earning a hundred times less than them. I'm willing to grant them more – it's part of our hospitality; they are our guests. But a hundred times more! I was getting 800 rupees a month and my counterpart 100,000 – and this in a country where the prime minister's salary was 4,000 rupees a month.'

When Pat and I had returned from Pokhara we'd found Charles and Christoph relaxing over tea in the Vajra's garden. Charles expressed astonishment that we should have enjoyed our trip. He loathed the countryside, and before our departure he had claimed that the only place worthy of a visit in the Annapurna region was Muktinath, which we had failed to reach. 'Oh, well, never mind,' he said, 'there's not much there – just a few old waterspouts; and the accommodation's terrible.' Needless to say, Charles had remained in Kathmandu during our absence, though in his imagination he was already on his way to London: Ascot and Claridges beckoned.

Christoph, in contrast, had been intensely active. He had just returned from a trip into the mountains to the west of Dhaulagiri, whose eastern flank Pat and I had skirted during the previous weeks. With him had been Marie de Poncheville, whom I now met for the first time. Marie was a journalist (and *une comtesse*, as Charles kept reminding me) and she had come to Nepal to write an article about the shamans they had visited. She was fortyish, stylishly dressed, and beautiful in a classical French way, with clear, tanned skin, brown hair and eyes, strong features and a large, sensual mouth. The expedition had been organized by Christoph, and on hearing Marie's description of it I made a mental note never to accompany him anywhere. They took five days to cover a distance for which most people allowed twelve, and this over terrain infinitely more difficult than anything I had experienced. In many places the path was non-existent, which meant traversing cliffs on tiny ledges. They even had to abandon a horse on their way back. Frequently they were on the go for twelve hours or more and Marie, who was the only woman on the trip, often found herself trailing far behind Christoph and their guides. She said she spent a good deal of time crying with pain. Even Christoph, who was renowned for his powers of endurance, admitted that the trip had exhausted him. From what I could gather, the shamans practise a religion which is based on magic and sorcery. All the important decisions affecting the community are taken in a trance, and the priests go for days without sleeping. To make sense of things, Christoph and Marie had to forsake sleep as well.

They were now about to make another journey into the hills, this time to the monastery of Tupten Choling, which was mid-way between Namche Bazar and Jiri, and about three days' walk from each for the average person (Brot once covered the whole distance in eighteen hours). In the days before the airstrip was built at Luckla anyone going to Namche and Everest had to pass through this region. Some still do, and those who intend to should read Hugh Downs's excellent book, *Rhythms of a Himalayan Village*, and see Christoph's film, *Lord of the Dance – Destroyer of Illusion*. One evening Christoph ran the film at the Vajra for a small audience of friends, many of whom were Tibetans who were in the documentary or who had helped him make it. Among them was Sang-Sang, a young monk whom Christoph introduced as the reincarnation of the father of the present abbot of the monastery, Tulshig Rimpoche. 'It is a difficult film,' explained Christoph before it began. In the sense that it was long (about three hours) it was 'difficult'; it demanded of the viewer both patience and concentration.

Lord of the Dance was about the festival of Mani Rimdu and the month-long preparations for it. As a piece of film-making it was outstanding, and many striking images still linger in my memory. There was the abbot, making his way on a white horse down a steep forested hillside like some Chaucerian pilgrim. There was the gloom inside the monastery, occasionally pierced by brilliant shafts of grainy sunlight that illuminated the shaven heads of the monks or fell on the stone floor. There were the macabre and terrifying masks worn by the monks during ritual dances. And there were the incongruous imports from the outside world: Chinese umbrellas, a green rucksack, a paraffin lamp . . .

One of the things which impressed me about Christoph as a film-maker was the sensitive way in which he went about the job. The first time he visited Tupten Choling he went alone and without a camera. The following year he took a film crew, but they were there simply to see what happened and to enable the monks to get to know them. No filming was done until the year after. Instead of leaving the monks with a thank you and a bag of rupees once the filming was over – the standard procedure among the makers of documentaries – they asked the monks whether there was anything they could do for them. The monks said they needed to re-roof part of the monastery. Christoph then set about raising some money to do this.

The other great event at the Vajra was the annual play, which was being rehearsed when I first arrived. It was long and gruesome. *Ling Gesar* was subtitled 'Episodes of the Superhuman Life of the Tibetan Hero', and I can't tell you much more about it than that. The first episode, according to the programme notes, was the 'Origin of the demons'; the twenty-sixth and last, 'Gesar appears as the Horpa's god Namthig and brings his plot to a horrific conclusion'. It was the noisiest play I have ever seen and the least intelligible. Sabine was magnificent as a male villain, and she played her part with Falstaffian gusto and great skill. My other two friends among the cast – a little French girl called Marie, and a tall Austrian girl called Sita (also a countess, according to Charles) – showed what critics condescendingly call 'promise'. One of the problems for the actors and actresses was language. Only two of the cast had been brought up speaking English, and the assortment of accents – French, German, Nepali, Tibetan, American – lent an air of bedroom farce to the most serious of scenes. It was like listening to Winston Churchill or Queen Elizabeth speaking French, only the other way round. All the same, it would have taken a cast of some brilliance to have made much of the script. I should mention that I met many people who were full of praise for other plays that the Vajra had put on in the past. I had obviously picked the wrong year to see one.

Shortly before I departed for Biratnagar the cast set off in a bus for Dharmsala, a town in the Punjab which had become home to the exiled Dalai Lama and many of his Tibetan followers. They put on several performances of *Ling Gesar*, which was apparently much appreciated. Charles, predictably, expressed horror that anyone should travel such a distance overland, especially at this time of year. He also did his best to dissuade me from going to Biratnagar. He said it was a foul place. He was, as I soon discovered, quite right.

6

The Far East

I LEFT THE VAJRA just before dawn fractured the western sky. Down by the bridge the dogs were strewn around like victims of a plague. One lay on its back in a culvert, its paws half-cocked and its muzzle pointed skyward; two more lay across the road and another three on a tin roof. All were as immobile as statues, twitching neither in their dreams nor in recognition of the passers-by heading up towards Swayambhunath. Once on the bridge I leant over the side to observe, by what little light the impending dawn permitted, the gravel beds and the grey-black river, which curled like a flayed eel around the western flanks of the city. Two dead dogs, one with a piece of rope round its neck, lay rotting in a small pool created by the gravel-diggers, and farther upstream there was an immobile and solitary pig. It had its eyes closed and its snout pointing towards the temple, to which it appeared to be addressing a somniloquy, the substance of which was a peculiar assortment of squeals, grunts and whistles. On the other side of the bridge were many more dogs, all asleep, and outside an old farmhouse whose walls were spattered with dung pancakes stood three cows, each tethered to a stake and chewing the cud absent-mindedly, as cows always do at the onset of a new day. The road up to Chetrapati was deserted, but I could tell which households were awake by the noises which came from them. The Nepalese are great spitters. They will spit anywhere and at any time, sometimes because they need to clear their throats, sometimes as a dramatic means of punctuating speech, and much of the time through sheer habit. It was the harsh sound of expectoration, not the crowing of cocks, which signalled dawn in Kathmandu.

In an hour or so the little roundabout at Chetrapati would be the scene of furious activity. Now it seemed strangely peaceful. A woman was doing her *pujas* in front of a small shrine of Ganesh, the elephant-headed god; a shopkeeper was opening his stall; an elephant lumbered by; and a man climbed on to his rickshaw, yawned loudly and pedalled off in the direction of Thamel. I followed him and found a taxi which took me to the airport.

I had been advised to befriend any Europeans on the flight to Biratnagar, as they would either be aid workers of one sort or another or army personnel heading for the Gurkha camp at Dharan, and they would almost certainly have a Land Rover waiting for them at the other end. I introduced myself to a white man with a smart suitcase. Rod was an Englishman and a civil engineer, and he was going to Dhankuta, a little way beyond which was the British-run agricultural station of Pakhribas, where I was heading. He said he was hoping to be met by a Land Rover and he kindly offered me a lift. (The other great advantage of taking a flight off the main tourist routes is that you pay at the same rate as the Nepalese. The flight from Kathmandu to Luckla, a distance of ninety miles, had cost me $60, whereas the flight to Biratnagar, which was 160 miles from the capital, cost only $23.)

We landed at the airstrip north of Biratnagar at midday, and an hour later we reached Dharan, where we stopped for a drink before climbing steeply into the Kosi Hills. At the top of the first ridge we came to a police check-post with a stunning view. Behind us, and far below, lay the plains of the Terai, cooking gently in the summer heat and shimmering like an enormous mirage. Little clusters of ochre houses were scattered across this endless, tedious landscape like breadcrumbs on a ragged carpet, and the knowledge that it stretched south for hundreds of miles into the Indian province of Uttar Pradesh, punctuated only by farmsteads and sprawling towns with belching chimneys, made one yearn to be out of sight of it and deeper into the hills. We soon were, and by late afternoon we had reached the end of the tarmac road and Dhankuta, where I parted company with Rod. I made my way down a cobbled street whose white-washed houses possessed handsome wooden balconies, on each of which were pots of red geraniums. It was a pretty street, full of clean, bright colours, like a painting by Raoul Dufy. Half-way down the hill I came to the prison – it had the words 'Female jail' written above one door and 'Male jail' above another – beyond which was the hotel that Rod had recommended. Its name was obscured by a plastic sign that ran the whole length of its façade. ICE BERG FLOODING DHANKUTA it said in large red-and-white letters, referring to a brand of Nepalese beer.

I was given a small room with three beds on the top floor of the hotel. I lay down on the cleanest of the beds and wondered what to do. It suddenly occurred to me that this was the first time I had ventured outside Kathmandu on my own. There is much to be said for solitude, though now I found myself rather at a loss. I descended to the café downstairs, but it was to early to eat, so I drank a tea and wandered round the town till dark. When I returned all the seats in the café were taken and I went up to my room again, where I inspected the mosquito net over my bed, which was torn, and read Conrad's *Heart of Darkness*. The former led me to ponder the most curious paradox: the efficiency of a mosquito net increases with the number of holes it has. The latter led me to contemplate the following passage: 'The conquest of the earth, which mostly means the taking it away from those who have a different complexion or slightly flatter noses than ourselves, is not a pretty thing when you look into it too much.' I jotted these lines down not because they provided a succinct summary of colonization, which they did, but because Nepal was one of the few countries in what we now call the developing world for which they did not hold true. I cannot tell you how refreshing I found it being in a country which didn't have a colonial past to blame for its present problems.

Most of the inhabitants of Dhankuta were Limbus, an ascetic-looking race with fine bones, sharp noses and pale complexions. About twenty of them, all male, were eating in the café when I went down. Some sat chatting in groups and others in a line at a long table watching a small television, which picked up an Indian channel presently devoted to folk music. I sat on my own. There were only two dishes on offer: *daal bhat* and 4-in-1 noodles. I chose the latter, which I had discovered could be considerably improved by the addition of chilli powder. Nobody took the slightest notice of me, and indeed I must have seemed a singularly drab specimen when compared with the Caucasians in the posters which were tacked to the walls. The four members of the pop group Kiss were made up like ghouls, and the lead singer sported a monumental leather codpiece and spiked knuckle-dusters. Having served me my noodles, the man who ran the hotel, a lanky individual in shorts and a checked *topi*, turned down the sound on the television and put on a cassette of Rod Stewart. 'We are sailing, we are sailing . . .' It went rather well with Conrad.

I went to bed early and would have slept immediately had it not been for the two girls in the room next door, who talked and laughed and shrieked with the various male companions who came up to see them during the evening. At first I thought they must be whores, but the chattering was so constant and the laughter so unabated that it seemed unlikely: they were having far too much fun. I passed them on my way out next morning. I had expected a couple of plump little things with big eyes and grins, but instead found two very tall, sophisticated Indian women in flowing saris.

It was only seven miles from Dhankuta to Hille, but the unpaved road was so scarred by gullies and potholes that it took the bus an hour and a quarter to get there, by which time my tongue was covered with teeth marks and my backside was severely bruised. There was no question of riding on the roof as one would simply have bounced off it, and I sat right at the back of the bus, which was probably the worst place to be. Soon after we left Dhankuta a flock of noisy school children got on. Like school children throughout the world, they immediately rushed towards the back seats. One of them, a swarthy boy in his early teens, jammed himself next to me and proceeded to crack jokes at my expense. What particularly infuriated me was the way he kept jabbing me in the ribs as if to remind me that I was the butt of his humour. All this was in Nepali and consequently incomprehensible to me. I doubt whether what he had to say was very witty: sarcasm appeared to be his main weapon. Some of his companions tittered – I suspect he was a local bully and they dared not do otherwise – but after a while a girl who had been observing this tourist-baiting walked smartly down the aisle, stuck her nose in the boy's face and delivered a sharp rebuke. She smiled at me graciously before returning to her seat, and the boy held his peace from then on.

In most parts of the world an incident such as this would be too commonplace to merit recollection. But this was the only time I experienced any rudeness in Nepal, and that in itself says much about the Nepalese. Incidentally, Nepal was one of the few countries I'd visited where I wasn't subjected to the tedious run of questions which goes something like this: Excuse me, what is your country?; What is your name?; My country is very beautiful, yes?; How many brothers do you have?; How many sisters?; What is your father's name?; How many children do you have? And so on. Thankfully there was none of this nonsense in Nepal. It is not that the Nepalese lack curiosity; nor is it that they are shy or reserved. They are a subtle people and they understand that there is more to someone than can be told through family arithmetic. Perhaps they know too that to ask you whether you like their country is rude, as such a question demands, in the name of diplomacy, an affirmative response, thus denying one the freedom to be honest. In any case, how could one not like it? I remember one old Gurkha telling me that the reason why the British liked the Nepalese had nothing to do with our special relationship with the Gurkhas; it was because the Nepalese, unlike many Indians and Pakistanis, had never wanted to emigrate to Britain. 'Have you ever met a Nepali living in Britain?' he asked. No, I said, after some reflection. 'Of course not,' he replied. 'The Nepalese who go abroad all come back here. You see, we think there's nowhere in the world as beautiful as our own village. We'd hate to live in England.'

Eventually, and none too soon, the bus reached Hille. It was market day and a great crowd thronged the main street. This was a frontier town, a child of the new road, exuberant and gaudy. Prayer flags on bamboo poles fluttered over tin roofs; plastic toys and washing bowls were on sale alongside wooden plough-shares and copper tureens. There were many Tibetans here, and scores of porters collecting goods to carry up the Arun Valley towards the Khumbu and Namche.

It took me half an hour to walk down the hill to Pakhribas Agricultural Centre. Inside the foyer of the main office were two photographs: one of the king and queen of Nepal; the other of Queen Elizabeth and Prince Philip.

Pakhribas was singularly – indeed, almost comically – British. The centre consisted of a nucleus of small buildings surrounded by 200 acres of terraced farmland. The buildings were modest, neat and functional, their brick walls painted caramel, their tin roofs a dull red, and they were linked by a maze of immaculately kept stone paths, which were bordered by shrubs and trees. In front of every tree was a green sign on which its name was written in white letters in English, Latin and Nepali. Just outside the entrance to the centre was a tennis court, and a little way inside a guest house. It had four bedrooms, a sitting room and the largest bath I had ever seen. Roses, poppies and marigolds bloomed in the trim little garden outside the front door. I was given toast and jam for lunch by the portly character who ran the guest house, after which I had a brief chat with Charles Borman, the director of the centre. We arranged to meet the following morning. In the afternoon I wandered round the farm, then spent some time in the library, where half a dozen Nepalese were perusing scientific journals and scribbling notes. I read an old copy of *The Sunday Times*. The day became progressively more miserable and by early evening the dense mist which had hung over the trees on my arrival had condensed into rain.

I was the only person staying in the guest house, but at dinner I was joined by a dourly pleasant Scotsman from a veterinary college in Edinburgh. He had arrived in the country a week before and he seemed somewhat non-plussed by his new surroundings. The food, at least, should have made him feel at home. We were served roast pork with crackling and apple sauce, accompanied by roast potatoes and green beans. Over dinner we discussed football and farm stock. My companion was enthusiastic about buffaloes, which he told me had smooth tongues, and extremely rude about Brahman cattle, which he claimed were exceptionally stupid. He was in a state of considerable frustration as the cattle on which he was to conduct experiments had yet to arrive at the farm. However, he turned up for breakfast the next morning in fine humour and announced that three cows had come during the night. His work could begin.

I took an instant liking to Charles Borman. He was a tall, thin man in his mid-forties with a strong, bony face and receding ginger hair. He had a gentle manner and spoke sparingly, amusingly and quietly. He had a natural modesty which meant that he was reluctant to talk about himself, and most of what I managed to find out about him came from a *curriculum vitae* in the library. In the early 1970s he had worked for his present employer, the British Overseas Development Administration (ODA), in the Solomon Islands, after which he had been an estate manager for Unilever in Cameroon and Ghana before returning to the Pacific, this time to work as director of agriculture on Tuvalu. Borman was unashamedly proud of the work which had been done at Pakhribas, though he immediately said that the bulk of the credit should go to his predecessor and the large and dedicated Nepalese staff. 'It's the best thing I've ever worked on,' he announced bluntly. 'We're actually doing what aid agencies should do. We're helping some of the poorest farmers in the world, and the benefits of the work we do here are both tangible and obvious.' He suggested I spend a couple of days walking round the area so I could see for myself.

Early the next day I set off with Madhab Rai, who had been given the task of taking me to a *panchayat* a few hours to the north-west of Pakhribas. Madhab was a young, stocky man with pronounced Mongoloid features, a wispy moustache and short, black hair which stood up straight like the hair of a cartoon character suffering from shock. He was quiet and shy and embarrassed by his English, which was much better than he thought. We picked up a porter outside the gates of the centre, then bought some provisions from a shop: rice, lentils, tea, sugar, onions, mustard oil, betel-nuts and cloves.

Madhab asked me what I wanted to drink, and I said stream water would do. 'You might get sick,' he commented anxiously, so I explained that I always carried with me a small bottle of iodine with which to render dirty water safe. As we left the shop I thought I heard him say, 'I have a bottle of Scotch. We can drink that tonight.'

'I can't,' I replied.

'Why not?' he asked. 'You don't like it?'

'Yes,' I said, 'but my liver can't take it.'

'Must be a very chronic disease,' he suggested. I assured him it wasn't. 'Oh, well,' he said, 'I'll have to drink it myself.'

For a bottle-of-Scotch-a-day man, Madhab struck me as rather timid. As soon as we reached the main village of Pakhribas, which was about twenty minutes' walk from the agricultural centre, he insisted we rush through to avoid trouble. It was election day and hundreds of men were gathered in the street. 'There may be fighting,' explained Madhab. Judging by the cheerful atmosphere that seemed unlikely, but Madhab predicted that sooner or later stones would start flying. The rounded hills which lay ahead of us were unlike any I had seen before in Nepal and they reminded me of the hills in Provence. On the summits were patches of scrub, abandoned terraces and groves of trees with dark green leaves. After a couple of hours we began to descend steeply through a landscape which was devoid of villages but liberally spattered with thatched farmsteads, around each of which were tiny terraces of maize, beans, pumpkins and other vegetables. The path had sunk deep into the red earth and at times it was like walking in a roofless tunnel.

Early in the afternoon we arrived at a farmhouse which was used as a seed distribution centre for the *panchayat* of Phalate. It was here, explained Madhab, that we would meet Kewal Dewan, a local farmer who would take me to look at whatever I wanted to see. Within a few minutes of our arrival seven children appeared and informed us that Kewal had gone to cast his vote in Pakhribas. There was nothing we could do but wait and chew betel-nut. After dark our porter cooked us a magnificent meal. 'Why don't you drink your Scotch?' I asked Madhab.

'My what?' he replied.

'Your Scotch. Your whisky.'

'I don't drink alcohol,' he announced. 'But there's the squash I was telling you about.'

Kewal turned up when we finished eating. We chatted for a while and he agreed to come and fetch us at six o'clock the next morning. We went to sleep in the loft and much later were woken up by someone banging at the door. It was a girl who worked for the agricultural centre as a 'women's motivator'. She lived 1,000 feet down the hill and she had come up, in the dark and on a filthy, rainy night, with the sole purpose of telling us that we could visit her the next day.

There are few things I find more enjoyable than listening to farmers talking about their maize and their cows, and the problems they have with pests and weeds, and one thing and another. However, I realize that many others view the world of farming with less enthusiasm than I do, and it would be an unkindness to recount in any detail the events of the day I spent with Kewal and the women's motivator, whose name was Parabata Rai. We did many things. Before breakfast we dropped some 1,500 feet at great speed to look at some rice paddies, and having done that we shot up again to have breakfast, after which we inspected some vegetable gardens, talked with various farmers, came across a wedding, discussed the yields of different crops, and finally made our way back to Pakhribas, where I arrived in a state of exhaustion and exhilaration.

There are many places in the world where you could walk all day and see only two or three different crops, but such were the variations in altitude here that the range of plants grown was enormous, and within a matter of an hour or so we had climbed from a tropical environment up to a temperate one. It was as though half a hemisphere had been concertinaed on to a single hillside. Broadly speaking, the hills of Nepal can be divided into three zones. Below 5,200 feet there is the rice zone, where most of the irrigated land is found and livestock are of secondary importance. Between 5,200 and 7,500 feet there is the maize and millet zone, where crops and livestock are knitted into a complex system of interdependence. Then above 7,500 feet farmers rely mainly on livestock production, though they still grow a few crops, the most important being potatoes, barley and buckwheat. An inventory of the fruit-bearing trees which Pakhribas was distributing to farmers in 1987 gives perhaps the clearest indication of the region's agricultural diversity. Among the citrus fruits were mandarin, lime, lemon and orange. Temperate fruits included apple, peach, plum, pear, walnut, persimmon, cob-nut, apricot, sapota and fig. The tropical fruits were mango, litchi, guava, jackfruit, pomegranate, avocado, pineapple and cardamom.

One of the first things which strikes anyone who spends time wandering round Nepal is the way in which the country has been carved up for the activities of foreign aid agencies. If you go to the Khumbu you will find the New Zealanders and the Austrians; round Jiri, the Swiss; in the far west, the Canadians; in Rapti, Mustang and Gorka, the Americans; in Dhading, to the west of Kathmandu, the Germans; and in the Kosi Hills, north of Dharan, the British. And of course there are the Chinese, the Indians, the Russians (present in Kathmandu, but no longer carrying out aid projects), the Japanese, the South Koreans, the Australians, and others too. However, it is the British who have been here longest, and to understand their work at Pakhribas and elsewhere in the Kosi Hills one needs to know a little about the history of Anglo-Nepalese cooperation, which really had its origins in 1814 when the two countries went to war.

In May 1814 a group of Nepalese soldiers attacked three police posts in Butwal District, killing an Englishman and some Indian policemen. A British force of 22,000 men, led by four generals, then invaded Nepal. According to Byron Farwell's history, *The Gurkhas*, two of the British generals were 'completely incompetent; they failed to reach even the outer ramparts of Nepal and were subsequently sacked'. The third general was 'not entirely sane ... and it was said that his mind was unsettled by alcohol and megalomania'. He was killed and so were almost a quarter of his troops. Only one column had any success, but it was to take a further two campaigns before the British forced the Nepalese to sue for peace. In 1816 the two countries signed the Treaty of Segauli, whose terms, not surprisingly, were much more favourable to the British than to the Nepalese. The latter were forced to give up their claims to an area of land roughly equivalent to the size of the state today, and they consented to the presence of a British Resident in Kathmandu. The British had been enormously impressed by the bravery and skill of the enemy, and the treaty gave them the right to recruit Nepalese soldiers. Since then the Gurkhas have played a significant part in virtually every war fought by the British (700,000 Nepali soldiers – approximately one-fifth of the country's adult male population – fought in the Great War of 1914–18). The vast majority of Gurkhas have come from just four tribes: the Magars and Gurungs, who are recruited at Pokhara; and the Limbus and Rais, who are recruited at Dharan. There are now some 7,000 men serving in the British Brigade of Gurkhas, and a further 75,000 serving in Gurkha regiments of the Indian army.

On retirement from the army nearly all Gurkhas return to their home villages. They are now men of substance, having earnt in a few years what their sedentary neighbours and relatives couldn't earn in a lifetime. They also continue to draw a pension till death. In 1987 the British army was paying pensions to some 15,500 Gurkhas who had retired since 1948. At £324 each a year, this means that British pensions to the Gurkhas alone come to over £5 million a year, and the amount of money coming into Nepal in the form of Gurkha salaries, pensions and related services is getting on for double that. You often hear people comparing this figure to sums spent on foreign aid projects, but it would be wrong to think of these receipts as a form of aid. For one thing, the money has been earnt, in the proper sense of the word. And for another, the pensions and salaries go direct to the soldiers: the money does not have to trickle its way through the hands of the Finance Ministry or any government department, as most aid money does. It is no coincidence that villages with a high proportion of Gurkha pensioners are invariably more prosperous than those where there are few or none. In some villages as much as four-fifths of the aggregate income stems from Gurkha wages and pensions.

This is all by way of introduction to the work which Pakhribas does. The project began in 1973 as a scheme to provide agricultural training for retired Gurkhas. However, it soon became apparent that the sorts of services it intended to provide were required by all farmers in the Kosi Hills, and in 1975 the centre's policy was changed so that it could offer technical assistance and advice to some 8,000 farming households in two 'target areas'. The aim of the project was: 'To raise the standard of living through improved agriculture, forestry and animal husbandry in our Target Areas with particular emphasis on the "poorest of the poor" farmers. The overall aim being to make all the farmers in our Target Areas permanently self-sufficient.'

This is standard stuff, much the same as you will find in any brochure on an agricultural aid project. Good intentions are one thing; good results quite another. The developing world is littered with failed agricultural projects, and all too often Western aid agencies have gone about things in a thoroughly Western manner, introducing their own technologies with little thought for the consequences their actions might have. To improve the standard of living of poor farmers means at least one thing: helping them to grow more food. If all available land is already under cultivation, then the increase in food production can only come by increasing yields. Either the farmer must grow more crops a year, grow better crops, or both. Thus the main thrust of agricultural development has been through the introduction of 'high-yielding varieties' (HYVs). These have undoubtedly boosted production, and without them there would have been no 'green revolutions' in Mexico, India, south-east Asia and elsewhere. But the HYVs have been a mixed blessing. Frequently one or a few HYVs have replaced dozens or hundreds of local varieties. They tend to be particularly susceptible to attack by pests and diseases, in part because they lack the resistance of local varieties, and in part because they are planted in 'monocultures', thus making it easy for pests and diseases to spread. HYVs also differ from traditional varieties in that they demand large quantities of artificial fertilizer (and sometimes water) if they are to fulfil the promise of high yields. Farmers and peasants who travel down the HYV path must not only buy the seeds, but must pay for pesticides and fertilizers as well. When the 'poorest of the poor' are induced into planting HYVs, they often become poorer, and a fair proportion of the world's peasantry is now enslaved by debt, some directly as a result of their flirtation with 'green revolution' farming.

According to Borman, the most important aspect of the work at Pakhribas was the provision of high-quality seed. However, he viewed artificial chemicals with great suspicion. 'We try to keep the use of fertilizer to an absolute minimum,' he said, 'and as for pesticides and weedkillers, we positively resist their use.' Many new varieties had been introduced, but the centre had taken care not to fall into the trap of making farmers dependent on inputs which they couldn't afford. The benefits which these new varieties had brought to the target areas were considerable. Between 1976 and 1986 farmers who had taken on new varieties had increased their yields of maize by 45 per cent, of wheat by 61 per cent and of soya bean by 52 per cent. The increase in production resulting from the use of improved varieties in an area which encompassed 4,200 households was estimated to be worth 17 million rupees a year ($790,000). The average increase per household thus came to over 4,000 rupees a year ($185).

There were many other aspects of the centre's work which impressed me. Special mention, perhaps, should be made of the help that the centre has been giving to women, whom until recently it had largely ignored.

Women have been taken on to the professional staff (the centre employs 340 people, only three of whom were British when I was there), and they have set up schemes to encourage farmers' wives and daughters to establish kitchen gardens. The costs have been negligible, but the benefits great. Women who decide to set up a garden are given a composite pack of seeds (which costs the centre 1 rupee) from which they can grow a whole range of vegetables. Not only have the gardens helped to improve the general standards of nutrition, they have frequently provided a surplus for the women to sell at local markets. The first gardens were established in the winter of 1986. By the time of my visit six months later 150 kitchen gardens had been set up, some of which I saw on my wanderings. They were all beautifully kept and highly productive.

Britain's annual aid allocation to Nepal is around £10 million a year. Of this Pakhribas takes but a small slice: £370,000 in 1984–5; £600,000 in 1986–7; and they were hoping for £1 million the following year. The centre receives its funds direct from the British government, which is unusual: virtually all bilateral aid projects (bilateral aid involves the flow of money from the government of a 'donor' country to that of a 'recipient' country) are administered by a ministry of the recipient country, through whom the money must pass. In Nepal it is the Finance Ministry, and one of the greatest frustrations for those working on aid projects is the way in which money gets held up there. It also tends to be filtered off by the 'line agencies', which are the government departments that oversee, or carry out, the work in the field: poor accounting and corruption are ubiquitous in Nepal. One of the reasons behind the success of the Pakhribas centre was its independence: all the money arrived, and arrived on time. When the British began talking about handing the whole thing over to the Nepalese government, none was more disturbed by the idea than those working at Pakhribas. This reaction was sad, though understandable. Sad, because there is little point in setting up aid projects unless they are taken over by the recipient country. Understandable, because of the financial 'difficulties' mentioned above. As it happened, HMG asked the British to carry on running Pakhribas for a while.

For those who have doubts about my objectivity – I have been fulsome in my praise of a British project, though of little else – I can dispel them, I hope, by adding a brief critical word about two other British projects. First, the twenty-seven-mile, two-lane tarmac road from Dharan to Dhankuta. This road was begun in the late 1970s and completed in the early 1980s, at a time when British aid was devoted to building up the country's infrastructure. Roads were seen as a high priority, both by HMG and the donor agencies. I was told on several occasions that the British ambassador of the time was particularly keen on roads: at least you could *see* that something had been achieved. I was also told that the main reason why the British built the road, which cost £18 million, was because King Birendra wanted one there. It is a wonderful feat of civil engineering and wide enough for two lorries to pass one another without either pulling into the side. In short, it is the sort of thing one expects to see in the Swiss Alps. During 1986 between 130 and 168 vehicles used the road each day. The last figures I saw were for March 1987, when around 110 vehicles used the road each day.

Cost-benefit analyses of roads are notoriously difficult to make. How does one price, for example, a saving of a few hours of a porter's time? (The bus takes five hours; you could walk it in twelve.) My own feeling – and I think that of many others in Nepal – is that the benefits of a road (and certainly one so costly and substantial as this) are few when compared with what could have been done with the same amount of money in other fields, such as health care and the supply of clean water. Roads in Nepal often cause great environmental damage (though this one hadn't) and they are extremely expensive to maintain, thus placing a further drain on resources. The British are providing £6 million for the Roads Remedial Works Unit, whose task is to look after the Dharan-Dhankuta road and to equip and train the Department of Roads to take over maintenance. They are also spending £7.7 million on the upkeep of the East-West Highway in the Terai. Roads represent a bottomless pit. The fact that Britain has refused a Nepalese request to build a new one up the Arun Valley – it will serve a Japanese-funded hydro-electric power scheme – suggests that the lesson has been learnt. The World Bank has agreed to do it instead.

Having built the road – whose purpose was to open up the Kosi Hills for development – the British then embarked on the Kosi Hill Area Rural Development Programme (KHARDEP), which I know about only through hearsay. It was an extremely ambitious project (rather like the RCUP), and the best I heard said of it was that it was like the curate's egg: good in parts (or as an Embassy handout put it, 'Our assistance in the Kosi Hills has shown mixed results.') The main phase of KHARDEP came to an end in 1985, and another phase began in 1987.

The Dharan-Dhankuta road, to borrow from Conrad, 'is not a pretty thing when you look into it too much'. We shall have to wait a few years to see whether the same criticism could be applied to KHARDEP.

'The Swiss are now a brave and warlike people,' wrote the inestimable Rabelais. 'But how do we know that they were not once sausages?' More appropriate, I think, would have been potatoes, which were served, both roast and boiled, with the beef we ate on my last night at Pakhribas. The two new arrivals, both of whom worked for the Swiss government, fell silent as they popped the first of the potatoes into their mouths. They masticated them slowly, with their eyes closed and brows furrowed in intense concentration, looking much like wine-tasters do as they pass judgment on a substance which is shortly to be expelled into a spitoon. The potatoes went down, rather than out, and the younger of the two turned to his companion: 'King Edwards?'

'Yes,' replied the other, 'Namche, I think.'

These men knew everything there was to know about the potato, and they proceeded to explain how they could tell that the ones we now ate were King Edwards, and why they thought they came from Namche. 'But what exactly do you do?' I asked. 'We're potato experts,' they replied bluntly. They spent their time travelling round different parts of Nepal, giving advice to farmers on what potatoes to grow and how to grow them. I asked them whether it was true, as some guidebooks claimed, that the potato arrived in the hills only in the mid-nineteenth century. No, it was nonsense. Colonel Kirkpatrick mentioned potatoes in his account of the country, and they were probably here long before that, although there were now many more varieties, some of which had been brought into the country by returning Gurkha soldiers. As far as Namche potatoes were concerned, they were a relatively recent introduction. Von Fürer-Haimendorf suggests that they came either from the gardens of Europeans in Darjeeling or from the garden of the British Resident in Kathmandu. I would like to think that Hodgson had something to do with it. Probably not: he never travelled up to the Khumbu.

The Swiss were eager to see the weekly film, so once we'd finished eating we set off to the largest of the centre's buildings, which was already overflowing with people. It seemed that everyone who worked for Pakhribas had turned up, along with their women and children. The film was called the *Karate Kid* and the opening scene reminded me of the Vajra play. A small, oriental gentleman (the hero) began by giving a colossal and muscle-bound white man (a villain) a tremendous beating-up. Having broken both the villain's arms and smashed his face with a car door, the hero dusted his lapels, readjusted his trilby and smiled inscrutably. All this was greeted by 'oohs' and 'aahs' and cheers of approval. After a quarter of an hour I left, driven away by boredom rather than violence. Films like this were shown every week at Pakhribas, passed on from the army camp at Dharan. There was nothing to stop parents from taking their offspring to see the most violent trash, yet theatrical performances of the great Shakespearian tragedies were banned in Nepal. (Apparently, they are banned because they show royalty in a bad light, in which case it is odd that Shakespeare should be 'taught' in schools.)

After breakfast the next morning I was given the visitors' book to sign.

An entry for 20–1 April 1985 read 'Timothy Raison, Minister of Overseas Development, London – "A memorable visit, for which I am very grateful."' One should never resort to plagiary in a visitors' book, as future guests, if they notice, will take this as the sign of a vacant mind. All the same, Mr Raison's sentiments were precisely mine.

7

Three Towns

'TERAI TOO HOT, TERAI TOO FLAT, Terai too much mosquito,' incanted the squat old Rai who sat next to me as the bus headed towards Biratnagar. I offered him a cigarette, which he took and passed on to the woman who sat beside him. 'I no smoke,' he explained, 'but old woman smoking. Very bad for her. Very bad for you too.' It wasn't often you saw a woman smoke in Nepal, at least not in public. I lit her cigarette and she cupped it in her palm, as though protecting it from the elements. It was a habit I associated with people who worked outdoors in temperate, windy countries such as Britain; I'd never seen people hold their cigarettes like that in the tropics. Watching this old woman smoke gave me acute pleasure; she treated the cigarette as I would an oyster. She smiled slyly with each deep drag and her eyes had a glazed look about them, much as vicars' eyes have when they greet the unfaithful in the street.

Shortly before we reached Biratnagar the old woman got off and we passed her stuff – two dehydrated hens with gaping beaks, some aluminium pans tied in a dirty cotton shawl, and a small sack of rice – through the open window. A vermilion sun was melting rapidly into the horizon and welding the brown fields to the opacous blue sky. An ox and cart rumbled by.

'In hills, no tips,' said my neighbour as we passed a factory which manufactured matches. 'In Terai, many tips. Very bad!'

This confused me. 'You have to give more money in the Terai?' I asked.

'No! No give!'

'Who do you tip?'

He thought about this for a while. 'Ah, no tip. Ships! Yes, many ships in the Terai.'

I let this pass, and I asked him what he did. He replied that he'd been with the British Gurkhas. 'Malaysia: put down rebellion – then Sumatra – then Hong Kong. Hong Kong no fighting: stopping Chinese. Seventeen year in Gurkha. My father fight in World War One.'

The old man lived in Biratnagar, a place for which he seemed to have an intense dislike.

'For you, no good. You leave tomorrow! Where you go?'

'Birgunj.'

'Where?'

Birgunj, I repeated. He shook his head. 'In Nepal, no place called that. How you spell?'

I wrote it down on the back of my cigarette packet – BIRGUNJ.

'Aha,' he cried. 'You go Birgunj. Very important you pronounce right.' He repeated the name with a great roll of the 'r'.

The bus pulled into a shabby park and we climbed into a rickshaw whose driver was so small and wizened that he had difficulty in getting the pedals to go round. I suggested to the old man that I should get down and walk, which would be no great sacrifice as I hadn't far to go; and in any case, with both of us in the rickshaw we couldn't go much above walking pace. 'No, no! I pay!' said the old man. I explained that it had nothing to do with money; I was simply feeling guilty about the rickshaw driver. The old man found this very funny. 'That how he make money,' he explained. 'He no care.'

When we reached the roundabout in the town centre the old man pointed to a policeman who was standing next to a statue of the king. 'If any ships, go to police,' he announced. 'Police work to ten o'clock.'

'Oh, you mean thieves?' I exclaimed.

'Yes!' he replied as I got down and thanked him for the ride. 'Yes! Tips! Watch out for tips!'

You know how it is when you turn up in a strange town after dark, and you're alone and the streets are full of people the same colour as their shadows, and you know nothing about the place or the people? You're covered with sweat and you're hungry and your muscles ache; your ears are full of the sound of jibberish and car-horns, and being white and a touch nervous you feel that everyone's eyes are fixed on you and you alone, and you wonder whether the man on the pavement who's staring at you now is a saint or a crook. Well, when it's like that the first thing you want to do is find a hotel, shut the door of your room, and lie down for a while with a cigarette and maybe a drink. You let the tiredness seep out of you, and as you smoke you study your new surroundings. When you're in this sort of state you notice everything: the nasty patterns on the wallpaper, the cracks in the plaster, the dripping taps, the stains on the sheets . . . In towns like this that's how the hotels always are.

Hotel Bardon, a large concrete building near the roundabout, came with back-handed recommendations which said more about its competitors than itself. 'Only hotel which isn't a knocking shop,' a Nepalese technician at Pakhribas had explained. 'It's where the Royal Nepal pilots stay,' another had said, as though that in itself was a seal of approval. It was a dismal place, though in retrospect I'm glad I spent a night there as it encapsulated the flavour of the industrial Terai.

I walked into the foyer and found a youngish man, an Indian, sitting reading a newspaper behind a large metal desk of the sort once found in dole offices in England in the days before there were many people on the dole. He greeted me by spitting into a metal wastepaper basket. He said they had two types of room: 'cheap room and not cheap room'. I said I'd take a not cheap room and he led me up a row of stairs to a long, wide corridor. On the way along it I caught glimpses through open doors of large numbers of people – they all appeared to be Indians – sprawled on vast beds, panting wearily like overheated dogs.

The walls of my room were a cold duck-egg blue and scarred by a mass of electric wires, some of them bare, which served an extraordinary array of appliances: two fluorescent lights, three ordinary bulbs, an air-conditioning machine, and a large fan which dangled from the ceiling. There was a plywood panel by the door with eight switches, one of which operated a light in a shower-room. The main room was as over-furnished as it was over-electrified, and most of it was taken up by two double beds, which were wedged together as though awaiting occupation by a very large family. They were made up with blue nylon sheets and pink quilts. There was also a newish settee with draylon covers, a small table with vinyl topping and a cabinet whose shiny blue surface was covered with cheap bits of god-wotery. Thankfully, there were no posters of actors or pop stars; instead there was one of Krishna as a young boy, and another of Laxma, the goddess of wealth. The latter had two pairs of arms, which presumably meant she could collect debts and count money twice as fast as mortal men (or women). The former sported an exceptionally soppy smile, much as Christ did in the paintings of my children's Bible, and he was decked out in a gold head-dress and an orange, braided jacket. His skin was blue and his lips purple. The poster reminded me of the cover for the Beatles' *Sergeant Pepper* album.

I sat on the bed, smoked a cigarette, fooled around with the switches, then joined a platoon of cockroaches in the shower-room. As soon as I turned on the water they marched smartly towards the WC, behind which they took refuge while I washed away the day's grime. They were the largest and most precocious cockroaches I'd come across: as soon as I turned off the water one landed on my shoulder and another crawled over my feet. Back in the bedroom I discovered an insect under the quilt the likes of which I had never seen before. It was about half an inch long and thin like a centipede, although with many fewer legs. When I poked it, it leapt into the air, bent itself double and made a loud noise like the crack of a whip. Once I'd spruced myself up I went for a wander in town.

Hitherto I had met not one person with a good thing to say about the towns of the Terai, and indeed the guidebooks hardly mentioned them. This had struck me as perverse, not least because the Terai was home to nearly half the country's population. The *Insight Guide* – which is by far the best available – devoted 151 pages to the Kathmandu Valley and only four to the Terai, most of which was about Chitwan. The only mention of Biratnagar, the second largest town in Nepal, came in the form of an aside:

Like Nepalganj to the west and Birgunj, Janakpur and Biratnagar to the east, Bhairawa's fortunes are built on the trade filtering between Nepal and India. Each of these towns consists of a collection of ramshackle concrete and wooden houses, a few factories, and a handful of rundown hotels. Their streets are left to fleets of often idle rickshaws.

There's little I can add to that. If I had to live in Biratnagar I suppose I would develop a liking for the place, but then one always tries to like wherever one lives, however devoid of pleasures it may be. With its atmosphere of disconsolate tawdriness, Biratnagar reminded me of a Soho pinball parlour. It was garish, seedy and entirely without charm.

I was hungry that night, having walked in the morning from Pakhribas to Dhankuta, spent five hours on the roof of the bus down to Dharan and another two inside the bus to Biratnagar. I hadn't eaten all day, and the manager at the Bardon promised to provide me with an enormous meal, which he said I would have to eat in my room. He rather overdid it. He brought me five different dishes, all of which had been cooked to a frazzle and tasted foul. My air-conditioner was so noisy that I slept with it off. The night was unbearably hot, and my mosquito net was no match for the local mosquitoes, which pestered me till dawn.

I left for Birgunj at six o'clock the next morning. The bus was very crowded but the driver wouldn't let me travel on the roof. We passed many statues of the present king and his immediate forebears; crossed several bridges with ostentatious signs saying they had been built by 'Nepal-USSR cooperation'; saw storks and egrets and kingfishers whenever we crossed rivers and streams. The landscape was unutterably dull, and I stared longingly towards the small and jagged Siwaliks to the north. I arrived at Birgunj an hour before sunset and set off in a rickshaw to look for Lorna Reid, a distant cousin whom I'd met briefly for the first time in Kathmandu. She was working for VSO (Voluntary Service Overseas) in a college on the edge of the town, and I found her sitting with a group of

Nepalese girls outside the main building. It was still over a hundred degrees and it took a long, cold shower to revive my spirits and anaesthetize the inevitable bus-induced bruises on my behind.

Birgunj was smaller than Biratnagar but otherwise similar. Another late child of the industrial revolution, it too was just a few hundred yards from the Indian border and populated largely by people of Indian origin. After dark Lorna and I set off for the town centre. Had I been on my own I would have passed another tedious evening, but Lorna, who had been living here for over a year, had developed a chary affection for the place which gradually rubbed off on me. She led me up and down the main street, which looked uncommonly like Brick Lane in London's East End, and we amused ourselves by studying the imported rubbish in the shop windows. The chemists promised great results for anyone prepared to spend a few rupees on various potions and perfumes, one of which was called Sex Appeal: 'Now you don't have to be born with sex appeal ... Irresistible to all women.' The most fascinating shop, however, was one which sold bathroom furniture. The man who ran it was a friend of Lorna's, a Newar from Kathmandu and an excellent character in every respect. He was greatly amused by a story which he'd just heard. Someone had told him that Queen Elizabeth and Mrs Thatcher had decided to take their own sofas with them whenever they went abroad: they were worried about catching AIDS from sitting on other people's. Sitting on things was the crux of this man's business, which was flourishing, thanks largely to the fact that commodes – the sit-up variety of WC – had become status symbols for the rich. Two years ago he'd sold six; last year, over a hundred. Commodes were considered particularly useful for old people who had difficulty getting up after squatting over the traditional pan-in-the-floor WC. So far there hadn't been a run on *bidets*. He had sold only one, which had been bought for the queen and installed in the National Stadium.

We ate well in a café by the bus station, after which Lorna introduced me to the sub-continent's equivalent of 'After Eights'. Unfortunately, I have forgotten what they are called and I cannot describe the taste of these gastronomic curiosities. Indeed, they have no single taste, as they consist of a large leaf on which have been placed a dozen or more different kinds of seed, herb, spice and gum. Once the ingredients have been daubed on the leaf, it is folded into a triangle and you pop it into your mouth. I popped mine out fairly smartly, but it took many cups of tea to wash away the unpleasant after-taste.

I left Birgunj the next morning at six o'clock, having decided to go to Pokhara rather than return immediately to Kathmandu. Although the journey lasted fourteen hours rather than the nine it should have taken, it was infinitely more enjoyable than the previous day's trip from

Biratnagar. The bus driver refused to let me on the roof, but at least we were soon back in the hills and away from the oppressive heat of the Terai. For the first thirty miles we headed due north over flat plains. Beside the road one could see where the old railway used to run – in places the metal rails poked out of the grass – and here and there were buildings which must once have served as stations. One stretch of road was being repaired and for five miles the bus stuttered along the floor of a dried-up riverbed. Then we climbed over the modest ridge of the Siwaliks and turned west at Hetauda to speed along a valley which gradually broadened out to reveal the wooded undulations of Chitwan National Park. Just after Hetauda we stopped at a village to pick up a wedding party which consisted of eighteen very smartly dressed men and seven women. The women all managed to squeeze on to seats which were already full, but the men had to stand. My notes remind me that the wedding party brought its own music. The nature of the music completely escapes me now, possibly because I could see neither players nor instruments, hemmed in as I was by a wall of standing passengers.

Hindu weddings are gay, colourful occasions and much more uplifting to witness than the po-faced affairs which follow traditional English marriages. The aftermath of the latter is memorable chiefly for the smutty speeches of the best man, the dreadful clothes which the bride's mother wears, and the sight of ancient aunts juggling cups of tepid tea. I was never invited to a Hindu wedding but I saw plenty of wedding processions on the streets. I recall one in particular, which I came across on a sunny morning in Kathmandu. A ten-piece brass band led the way in front of a taxi in which the happy couple travelled. I suppose they were playing a wedding march, in which case the Christian equivalent is not to be sniffed at: this sounded more like a baleful chorus of cats than anything else. However, it was entirely redeemed by the trombonist: every few minutes the rest of the band would fall silent and he would play a marvellous jazz solo.

The wedding party got off the bus at Narayangath. From there to Mugling was an hour's journey but we took three as we had two punctures and had to wait for spares to be found. We ate a late lunch at Mugling, then turned west along the winding road to Pokhara, where we eventually arrived at eight o'clock. We were greeted by a downpour and by the time I got to a hotel near the lake I was soaked to the skin and as cold as a herring.

In every country in the developing world – or, at least, in all those I have been to – there is one place to which travellers flock for relaxation and where they find a combination of peace and comfort not to be found elsewhere. In such places a sort of lazy hedonism prevails. Nearly always these places are beside water; nearly always the locals have provided lodges and hotels where Western food is to be had and Western music heard; and nearly always there is a cheap and easily available supply of hashish. Such places as these become sites of pilgrimage, and you can be fairly sure that sooner or later every traveller pays homage to them. In Kenya there is Lamu, a small island ringed by lagoons and coral reefs; in Senegal there is St Louis, a shabby old French town also on an island; in India there is Goa; and in Nepal, Pokhara.

Pat and I had spent the tail-ends of two afternoons and two nights in Pokhara. On our first visit we hired a rowing boat and paddled idly around Phewa Lake, whose eastern shore was lined with lodges and restaurants. In the failing light of early evening the water was a soupy pea-green and egrets whirled like snowflakes against the heavy grey-blue storm-clouds. It had been a hazy day and none of the great mountains to the north had been visible. When we returned from the Kali Gandaki a couple of weeks later it was pouring with rain and this time we couldn't even see the terraced foothills beyond the lake. However, by the next morning the storm had blown itself out to reveal a landscape of astonishing majesty. Macchapuchhare – the fish-tail – loomed over the lake, and mountain after snow-capped mountain towered into the sky as far as one could see, both west and east. As we made our way from the lakeside to the bus station we walked crabwise, unable to take our eyes off the breathtaking panorama. I don't know how one describes a landscape such as this without resorting to a string of clichés, so I shall save myself the bother of trying, and quote instead from a travel piece in the *Times of India*: 'It is a sight for the gods which few mortals have been privileged to see ... The whole of Nepal is like a pretty woman, with a blush ever ready to erupt, but even there within, Pokhara is like a prettier woman among them.'

I had left Pokhara at the end of April under the impression that it consisted of little more than the tourist settlements by the lake and a collection of scruffy streets near the bus station. How wrong I was. On my return from Birgunj I spent three days here, much of it wandering round what I now discovered to be a substantial town which boasted a lively commercial centre, a Gurkha camp, and a large community of Tibetan refugees in addition to 50,000 or more people of Nepalese origin. The bus station's relationship to the rest of the town was that of a kneecap to a body. The tourist lodgers by the lake occupied the position of feet. Its left ear was the Annapurna Regional Museum, whose resident entomologist was an admirable Englishman called Colin Smith.

The museum occupied a small building on the university campus. It was largely devoted to wildlife and geology, and most of the exhibits, as one would expect, came from Nepal, though here and there were bits and pieces from other parts of the world: some Greek marble, a chunk of lava from Iceland, shellfish from Malaysia ... The walls of the main hall were covered with a mural of little artistic merit but sufficient accuracy to enable one to identify the mammals, birds and flowers which it depicted. In another room there were some charming old wildlife maps, printed on canvas, of Africa, Asia and Europe. Nepal was represented by the tiger and the rhinoceros; Britain by the otter, red deer, lobster, herring, ermine, grouse, gannet and fulmar. However, the museum's *pièce de résistance* was its marvellous collection of butterflies and moths. I was surprised by the numbers of specimens, captured in Nepal, which I recognized: peacocks, brimstones, commas, cabbage whites, red admirals, painted ladies, tortoiseshells, swallowtails – all can be found in Britain too. I met Mr Smith, the founder and keeper of the collection, on my way out. He had a long, tousled beard, a disorderly mop of hair and a pair of ancient spectacles balanced on a prominent nose. He was as stringy as a vine, and it was hard to tell how old he was: somewhere in his fifties, I imagine.

'Must close!' he exclaimed as soon as he saw me. 'Yes, I'm afraid I've got to go. I have to pay for a bed. I haven't seen the bed, you see, but I'm the one who's got the money for it. Somebody else has seen it but they haven't got the money. No, I've got it. So I've got to bicycle there now.'

'Wonderful butterflies you have,' I said.

'Ah,' he replied, taking a closer look at me. 'Ah, yes! Well,' he reflected, 'no hurry really.' And for the next quarter of an hour Mr Smith told me about his butterflies. He spoke at great speed, and it would have required a stenographer of genius to record all he had to say. He began by telling me how he had got hold of some butterflies from Sarawak. Apparently, they had been collected by the curator of a museum there. The curator had only stayed for three years, after which he had emigrated to South Africa. On his death his family had found 10,000 butterflies in his attic, all wrapped in newspaper and stinking of naphthalene, a moth-killer. 'Now my brother has this collection,' explained Mr Smith, 'and he gave me some that he could spare.'

When Mr Smith first came to Pokhara he had a job as a teacher. He thought butterfly-collecting would make an interesting hobby and at weekends he used to go into the countryside with his net and catch whatever he could. Twenty-one years ago he started this museum. The Natural History Museum in Kathmandu then gave him a two-year contract to collect butterflies. In the end he spent six and a half years collecting for them.

We left the building together and Mr Smith climbed on to his bicycle. 'I'm really very excited,' he said. 'The other afternoon I found a very rare butterfly. There's only one other record of it in Nepal. Most exciting!'

'What's it called?' I asked. He replied in Latin.

By odd coincidence the other long-time English resident of Pokhara was also a collector of sorts. Colonel Jimmy Roberts founded Mountain Travel, Nepal's first trekking agency, in 1965. I went to see him on my first visit to Pokhara as I wanted to hear his views on the rapidly expanding tourist industry. Colonel Roberts had a strong, ruddy-brown face, heavily wrinkled by a life spent outdoors. I explained that Brot Coburn had suggested I see him. 'Oh, Brot,' he said, pronouncing his name as though he was a Swedish sandwich. 'How is Brot? He's a good boy.' Colonel Roberts said he'd be happy to talk to me, but he suggested I should see more of the country first. Before I left he showed me round the bird-cages in his garden. He had some spectacular Himalayan pheasants, some cranes and some peacocks. Unfortunately he was away on the other occasions I dropped by.

Pokhara was an enervating place, and it was easy to understand why so many travellers came here for a few days and ended up staying weeks. It was the sort of place which induced your brains as well as your limbs to have a rest, and I soon abandoned the idea of looking at any of the local aid projects. I swam in the lake every day, went for slow, contemplative walks, wrote letters and read. I also found Mek, who was sitting with friends near the grass airstrip. Since we'd seen him he'd taken a small group of tourists up to Annapurna base camp. 'Not like you and Miss Pat,' he said, which I took as a compliment. We spent the afternoon together, and when I went to get the bus back to Kathmandu at six o'clock the next morning he was waiting to say goodbye. He was rather downcast as the trekking season was drawing to a close and he was out of money. If you go to Pokhara, please hire him.

8

Jiri — Making up for Lost Time?

$\mathbf{D}$ERVLA MURPHY'S *The Waiting Land* is a delightful account, written in the form of a diary, of the six months she spent in Nepal during 1965, mostly in the company of Tibetan refugees in Pokhara. Contemplating her departure, she wrote that it was 'wretchedly certain' that if she ever did return to Nepal she would find that 'all will be changed, changed utterly', especially in such places as Kathmandu and Pokhara. Here are a few lines from her elegiac and prescient epilogue:

The West has arrived in Nepal, bubbling over with good intentions (though the fire that keeps them bubbling may be fed on expediency), and soon our insensitivity to simple elegance, to the proud work of individual craftsmen, and to all the fine strands that go to make up a traditional culture will have spread material ugliness and moral uncertainty like plagues through the land. Already our forward-looking, past-despising 'experts' are striving to help Nepal 'to make up for lost time' by discarding the sound values that lie, half-hidden but still active, beneath 'pagan superstition' – and that would provide a firmer foundation on which to build the new Nepal than our own mass-production code, which makes a virtue of unnecessary earning for the sake of unnecessary spending ... Perhaps nowhere in Asia is the contrast between a dignified, decaying past and a brash, effervescent present as violent as in Nepal; and one knows that here too eventually, the present will have its shoddy triumph.

If we are searching for an epitaph to inscribe on the tombstone of the twentieth century those last few words might do: 'The present will have its shoddy triumph.' The statement has the beauty of being too imprecise to refute, and it hints at the contradictions contained in the idea of progress, in whose name have been performed deeds both wondrous and terrible. Nowhere was I more aware of the present's shoddy triumph than in the small town of Jiri, yet there were few places for which I developed such a strong affection. There is no paradox here: I have always found myself compellingly attracted to boom towns. What I loathe is the sight of an old place – a repository, if you like, for Murphy's 'proud work of individual craftsmen' – gradually being destroyed by the evanescent creations of today. But if the latter are simply accreted round what formerly existed, as barnacle-spat are on the piles of an old wharf, then past and present can co-exist on equal terms and the future can grow from a symbiosis between the two. Modern Jiri is very much a child of the new age, the half-caste offspring of an impoverished Nepalese mother and a wealthy Swiss father. It reminded me of the wide-boy made good in the city slums: bejewelled, snazzily dressed, ever eager to impress with the flashy car and the roll of bank notes.

Thirty years ago Jiri was a small village, though passing travellers might have considered such a description a rural conceit. It consisted of a huddle of farmsteads near the head of a wedge-shaped valley a little over mid-way between Kathmandu and Namche. It lay a short walk north of the main trail, secluded, insignificant and no different from thousands of other hamlets scattered across the heaving, deep-ravined mountains which form the geological prelude to the great fugue of the high Himalaya. For hundreds of years, maybe thousands, the rhythm of life here had been determined by the rhythm of the seasons. Jiri's history was a peasant history: repetitive, unremarkable, utterly predictable. 'One generation goeth and another generation cometh; and the earth abideth for ever.'

The bus journey to Jiri was exhausting. We left Kathmandu at five o'clock in the morning and there were as many people standing as sitting. For the first five hours we proceeded noisily northwards as we followed the road which linked the capital with the Tibetan border. The bus windows were so filthy that it was impossible to get anything more than an impressionistic idea of the landscape through which we passed, although the tilting of the bus confirmed its topographical exuberance. I felt like a bubble trapped in a spirit-level.

At Lamosangu we left the main road, crossed the Sun Kosi on an iron bridge and began the first of two long and steep ascents. Half-way up the first hill the bus stopped and those who wanted to get on the roof did, which was about twenty of us. The next seventy miles took seven hours if one included the hour's stop for *daal bhat*. However, the time passed quickly enough: the weather was fine, the views magnificent, the company enjoyable. The countryside was rugged, heavily cultivated and full of strong colours: the blue-green pines looked as though they had been applied to the red earth by *pointillist* brush-strokes. The Sherpa next to me chatted enthusiastically about his plans for the summer. The trekking season had now finished and he was returning to his home a day's walk from Jiri. He had bought a ghetto-blaster for his wife and new toys for his children. Last year he'd taken the family on holiday to Kashmir; this year he thought they might go to Darjeeling.

By the time we caught sight of Jiri the sun had disappeared behind us and a thin drizzle had cast a grey, diaphanous veil over the town and the valley. We stopped at the police check-post at Jiri Bazaar, a mile or so from the main town, then the bus sped down the hill and scattered dogs, goats and children as it rumbled along the length of the main street. At the far end there was an open expanse of gravel where the bus turned, and a large white milestone on which was printed: 'JIRI O KM'. The bus returned to the main street, by which time scores of people had come out of their homes to welcome friends or simply to observe the interesting spectacle of a bus disgorging its disorderly and dishevelled contents.

I walked down the street and went into the Cherdung Hotel. There was nobody there, so I sat on a wooden chair at a wooden table in the dining room, lit a candle and smoked a cigarette. The wooden walls were devoid of decoration except for a photograph of the king and queen and a British bus poster, which gave the times of departure and arrival for the National Express 'Rapide 512' (Hereford-Gloucester-Cheltenham-London). Eventually a young girl, somewhere in her early teens, arrived with a plump boy of similar age and a much smaller youth who grinned broadly and fizzed about like a bluebottle on a window pane. The girl's parents, who owned the hotel, were away in Kathmandu, so these three were looking after the place during their absence. The small boy – he was a Sherpa from the Khumbu – showed me up to a room on the first floor and announced that dinner would be served as soon as they'd cooked it. The competence of Nepalese children is staggering; if all the adults were to die tomorrow they'd manage perfectly well on their own.

I met the only other guest – a Gurkha soldier, recently retired from active service – as I waited for dinner. He had been born and brought up in Dharan and he was leaving the next morning for Kathmandu, from where he was going to catch another bus home. His reservations about living in this part of Nepal were few. 'I love it,' he said, 'but the walking is terrible – either straight up or straight down.' He was in charge of one of the twenty-five Gurkha Welfare Offices in the country, and his main task was to help old soldiers who had fallen on hard times. He was allowed to give distressed individuals 500 rupees ($23) straight away; if a greater amount was required he had to send a report to Dharan. He was an articulate, kindly, intelligent man and as he took his pre-prandial *rakshi* – 'I never eat here,' he announced bluntly, 'the food is not so good' – he told me where he'd served: Singapore, Australia, England, Hong Kong, Malaysia, Fiji and the Falklands.

'How were the Falklands?' I asked.

'Terrible.'

'Why?'

'Very cold, very wet, and we had to carry a hundred and ten pounds of equipment on our backs for hours on end through dreadful bogs. Really terrible!'

'What about the fighting?' I asked.

'No problem,' he replied. When I pressed him further he just shrugged his shoulders, as if to say there wasn't much to tell.

When the old soldier left, the *daal bhat* came; and soon after so did a New Zealand girl who introduced herself as Jillian. She was slightly built and pretty, with straight, shoulder-length brown hair, brown eyes, a freckled complexion, a sharp nose and an expressive mouth. She reminded me of Botticelli's 'Head of Flora' in his 'Primavera'. She'd arrived two nights ago, and she told me in her pleasant drawl what she'd seen so far. She was staying in a hotel along the street and she said that we were the only travellers in town tonight.

I went to bed early, which was just as well, as sleep in Jiri was impossible after five o'clock in the morning, which was when the first of the two daily buses to Kathmandu signalled that it was ready to leave by honking its horn for a good five minutes. This was followed by half an hour of shouting and arguing, then as soon as light appeared in the sky the buses revved up and made a cacophonous exit past my window. This was the cue for a man opposite to begin his work, which consisted of fashioning tureens out of copper sheets with the help of a hammer.

Before breakfast I wandered a little way along the trail which led east towards Jumbesi and Namche. It began at the end of the street and climbed past a small shed beside which three men were dealing with a buffalo they'd just slaughtered. The beast's head had already been severed and they were attacking the body with speed and skill. Its entrails slithered out on to the wet grass, like spaghetti escaping from a colander, and its liver was poured into a plastic bucket. I sat down on a rock some way above and surveyed the town beyond. Its backbone was the wide main street, under the west end of which ran the Jiri River. The street was about 200 yards long and lined by two-, three- and occasionally four-storey buildings, most of them made of stone and wood and constructed during the last decade. The houses on the north side were raised higher than those on the south side, thus affording their upper floors a view over the roofs opposite and down the valley. The shops on the ground floors were now open and outside one some porters were having their loads weighed before climbing up to where I sat and setting off on the long journey towards the Khumbu. They had about five days to go if they were heading for Namche.

Immediately below the main street and to the south was a collection of a dozen or so solid, handsome, wide-eaved buildings built of grey stone. This was Jiri Technical School. Farther down the valley there were some large farm buildings on the left bank of the Jiri River, and on the right bank was the airport, which consisted of an oblong grass field, delimited by lines of white stones and just large enough to allow four-seater Pilatus Porters, which were supposed to come twice-weekly, to land. Beyond the thatched shed which served as the airport 'terminal' the valley billowed out, then the hills on either side pressed in like a sphincter, to leave space only for the river to pass on its short journey to join the much larger Khimti Khola River, whose waters flowed south to meet the Tamba Khosi. This in turn led to the Sun Kosi, a large river which, a hundred miles to the east, and a little way to the west of Dharan, met the Arun. And so on down to the Ganges and the Bay of Bengal.

The valley bottom presented the most pleasing of pastoral scenes. A herd of Swiss cattle, creamy-yellow and grey, grazed the lush green grass which here and there was streaked yellow with ragwort. To the north of the town there was little flat ground, though there were a few largish terraces from which corn had recently been harvested, and on the western flank of the valley there were some smaller ones, planted with either maize or millet – from where I sat I couldn't tell. About a third of a mile up the valley I could see a monastery, which was surrounded by bamboo poles festooned with prayer flags. A little way beyond, mountains rose dramatically into cloud.

After breakfast I walked down to the technical school. It was just before nine o'clock and the students – most of whom were young adults – were sitting outside the main office awaiting the arrival of the principal, Mr Jeevan Raj Adhikari. The girls wore blue sari-like dresses and the men looked smart too. A teacher told me that Mr Adhikari would be taking morning prayers and he suggested I come back later, which I did.

Mr Adhikari was a short, stubby man with the countenance of an eagle. 'You a Brahman?' I asked once we'd dispensed with the introductory pleasantries. 'Of course I am,' he replied. 'Look at my nose! You can always tell us by our big noses.' His English was colourful and convoluted, and he answered all my questions about this Swiss-funded school and about the general business of aid with refreshing candour. Before lunch he showed me round the school, then took me down, at my request, to see the hospital and the farm, which had also been set up by SATA (the Swiss Association for Technical Assistance). Both had been handed over to HMG, and I shall reserve most of my comments about them till later; suffice it to say now that they provided a sad spectacle. The farm buildings were ill-kempt and dilapidated, the cattle looked mangy and lustreless, and there was little to suggest that this was an agricultural research centre of some importance. Though very small, the hospital had once been famous throughout the Himalaya, and people used to come here from as far away as Delhi to be treated for TB. One section dealing with mothers and babies was staffed by girls from the school; it looked impressively clean and well-organized. As for the rest, it was grubby and neglected. The X-ray machine had broken down, and all but two of the twenty-odd beds were empty. The two doctors who were supposed to work here had private practices in Kathmandu, and they made only occasional visits. It was run for the rest of the time by a young man who had no medical qualifications. He said he was expecting one of the doctors to come in ten days' time. Someone told me later that they came only to draw their pay.

That afternoon Jillian and I set off to visit a cheese factory which was bedded into a mountainside some 1,500 feet above and behind Jiri. It was hidden from view by a fir copse, and our progress was erratic as we kept changing our minds and directions. Twice we had to wade across bubbling, ice-cold streams and by the time we began climbing in earnest the rain had come. It was of the slanting, swirling variety and my umbrella was of little use. Thunder, lightning and hail forced us to quicken our pace. Although Jillian had already spent six months wandering around south-east Asia, she had done little trekking. However, she proved herself to be considerably less frail than she looked, trotting cheerfully along in a pair of flip-flops and chatting incessantly as though this was an everyday stroll. It was a muddy, wet, exhilarating walk, and our first glimpse of the factory came only when we were within a hundred yards of it. That it was called a factory required a semantic sleight of the same order as the one that deemed Jiri a town. It consisted of several small farmhouses, one of which was devoted to the manufacture of cheese.

We found four lackadaisical young men in Western dress in a dingy room which appeared to be their sleeping quarters. They behaved as though they were resting after a heavy drinking session and gazed at us blearily, uncertain what to make of our sodden appearance. One of them stood up after a while and led us to an office where the director of the factory was writing in a large ledger. Though friendly enough, he was somewhat perplexed by our presence and surprised that I wanted to hear about the cheese factory. As soon as I sat down I felt like an imposter and I was eager to get away: it depressed me to think of these womenless men stuck up this God-forsaken hill while outside it was pissing down as though it would never cease. Anyway, I asked the director a few questions and he trotted out facts and figures which I dutifully consigned to my soggy notebook: '17,000 kg cheese to Kathmandu each year – 47 farmers paid every 15 days – 700 litres of milk a day in peak season – Milk comes from a yak cross – Farmers get 5 rupees a litre – Fat content 6 per cent. Manager Swiss-educated – speaks fluent French.' Before we left I bought a kilo of cheese for 90 rupees. Yaks' cheese is a beautiful cheese, and this one was as good as any I had tasted. There is nothing quite like it in Europe, which is a pity. It is pale yellow, like a good farmhouse Cheddar, though harder and drier. Its flavour is tart yet subtle. It is the sort of cheese which would go very well with fruitcake or apple pie.

The rain had slackened by the time we left and half-way down the hill the mist cleared to reveal a gang of blue-black clouds emptying themselves on the distant hills. We reached the monastery in late afternoon and a boy led us inside and introduced us to the head *lama*. Neither of them could speak any English, but the *lama* invited us to sit and we stammered away at one another for half an hour. The monastery had been built ten years ago and had it not been for the frescos inside the porch unsuspecting passers-by would have taken it for a nondescript private house. Inside it was magnificent in a sickly sort of way; post-box red, buttercup yellow, dark blue and a variety of greens, including one the colour of confectionary marzipan, predominated, and not a scrap of wall, beam, column, lintel or door was left unpainted. Many of the paintings looked to me like jumbled-up versions of the Last Judgment: gods, demons and animals were scattered across stylized landscapes in which the hills were topped with snow and cattle grazed fertile valleys.

Ngawang Sherap was a cheerful, round-faced, purple-robed man with a blur of grey stubble across his head and cheeks. He divided his time between reading a text on waxed paper and asking us questions which we didn't understand. At one point I said '*choina*', which means 'there isn't', but my pronunciation deceived him and he thought I said I came from China. 'You China? You China?' shrieked the boy excitedly. From what we could gather there were twenty-five monks here, but all except the *lama* had gone off for two weeks' holiday. I gave him a lump of cheese before we left and he handled it with the reverence it deserved.

Early evening in Jiri was a time of anticipation and excitement, no less for us than for the local inhabitants. Each day brought one or two new Europeans, either by bus from Kathmandu or by foot from the trail to the east. The former, fresh from the city, were always eager to set off to the hills, and they'd leave first thing the next morning; the latter, having spent weeks or months in the hills, were also keen to get away, and they'd take the first bus to Kathmandu. I skimmed through the visitors' book in the Cherdung and there wasn't a single entry over the past four years for anyone who'd stayed more than one night. (One of the names I came across belonged to a man I'd known at university some fifteen years earlier. Ian Tattersall was a climber and under a column headed 'ambition' he'd put 'immortality'.) That night we were joined by three new arrivals: two English girls and a Swiss potato expert. The girls looked (and sounded) as though they'd just stepped out of the hair salon at Harrods. They were immaculately turned out, and it was hard to believe that they'd just spent three weeks trekking in the Khumbu. They found it hard to believe as well. 'We're amazed at ourselves,' said the one with blonde hair, who'd spent the past three years working as a stockbroker on the Paris *bourse*. 'We've never done any exercise in our lives till now.' They'd been away from Europe for five months, and after spending time in Burma, Thailand and the Philippines they'd flown to Kathmandu with the intention of travelling up to Tibet. 'But we heard they were bringing foreigners out in body-bags,' said the one with auburn hair, 'so we decided to go for a trek instead.' At Namche they'd met the son of George Mallory, the climber who achieved something close to immortality by disappearing without trace on Everest in 1924. The girls said his son was much given to lecturing everyone he came across about the dangers of mountain sickness.

The potato man was also here just for one night, though he'd stayed at the Cherdung many times before, and indeed he knew most of central Nepal well. I asked him whether he'd come across a tribe called the Chepangs, whom I was soon going to visit in the hills to the west of Kathmandu. He said he hadn't, though he'd heard of them. 'If you ask people in Kathmandu about them,' he said, 'they'll tell you that the Chepangs are ape-men.' It was typical, he continued, of the prejudice with which people in the cities viewed those in the countryside. He recalled working on a farming project in Dhading District on which all the HMG staff were Brahmans from Kathmandu: 'They hated leaving the city, these Brahmans. There was one time when two of them were supposed to accompany me to a Tamang village. They kept saying, "We mustn't go there. The Tamang are wild, dirty people; they're thieves; we won't be able to get good rice with them." It's very sad: you come across that attitude all the time out here.'

After dinner the potato man went off to see 'an entertainment' at the technical school while the girls mused over their return to civilization. The fact that there was no running water in the hotel (you had to get it from a stand-pipe in the street) and that the electricity was erratic (the lights came on only for about half an hour that evening) did nothing to diminish their pleasure. They discussed at great length all the different things they intended to eat when they arrived in Kathmandu the next evening. Chocolate cake was top of their list. A couple of weeks later I met the blonde-haired girl in a bookshop in Thamel. She said they'd been doing some first-class eating.

The next morning Jillian and I joined the crowds trooping up the road to the weekly market at Jiri Bazaar, which was held on a sloping piece of grassless ground between two rows of solid old houses. It was a fine sight, and we spent several hours there. A constant stream of peasants and merchants descended on the market, the women colourful as jungle parrots, the men drabber, though smart too, in traditional *sural* and *daura*, baggy-seated jodhpurs and double-breasted shirts. The occasion was both commercial and social; the atmosphere that of a large family gathering. At the top end, near the tarmac road, was a medicine man with a collection of fifty or so jars full of roots, herbs, powders and resins. Every now and then his assistant banged a drum, and once the crowd had been augmented he indulged in a short bout of ululation, then got down to the business of selling his wares. A little way below the medicine man, women sold *dokos* and baskets made out of bamboo. Beside them were the ironsmiths, who sat cross-legged in front of neatly laid out rows of axe-heads, hoes and trowels. Then there were the fruit sellers, the vegetable sellers and the stalls selling saris, shirts, *surals* and other clothes. There was also a separate patch where rice, lentils and beans were sold, and another, run by a noisy gaggle of women, devoted to lurid-coloured wools and haberdashery. Most intriguing of all were the men who weren't specialists, but who sold a great assortment of bits and bobs found nowhere else in the market. One of them had laid out on a hessian sheet the following items: candles; tobacco leaf; 'coldgate' toothpaste; 'glucose' biscuits; turmeric; betel-nut; roundworm lotion; little metal aeroplanes (brilliantly painted with the letters USAF-B82 on their sides); snuff; children's marbles; chocolate made in Bombay; horrid sickly sweets; *bedis* and cigarettes; green, orange, blue and red plastic bracelets; plastic ear-rings; and a goat.

We left around midday and walked down a trail into a forest, where we found a sheltered and sunny glade and ate some lunch – bananas and yaks' cheese – in the company of three women who were selling glasses of *chang* for 1 rupee to people making their way towards Those, a town on the Khimti Khola. A young Gurkha soldier on leave stopped to talk to us. He had a small badge on his *daura* (a photo of King Birendra), a gold watch, a gold bracelet, and a large radio. He complained, in perfect English, that he and his compatriots were paid less than British soldiers of the same rank. I agreed that if that was the case it was most unfair. After lunch we made our way down to the river, where I washed my hair and beside which we dozed till late afternoon. On our return to Jiri we were greeted by two men who were relaxing outside the technical school's site office. We sat down and chatted for a while about this and that before I asked them if they knew someone called Prem Dulal, whom an acquaintance in Kathmandu had suggested I find. 'That's me,' announced the smaller of the two men, a quietly spoken Chhetri with a thick, droopy moustache and lively eyes.

Prem had lodgings in a house near the Cherdung and I accompanied him there once it got dark. For the past five years he had been employed by SATA as the chief site engineer at the technical school. When he first came here there was no tarmac road, no electricity and fewer than ten houses on what was now the main street. We talked about how Jiri had changed, then he showed me photographs of his wife and children and some of the buildings whose construction he'd overseen: the national park centre at Namche; a house for Boris Lissanevitch in Kathmandu; an office for the Nepal Australia Forestry Project at Chautara. Prem was one of those men – by no means common in the building trade, especially in Nepal – whom one knew instantly to be honest, incorruptible and devoid of racial or caste bigotry. In fact, he was one of the nicest people I've ever met.

I returned to the Cherdung to find that the evening tide had washed ashore some interesting jetsam. Two English teachers from Buddhalikantha School were sitting over supper with a woman who worked at the Australian Embassy in Kathmandu. They'd come in a jeep and brought with them a hamper of food, the sight of which had me salivating copiously. It included a large onion quiche, a small slice of which I ate, a bottle of good red wine, some fresh fruit and a jar of Fortnum and Mason's mustard. Jillian and I had intended to eat at the hotel, but we changed our minds as soon as we met an American arrival. He was a loud, arrogant man, incapable of keeping his mouth shut and eager to tell anyone who'd listen about his experiences on the way up to Everest base camp. He was a sort of mountaineering groupie and he talked of great climbers as normal men might of Marilyn Monroe or Nastassja Kinski. He seemed to think that Nepal existed solely for the benefit of hearty types such as himself.

We went to eat at Jillian's lodge, and there found two Australian couples who'd arrived on motorbikes, a timid and respectable English couple who'd just descended from the hills, and a French couple who'd come on the bus from Kathmandu. The Australians were true bikers: leather-clad, tough, greasy and crude. They had shipped their bikes from Australia to India and they were now making their way overland to Europe. I particularly liked the French couple, neither of whom could speak much English. With the monsoons approaching this was the worst time of year to begin the trek up to Everest base camp, but that didn't seem to bother them. *'On a du temps,'* explained the girl. *'Il faut essayer.'* They were singularly ill-equipped, yet they seemed more concerned by the prospect of eating *daal bhat* than by their lack of sleeping bags and waterproofs.

'This town no good,' announced a young man playing cards in Those's

Sunlight Hotel. 'Everything finished. Bazaar gone.' Having said this, he dealt a hand to himself and his three companions and the game continued in desultory silence.

It had taken us three hours to walk here from Jiri. Now it was midday, the sun shone brightly and Those had drifted into siesta. The air was full of the buzz and hum of bees and flies and it sounded as if someone was slowly running a bow across the bass strings of a cello. A pair of swallows dipped in and out of the door with food for their piping nestlings; a cuckoo called in the trees beside the river; and mynah birds hopped about in the hotel garden, beyond which a group of old women, wizened, knotty and mahogany brown, sat on their haunches, cackling at one another like querulous turkeys.

After lunch Jillian and I wandered round the town. There was little to suggest that Those had once been a great industrial centre – 'famous all up and down Nepal,' as the card-player put it. I quote from a book by the Swiss geologist Toni Hagen:

In the mountains above Those in the region of Jiri there are about 4 million tons of iron-ore with an iron content of 68 per cent. The iron works were opened in 1893, smelting began to flourish, and by 1924 there were 18 smelting-furnaces in operation. With 15 furnaces (fuelled with charcoal), operating for a period of 20 days a month, 14 tons of pig-iron were produced annually. Hydro-electric power was installed to run an electromagnetic separator and various lathes and drills. They produced fire-arms, chains, hammers, plough-shares, shovels and spades, pick-axes, crowbars, *kodalis* (a form of hoe), horseshoes and oil or butter lamps, which were sold within an area of 5-days' walk in the environs of Those ... In 1936 the main customer, the Maharaja of Nepal, lost interest, for it was more economical to buy the rifles (of infinitely superior quality) from abroad. In 1967/8 only two furnaces remained and most of the blacksmiths had gone to Kathmandu or India.

There is nothing remarkable about the rise and fall of Those; precisely the same thing has happened to hundreds of small towns in Britain and throughout the Western world. One thinks, for example, of the lead-mining towns of the Yorkshire Dales or the towns of the coal-rich hills in County Durham. A mineral was found, exploited, refined; peasants became industrial workers; a period of prosperity was eventually followed by a period of decline; the mines closed, smelt-mills were abandoned, people drifted elsewhere.

The decline of Those's iron industry was to some extent – and for some time – compensated for by its prominence as a market town. Before the construction of the tarmac road to Jiri, Those had the largest bazaar between Lamosangu and Namche. Now virtually everyone, whether porter or tourist, went via Jiri; in Those passers-through were few and far between. Many of the fine buildings on Those's main street were locked up, and looked as though they had been for years; and in the fields behind, magnificent stone mansions with carved windows and pantiled roofs were falling to ruin. There is something particularly beautiful about the death of a town, just as there is that of an ancient tree. First the branches sag, then they fall and rot away; the trunk may stand for years yet, but eventually it will be toppled by death, and often its death will be egged on by the new growth around it. Neither nature nor history has time for the old and redundant. One life ends, but sooner or later another begins: seeds turn into saplings, saplings to trees, and the whole cycle repeats itself. In Those one saw the signs of the new future as the stones of ruins were dressed and laid to make foundations for new buildings. Near the hotel a bank had recently been constructed, and in its gardens were neat rows of roses; by a small stream, in the shadows cast by a roofless old farmhouse with sagging lintels, two new buildings were going up. The only signs of Those's iron age were to be seen in the spoil-heaps on the hillsides; in the great chains of the bridge across the Khimti Khola, under which the village boys were swimming and splashing when we left; and in the few shops which remained open, where one could buy nails and hammers and remarkable oil lamps shaped like cockerels.

As usual, rain came in the afternoon. We ran into small squalls on the climb up the hill behind Those, and had we not stopped so long for tea in a small shack owned by a Sherpa we would have made it back to Jiri before the main deluge. As it was, we were caught on the airstrip with a score of other people, and the storm was so ferocious that we were forced to shelter under the eaves of the hut by the river. Within an hour the Jiri had turned from a clear, shin-deep stream into a violent torrent the colour of Guinness. It must have risen six feet, and its power assured us a constant supply of electricity that evening, which we spent in the company of Prem, Mr Adhikari and five others from the technical school. We began the evening in the café on the main street, then retired to a hut on the campus, where we were offered *tongba*, an alcoholic gruel of fermented millet to which is added boiling water. It is a drink which requires some patience, or at least skill, as it must be sucked slowly through a bamboo straw without disturbing the grainy sediment. Jillian didn't make much of it, and I resisted it on the grounds that once started I would continue to excess. The others argued that that was precisely the idea, and they became increasingly expansive as the evening progressed.

There is nothing the Nepalese enjoy more than good conversation, and there were few subjects that evening which we didn't touch upon. The time had come, so to speak, to talk of shoes and ships and sealing wax, of cabbages and kings ... And, of course, of foreign aid, which is a subject which lends itself well either to ridicule or to serious discussion. While some polite things were said about the Chinese efforts here – 'They are almost untouched by corruption compared to the rest,' suggested one – and some reasonably kind things were said of the Swiss (all these men were working for SATA), the Americans, the British and the Japanese came in for some rough criticism. One of the men here had observed the behaviour of the British contractors who built a stretch of the East-West Highway. 'They spent half their time drinking beer and half the time chasing our women. They also made a very bad job of the road.' The tales they told of American aid projects were all familiar, though what they seemed to find particularly galling was the way in which the American experts behaved while in Nepal. 'Three Americans drove up here one day in an eight-cylinder car,' said one indignantly. 'They brought all their drinking water from Kathmandu and all their food – it was as if they feared catching the plague by eating what we have.' And if I wanted to see what the Japanese were up to, they suggested I should walk a little way along the Jiri River and look at an irrigation system they'd installed.

As it happened, I'd already seen it. At a point where the river plunged down a steep slope the Japanese contractors had built a concrete race along the hillside to take water into a tank, beneath which were two large turbines. It was a lift-irrigation scheme designed to pump water up to some small terraces farther up the hill. The pipes were already in place, but since it had been built three years ago not a drop of water had been diverted from the river. Last year some Japanese landed at Jiri in a helicopter, looked around the site, then flew off without so much as passing the time of the day with the *pradhan panch* or anyone else in the town. No one knew what was going to happen. As was so often the case, the only people to have benefited from the scheme (so far) had been the Japanese contractors and presumably the Japanese firms who had made the turbines. 'Even the screws they used came from Japan,' said one of my drinking companions in disgust.

It rained that night almost without cease, and on and off for much of the next day, most of which I spent in or near Jiri. The evening was enlivened by a plentiful supply of electric light and the arrival of a couple who came from Esher, a commuter town to the south-west of London. The man was a fanatical fly-fisherman, so we spent a happy hour talking about trout and the business of catching them.

Jillian and I left the following morning. For some reason (or, more likely, for no reason at all) the bus driver refused to let anyone on the roof, and consequently the journey was exceedingly tiresome. Two people were sick within an hour of leaving and the only way to escape from the smell of vomit, stale sweat, sickly *bedis* and unwashed feet and crotches was to hang one's head out of the window. We stopped for lunch at Lamosangu and I left Jillian there as she wanted to visit a village near the

Tibetan border. I continued south, and we reached the Kathmandu Valley as the sun was setting. In the soft, dusty light of evening the old city of Bhaktapur, with its pagoda roofs and its harmonious blend of wood, mud-brick and copper, looked extraordinarily beautiful. It was as though a faded medieval tapestry were tacked on to the pale tea-rose sky. In the foreground a farmhouse was on fire, and orange flames licked like liquescent dragon's tongues across the thatched roof. One thought of Chaucer's England and Rabelais's France; of a world of intense, violent passions and brilliant colours, where sin was plentiful but so were grace and forgiveness . . .

So what of the Swiss involvement in Nepal?

They had certainly dipped their fingers into many different pies. They'd set up cheese factories in the hills; they had helped to create craft industries for Tibetan refugees; they had involved themselves in work to increase potato production throughout the country; they'd given financial and technical support to various industrial concerns; they'd set up the Jiri Multi-purpose Development Project (JMDP); they'd funded the building of the road from Lamosangu to Jiri; they had helped establish the technical school at Jiri – and more besides. But what precisely had they achieved? A list of projects tells us so little.

By now I was beginning to have serious doubts about my ability to judge the success or failure of the projects I saw. Certainly, there were many things happening in the country which involved great squandering of money and provided few or no tangible benefits to the peasantry. In this category one could include the Japanese irrigation scheme at Jiri, the RCUP forestry projects at Tukuche, the Austrian hydro-electric plant near Namche. Few would deny that these projects were, when all is said and done, very stupid. They had been ill-conceived and ill-executed. Then there were the projects which seemed to work so well that whoever judged them, and on whatever terms, would probably conclude that they were worth while. Pakhribas apparently deserved the accolade, and so did the Nepal Australia Forestry Project, which I was to visit shortly. However, the vast majority of aid projects could neither be wholly condemned nor unreservedly praised. They were, like the curate's egg, good in parts; which meant, of course, that they were also bad in parts.

A bad project to one person might be a good project to another; it all depended on which part of the egg they chose to dip their spoon into. I found this to be especially the case with the Swiss projects at Jiri, which I discussed not only with the people I met there, but with others who worked at the SATA offices in Patan. One official described the JMDP, which was begun by SATA in 1958 and handed over to HMG in 1971, as a 'partial success'. Three others condemned it bluntly as a failure. Initially this project was conceived solely in terms of improving livestock management, but it soon turned into the first of Nepal's 'integrated rural development' projects. It tried to tackle everything, from agriculture and forestry to health and education. It was under this scheme that the farm and hospital had been established. The SATA official who viewed it as a partial success based his judgment on the fact that the local people in Jiri were better off – albeit marginally – as a result of it. 'Before the JMDP the Jirils were terribly exploited by a few rich people,' he said. 'They were chronically poor and ill-educated; they had nothing. But because of this project some had the opportunity to study at school; some became nurses, administrators, accountants ... They were no longer under the thumb of the rich. Had it not been for the Swiss, they would have remained oppressed to this day.'

Those who claimed the project to be a failure pointed to what had happened since the Swiss had handed it over to HMG. Both the farm and the hospital had gone into decline. The former was doing little to help farmers in the district; the latter provided only the most rudimentary of services for the sick, and indeed the technical school had a vehicle on permanent stand-by to whisk anyone in urgent need of treatment down to Kathmandu. The doctors, as I have said, were more interested in their practices in the capital than they were in treating the sick at Jiri, for which they were being paid. Blame for this sad state of affairs was directed both at SATA and at HMG and its employees. The Swiss were blamed for the inappropriate scale of development. It was argued that they should have realized that once they pulled out, HMG would be unable to carry out basic maintenance on the buildings, which were now falling to bits. There was also no money to buy fuel for the hospital generator. The X-ray machine no longer worked, nor did the hospital telephone. As for the HMG employees, many were said to be lazy, corrupt and inefficient. 'If you're honest and hard-working,' said one Nepalese official, 'it's terribly frustrating, because you're surrounded by people who don't care.' Why, I asked, do they get the jobs? 'Simple,' he replied. 'For every job on offer there's a long queue of excellent people waiting outside the front door clutching their CVs and eager to help make things work in this country. But while they're waiting, the crooks slip in through the back door ... Perhaps they pay a small bribe, or maybe they have family connections. They're the ones who often get the jobs. And when they've got them – well, that's it.'

Obviously, the primary aim of the Jiri project was to raise the local standard of living, whether by helping farmers increase yields, by restoring eroded land or by setting up cottage industries. However, Jiri was a five-day walk from the Kathmandu Valley, which meant that it was effectively isolated from the country's economic and administrative heart. Many of those involved saw this as a major problem, and HMG asked the Swiss to undertake a feasibility study for a road to connect Jiri with the one which already existed between the valley and Kodari, a town on the Tibetan border. The study concluded that a road would bring many benefits if its construction were accompanied by further projects to 'develop' the hills. In 1972 HMG asked the Swiss to participate in both the road project and a development programme. They agreed. Construction of the Jiri road began in 1974; it was completed eleven years later. The Integrated Hill Development Project got under way at the same time, and it will run until 1990.

Whatever one thinks about the need for a road to Jiri, one cannot but admire the way in which its construction was organized. The Swiss, who contributed 220 million rupees towards the construction cost of 250 million, did their best to ensure that the project was labour-intensive, and everything possible was done to spend money in such a way that it stayed in the area through which the road passed. At one time 9,000 labourers were employed. The fact that less than one-third of the 250 million rupees spent actually stayed in the project area says more about the nature of road-building than about the Swiss way of doing things (27 per cent made its way back to Kathmandu, and 41 per cent went abroad). The road is not only among the best designed in Nepal, and the least damaging from an environmental point of view, it is one of the cheapest so far built in the country. The two-lane road from Dharan to Dhankuta cost 8.4 million rupees per kilometre; the one-lane road from Lamosangu to Jiri 2.2 million rupees per kilometre. The British would say (indeed, they did say) that their road was wider (true) and built on much more difficult terrain (doubtful).

Juggling around with facts and figures can be rather a futile occupation; so let us drop them forthwith and allow Mr Adhikari, revived after a long day's work by the hot *tongba*, to interject. 'Development,' he announced, raising a stubby forefinger portentously, 'is not just a matter of building roads, or schools, or clinics, or power stations. No – the crux of development is about attitudes. The main problem in this country is that people's attitudes are all wrong. Only when educated people change their ideas will projects succeed.'

On paper it may seem that Mr Adhikari was sliding into metaphysics; but having spent time with him looking round the school I knew precisely what he meant. On that first morning he had recounted the whole history of the school: why it had been set up, how the buildings had been built, who the students were and so forth. It was one of a string of schools across the country whose purpose was to provide basic training in skills which were urgently needed in the countryside. At Jiri they fell under three headings: agriculture, construction and health (which was largely midwifery). The trainees worked on the school farm, maintained the buildings and ran the ante-natal clinic. Outwardly, the whole place was impressive. On the conclusion of my visit I murmured something to the effect that the school was obviously a success. 'Well,' said Mr Adhikari, 'we don't know yet whether or not the school is a success.' He explained that the students spent three years here, then a final year back in their villages putting into practice the skills they had acquired at Jiri. After that, most would probably end up working in HMG posts, or they could set up their own businesses if they wished. The school opened in 1984, and so far there had been 161 trainees. At the time of my visit none had completed the course. 'We'll only know whether it's a success once the trainees are back in the field and working. Then we'll really see what attitude they have.'

Prem said that during the five years he'd spent at Jiri he'd noticed a change in the way the local people viewed development projects. 'A while ago if the local people saw foreigners coming they thought: "Aha! Here comes money." They became lazy because things were given to them. Their attitude changed with the road. They realized they had to work themselves if they wanted something.' The Swiss, suggested Prem, had understood that there was no point in pursuing projects which didn't require local people to help themselves. 'Now they're teaching people how to fish,' he said. 'They're no longer just giving them fish on a plate.'

9

How the Chepangs Got Their Name

I FIRST MET TRAILOKYA SHRESTHA, a chunkily built, bespectacled Newar in his late thirties, when he turned up at the Vajra one afternoon, having been alerted to my presence there by friends in London, whence he'd just come. I was surprised when he announced, over tea in the dining room, that his visit to Britain had been his first: he spoke perfect, colloquial English and even his humour and mannerisms seemed Anglo-Saxon. He had been to a conference in Belfast, and on its conclusion he and some others had driven back to London from the Scottish port of Stranraer. He eulogized about the leafy, green countryside, the hills of the Lake District, the lushness of the sheep pastures, the stately homes and their oak parks, the worn neatness of the villages. Listening to him I was filled with a curious nostalgia: he seemed to be describing the pastoral England of long ago – the England of Keats and Elgar, not the suburban England of today. And London, I queried? 'Oh, marvellous!' he exclaimed. 'A marvellous city!' He'd seen all the sights – on one of those open-topped tourist buses, I think. 'But I was very disappointed with Buckingham Palace,' he added. 'It was so small.' Compared to some of the Rana palaces, I suppose it was.

After tea we wandered across the river to his home in Chetrapati – he had a flat in a small Rana palace – and he told me about the Chepangs, whom an organization he worked for as a volunteer, Service Civil International, had been trying to help. He said they lived in a state of dreadful distress in the hills to the west of the capital. Would I like to visit them? We could leave any time, as long as it was before the monsoons: once the heavy rains came the rivers would be too high to wade through.

This conversation had taken place a while ago now, and in the meantime Trailokya had introduced me to Panna and the untouchables along the riverside, and I had been on my trips to the Kosi Hills and Jiri.

I'd also done my best, when in Kathmandu, to find out more about the Chepangs, but I came up with remarkably little. Few people seemed to have heard of them, and most of those who had dismissed them as 'ape-men', just as the Swiss potato man at Jiri suggested they would. They were savage, dirty, fierce and primitive, I was told. They worshipped stones, ran around naked, lived in caves and hunted with bow and arrow. That the Chepangs were viewed with contempt didn't surprise me in the least. This country is so full of prejudice that after a while one expects and accepts it.

Anthropologists have spent little time with the Chepangs, and consequently written information about the tribe is sketchy. The first person to attempt a description of them was the admirable Brian Houghton Hodgson, who spent a few days with a group of Chepangs in the 1850s. They were, he wrote, 'not noxious but helpless, nor vicious but aimless, both morally and intellectually, so that no one could without distress behold their careless unconscious inaptitude.' Hodgson found them living entirely upon wild fruits and the produce of the chase: 'It is in the very skilful snaring of the beasts of the field and the fowls of the air that all their little intelligence is manifested.' He attributed their 'wretched condition' to 'the savage ferocity which broke to pieces and outlawed both the Chepang and the Kusunda tribes during the ferocious ethnic struggles of days long gone by'. The lapse of a few generations, wrote the British Resident, 'will probably see the total extinction of the Chepang'. Fortunately, he was wrong: at the last rough count there were some 35,000 Chepangs, which meant that their numbers far exceeded those of the better-known (and more intensively studied) Sherpas and Thakalis.

There was nothing in Hodgson's paper to suggest that the Chepangs were fierce, and indeed most accounts by outsiders reported their timidity. For example, Dor Bahadur Bista noted in his book *People of Nepal* that 'Chepangs seldom indulge in violence. But since they are all illiterate and ignorant, and most of them shy and timid, they are exploited by Brahmans, Chhetris and even Tamangs.' C. L. Gajurel and K. K. Vaidya, in their book *Traditional Arts and Crafts of Nepal*, suggested that we would be hard pressed even to locate the Chepangs of the higher hills:

The primitive Chepangs do not appear before us. If they happen to encounter us, they run away from us as fast as their legs can carry them. If we visit their settlements, they even leave their children and run away but watch our movements from a distance. They come back and take care of their children only when they are sure we are far away from them.

They added that the Chepangs 'who have come down to the agricultural age are refined and friendly'.

Trailokya and I left Kathmandu by bus at nine o'clock in the morning. By midday we had reached Malhaiku, a small town on the Trisuli River mid-way between Kathmandu and Mugling. We ate some *daal bhat* in a shack by the road, found a guide, then set off on foot up a river which flowed down from the hills to the south to join the Trisuli. In places the riverbed was well over a hundred yards wide, but the river itself only occupied a small channel and it meandered to and fro between the terraced banks as though searching endlessly for some means of escaping its boulder-strewn captor. There was no sense in keeping to one side of the river or the other, and we walked in a straight line, splashing back and forth through the water. Trailokya was not a great walker so our progress was gentle, which suited me, as it was exceedingly hot and I was continually stopping in the river to splash cold water over my head and shoulders.

Around mid-afternoon the path led a little way up the hillside to our left and we rested in the shade of a *swami* tree. Others making their way up-river stopped to sit with us: two Brahmans, three Chhetris, two Tamangs, a very chirpy Magar boy and a garrulous (untouchable) blacksmith. The latter explained that whoever planted a *swami* tree immediately rid him or herself of a hundred sins. This struck me as a fine means of atonement. When we stood up to go they all got up too, and we continued on our way together. An hour later, back by the river, Trailokya and I stopped again, and so did everyone else. 'They must like company,' suggested Trailokya, who was amused by their behaviour. While we were sitting there six men and six women came round a cliff and trudged past us in a line. The men were dressed in rags; one of the women was bare-breasted. None of them were talking and they avoided looking at us until Trailokya hailed them. He asked them if they were Chepangs, and they replied that they were. They stared at us suspiciously while Trailokya explained in Nepali why we were here. One of the Chepangs translated for the benefit of those who didn't speak Nepali. 'He's saying it's all right, I think,' said Trailokya. 'They were worried in case we were from the government.' Once the translation was complete they all relaxed and the spokesman said they'd come and find us the next day.

A little farther on we left the river again and wound our way through emerald-green rice paddies, beyond which was a verdurous wood. A small spring spurted out from a tangle of roots into a wooden trough and we stopped to slake our thirst. The air was lovely and cool and moist, and we savoured it in silence. Above our heads the lower boughs of the trees were covered with purple orchids, which hung like tassels from a pelmet.

It was dusk when we reached Talti Mahadevsthan, a village of 600 people perched on a tongue of land on the south bank of the river. We found three policemen sitting outside the police station and playing cards on a flat piece of almost grassless ground. Trailokya explained why we had come and they nodded unenthusiastically. The senior of the three was the unhappiest-looking man I'd ever seen; just watching him made me want to cry in sympathy. He had a large mouth which drooped at both corners, as though in imitation of his moustache, and his small brown eyes told of a life full of anguish and boredom. He said that we could sleep in the redundant health centre, a tin-roofed building next to the policemen's living quarters. He gave us a key and we dumped our stuff there. There was a table in the centre of the room and two beds beneath the shuttered windows. The walls were covered with posters: one produced by Unicef about the treatment of child diarrhoea; others on nutrition and vaccinations. It was dark now and we were led down to a house in the village where a woman presented us with *daal bhat* and fresh chillies, which we ate with our fingers sitting on the mud floor by the dying embers of the hearth. The woman watched us eat and some chickens came indoors to inspect us too.

Afterwards we rejoined the policemen, to whom Trailokya chatted while I lay on my back, smoking and watching a sliver of moon make its way slowly into a thick mass of stars. I felt dirty but deeply relaxed. There were many bats flitting around the trees beside us, and a cuckoo began calling: *keho, keho* – who's there? who's there? Then it fell silent, realizing, perhaps, that though the heat of the day had yet to pass, the light already had. I was almost asleep when we were joined by Dibya Kanta Senghai, who until the elections this year had been the local *pradhan panch*. He was a Brahman. I couldn't see much of him as it was dark, but I liked his voice, which had a rough resonance like an oboe with a sore throat. He spoke for a long time, and every so often Trailokya would interrupt him to translate for me. 'He says the Chepangs in the village over there will be starving soon.' I observed Trailokya's silhouette waving across the valley towards Shimthali. Then later: 'He thinks some will die if they haven't already.' Have they no food at all, I asked? 'They're eating nettles and something called *githa*, a tuber, a bit like a potato, which they dig up in the forests.' After Dibya left I suggested we bring our beds outside and sleep in the open. Trailokya communicated my wish to the police. 'They say it's too dangerous,' he said. 'They say that the Chepangs are hungry. They might come across the river and raid Talti tonight.' So we slept indoors.

I woke up at dawn to find that Trailokya had already risen and gone down to the river to wash and pray. I washed too, but with last night's drinking water, or what little was left of it, then went to sit on a wooden plank which had been nailed between two trees outside the police station. I could hear the policemen mumbling and spitting in their sleeping quarters. The sun peeped over the ridge behind us and its rays gradually moved down the hill on the far side, like yellow fingers working their way sensuously down a lumpy green back. Shimthali was still in shadow and I listened as the sounds of early morning – dogs barking and people shouting – floated across the valley. Below the village there was a heap of thin, green terraces, piled up one upon another like the steps of a pyramid, at the foot of which was the riverbed. The water was making erratic progress between bleached boulders and in the same direction flowed a trickle of people, mostly Chepangs, making their way down towards Malhaiku. Sometimes one walked alone; more often they were in groups of three or four. Most of them, we discovered later, were off to buy maize with loans they'd just received from one of the Brahman landlords.

When Trailokya returned from the river I went into the police hut and presented my passport and travel permit to the chief, who lay in bed smoking. He looked at my permit, managed a wan smile, then waved me away. After breakfast we descended to the river, crossed it, then climbed up through the terraces to Shimthali. It was difficult to imagine anyone going hungry here. In the mind's eye starvation goes hand in hand with barren, sun-baked, wind-raked landscapes. Here was a scene of such lushness, such beauty, that I felt paradise must be like this: the rice paddies were as green as the wings of a love-bird; the maize higher than a man; and each of the mud-and-thatch houses had a pleasant rotundity like the belly of a well-sated Buddha. On the edge of the village we stopped to talk to a man who introduced himself as Buddhi Bahadur Chepang. He was tiny, dark and looked much younger than sixty, which was how old he thought he was. His eyes were small and set well apart in a wide, flattish face and his lips were fleshy and considerable. He squatted with us and told us that he was on his way to get a loan to buy some maize for himself and his wife. They hadn't eaten for two days, he said, grinning broadly as though he had told a good joke.

We asked him if he had any land. Very little, he replied. He explained that the government, through the *Praja Bikas Samiti*, which was set up on the king's decree to help Chepangs in the 1970s, had settled sixteen Chepang families here a few years ago. They had all come from areas which had been devastated by landslides and each family had been given a house and a little land round the village. Buddhi, who had been here for many years, had applied for land himself in 1984 after the river had washed away most of what little he had. Nothing had happened. Last time he approached government officials he was told that his application papers had been lost.

So who owns this land, we asked, pointing to the terraces below us? Nearly all of it belonged to either the villagers, Brahmans or Gurungs, the latter being a hill tribe; a few terraces had been given to the immigrant

Chepang families. There were about 200 people living in Shimthali; most were Chepangs, although there were two Brahman and several Gurung families.

Then Buddhi told us the story of how the Chepangs had lost their land. A long time ago, he said, the Brahmans and Chhetris used to come up to this valley to graze their cattle. His people, the Chepangs, had owned all this land here and all the forests. At the time they attached little importance to the land, and they were happy to let the Brahmans use it. 'This is what my father told me,' said Buddhi, 'and it was what his father had told him.' One year the Brahmans said to the Chepangs, 'Look, we bring our cattle here, and they leave all this good dung on the fields and it's all being wasted. Couldn't we grów some pumpkins on it?' The Chepangs agreed, and the following year the Brahmans grew pumpkins. Whenever the Brahmans came they would flatter the Chepangs. 'You see,' explained Buddhi, 'we've always been very susceptible to flattery; we're always happy when people say nice things about us.' Some of the Brahmans asked the Chepangs if they'd join them in ritual brotherhood, or *mit*. This was – and is – a custom whereby two men swear brotherhood with one another in front of a temple. Afterwards each can ask the other to give him something. The Chepangs had been flattered by the Brahmans' friendship, and many agreed to become ritual brothers. After the ceremonies the Chepangs would ask for something small – maybe some food, or some maize beer; the Brahmans would ask for land. 'So that's how the Brahmans took our land,' concluded Buddhi. 'They cheated us out of it.'

While Buddhi was telling us this story the village's eldest Brahman arrived. He nodded at us, readjusted his yellow *topi* and listened. 'Yes, that's right,' he said cheerfully once the story was over.

We asked Buddhi about the Chepangs' beliefs, and he said they still practised the religion of their grandfathers, which he called *raitabare*. At a certain time of year, and always on a Sunday, they slaughtered an animal, preferably a chicken, over a rock or a twig in their house. They also worshipped Bhimsen, an agricultural deity, at the same time as the Hindus celebrated the festival of Dasain. 'They're very influenced by Hinduism,' interjected Jairaj Senghai, the old Brahman, as though eager to confirm the civilizing influence of the non-animist newcomers.

Jairaj was impatient to lead us farther into the village and we followed him to a particularly handsome house, where we found a family of Chepangs sitting on a raised platform below the thatched eaves. We sat down beside them and soon afterwards were joined by Dibya Senghai, the ex-*pradhan panch* whom we'd met the evening before. A most curious conversation ensued, for here were two Brahmans – the landlords, the money-lenders, the oppressors in the eyes of the Chepangs – quietly discussing with us, and the Chepangs, the problems which the latter faced, and which all agreed were in some way attributable to the power of the Brahmans.

One of the Chepangs explained that his father had incurred a debt of 240 rupees to a Brahman, and he'd had to serve the Brahman as a virtual slave for fifteen years in order to pay it off. Jairaj nodded, confirming the truth of the story, but Dibya was keen to discuss the wider issues of development. The problem, he said, was that the landowning Brahmans were poor themselves; the land was infertile and every year the river washed more of it away. They all wanted to leave, and he himself was selling up soon and going down to Chitwan. He argued that once the Brahmans departed things would be even worse for the Chepangs: there'd be no one here to lend them money or provide them with work in the fields with which to pay off their debts. If only the government would build a road up to Talti, said Dibya, then things would be different. They should develop the area, he insisted, then the Brahmans would stay and the Chepangs could share their new-found prosperity. Jairaj listened to this but said nothing, and Dibya departed. Later we discovered that in the 1982 elections Dibya had lost to a Chepang. This was hardly surprising as the Chepangs far outnumbered the Brahmans in the *panchayat*. However, the Brahmans, who held all the administrative posts, were incensed at the rejection of one of their leaders. The result was declared void, the counts tampered with and the elected Chepang displaced in favour of Dibya.

Once Dibya was out of the way Jairaj delivered a short speech, which he prefaced with some vigorous spitting. 'Many people may leave,' he said, 'but I never will. I played with the Chepangs when I was a child, when my family first came here; I slept with them; I ate with them; I grew up with them; they helped me when I had my first cattle, and it was through my cattle that I prospered. I owe a lot to them. When they suffer, I suffer too; my heart beats with their hearts. I couldn't leave and I can't see them starve: I always lend them a little money when they need it.' He spat again and scrutinized the faces of the Chepangs, as though he was awaiting confirmation of his declared solicitousness towards them. Some of them nodded. 'These people are very innocent,' he continued, 'they're very honest. Yes, I love these people.'

Jairaj then explained how the Chepangs got their name. There seemed to be various theories, but the one which he favoured, and which seemed to please the Chepangs present here, was that the Chepangs were born out of the communion of a dog (*che*) and a rock (*bang*). The former pissed on the latter, and thus began the Chepang race. (The anthropologist Navin Rai gives a rather different explanation for their name: 'They call themselves Chyobang or Chebang, *chyo* meaning, "on the top" and *bang* meaning "stone", in other words, "the people living in the hills". The

Chepangs claim their ancestors lived in rock shelters and caves, and most believe they originated from stone.')

Trailokya asked the Chepangs who lived in the house where we now sat – they belonged to one of the rehabilitated families – what they had to eat. Hardly anything, replied one young man. 'Maybe this house looks good to you,' he said, 'but all we have is this.' He went inside and returned with three small tubers which had been blackened in the ashes of a fire. This was *githa*. He began peeling one of the tubers and everyone laughed. The *githa* season was almost over, so even this source of food was difficult to come by now. A Chepang woman explained that *githa* used to be plentiful in the woods by the river, but they had become much harder to find since the landslides and floods of 1984. *Sisnu*, nettles, were also scarcer than they used to be, partly because their habitat had diminished, partly because they had been so intensively sought during the past years.

Opposite where we sat was a buffalo shed, open at each end, made out of bamboo, and thatched roughly with the leaves and branches of trees. Above the buffaloes and the pigs was a platform. Two Chepang families, one of seven people, the other of five, lived here, one on each side of a central divide. They slept on the platform and they cooked below, among the animals. We asked what the Chepangs who lived in the shed – it belonged to Jairaj – thought about the new arrivals being given much better houses. 'They're too poor to think,' said the man with the *githa*. 'They're too busy worrying about eating to think about injustices.'

This man's mother, a marvellous old sack of bones, now appeared from the house. Luti Maya Chepang said she was somewhere in the region of eighty or ninety years old, though her movements were those of someone half her age. It was difficult to get much sense out of her, and as our questions were translated to her she greeted each with great guffaws of laughter. To our astonishment – and to the amusement of her offspring – she proceeded to tell us that life now was very good indeed, much better than it had been when she was bringing up a family. She'd had eleven children, four of whom had died when young; her husband had succumbed to goitre twenty-two years ago. She said that nowadays her son could always borrow a little money to buy food, something which was unthinkable in the old days. When he was a child the family had lived off roots and leaves; if they were lucky she had been able to give them some maize gruel twice a month. She instructed her son to go and get some of the leaves they used to eat. He returned with a branch and she roared with laughter. This is what they were brought up on, she said, plucking leaves off the branch. It was animal fodder.

Before Jairej led us away, another young man appeared with a bow and for our entertainment he fired a couple of arrows at a nearby tree. He explained that the men sometimes went after deer, but they were difficult to find now, and it was a long time since they'd killed any.

At the top of the village we were shown some of the projects which had been set up by *Praja Bikas*. There was a shed where some Chepangs had been trained to weave and another where they'd been taught to make baskets out of bamboo and plastic. One man, Krishna Bahadur Chepang, showed us the results, which were horrible. After the one-month training course he and his brother had borrowed 400 rupees to buy the plastic. They'd had to go all the way to Narayangath, a town in the Chitwan Valley, to get it. They'd made eight baskets so far, but sold only one. Each took two days to make. He said nobody wanted to buy them here and a *Praja Bikas* official had told him he should travel to Kathmandu to sell them. But he didn't have any money to take the bus, he knew no one there, and he now realized he could never recoup the money he'd spent. The interest rate was 60 per cent a year; so he already owed 20 rupees in interest, which he didn't have. He hadn't any food for himself or his family, and until the harvest began in six weeks' time there wasn't much hope of earning any money.

Most of the Chepangs here hadn't eaten for several days, but they said no one had died of hunger yet. They didn't even talk of their present plight as though it were anything out of the ordinary: food shortages always occurred at this time of year, and it was simply a matter of hanging on till the harvest, when there would be work and food.

Just before we left Shimthali we stopped at a house where a woman sat with three small children. She said she had some maize for the children but no food for herself or her husband. One of the children had her left nipple in his mouth and he stared at us with large, doleful eyes. He didn't suck at all, and even when she stood up and showed us inside the house – they slept on the bare mud floor and there was no furniture of any sort – he retained the nipple in his mouth. She was an animated, handsome woman and I found her very attractive, a fact which I passed on to Trailokya.

'That was odd,' he mused once we'd set off from the village. 'When I told her you thought she was beautiful she couldn't work out what I meant. I don't think anyone had ever told her that before.' That made me feel sadder than almost anything I'd heard that morning.

It took us a couple of hours to walk to Bangarang. Again, we followed an almost dry riverbed, a tributary of the one we'd come up the previous day. The river had cut a deep, narrow gorge, the sides of which were densely wooded. It must have been humid here, for ferns grew in profusion and the lower boughs of the trees were seamed with orchids. Here and there the glossy, spatulate leaves of palms rose above the hazy canopy of oak and sal; they were so different from the surrounding foliage that it looked as though they had been whimsically transposed upon the rest with the sole intention of startling passing travellers. We were accompanied by Krishna, the basket-maker – he explained that he had business to attend to at Bangarang, although later we realized he simply came for the walk – and by a cheerful youth in a loin cloth who carried a bow and a clutch of arrows and pointed out footprints of deer whenever we came across them. To my annoyance, our Brahman guide, an insolent young man to whom I'd taken a severe dislike, was still with us. He was for ever demanding cigarettes, and I was glad to have the Chepangs with us as it meant I could give them cigarettes while ignoring him. They always received them with cupped hands and a graceful bob of the head, but after a few drags the Brahman would harry them into relinquishing them. Half-way to Bangarang we sat down and I produced two bags of nuts and two packets of 'glucose' biscuits. As the guide had just eaten *daal bhat* at Shimthali I felt justified in offering him nothing and split what I had between the rest of us. He stared at me malevolently, which pleased me as it meant the message was getting through. 'Bloody Brahmans!' I muttered to Trailokya. 'Yes,' he laughed. 'Bloody Brahmans!' Racism, as I said, is endemic. Apologies to my many Brahman friends.

Bangarang was too scattered to be a village in the real sense of the word. There were some twenty houses dotted over a hillside, and we stopped at the first we came to. It belonged to a relatively prosperous Chepang family, the head of which, a fit-looking man of late middle age, greeted us cordially and ordered a young girl to fetch rush mats for us to sit on. He announced that I was only the third white person to visit the village within living memory, which went some way towards explaining why I had become an object of considerable interest to the children, who gathered to stare at me and smile warmly.

Over the past fourteen years the river had taken twenty-six ropanis (a ropani is about one-seventh of an acre) of this family's best land, leaving them with only six. Many families – though not this one – had left here after the landslides of 1984 and moved down to Shimthali. Our host owned a pair of buffalo and twenty-four goats, and despite his loss of land he considered himself a man of means. The women of his family made bamboo *dokos*, which they sold for 10 rupees each at Malhaiku, as well as fishing nets and other odds and ends. They also hunted occasionally in the forests, but hunting was difficult as game was far less plentiful now than it had been in his youth. 'I am old,' he said, 'but I have very energetic sons and I feel secure.' He suggested that many Chepangs didn't like working hard, but that was probably because they were paid so little, and in any case they found it demeaning working for Brahmans. If they worked for themselves they were industrious.

Krishna had a young brother called Tek who'd also come to Bangarang today. He had a little land here, and some at Shimthali, though not enough to provide for his family. He was a bright individual, and articulate about the problems which he and the Chepangs faced. So far most of the Chepangs we'd come across seemed resigned to their poverty, accepting the oppression of the Brahmans almost as though it were the will of the gods. Tek talked about the Chepangs much as a historian might, weighing the legends and myths about the tribe against the reality of their lives. One by one he dealt with what he considered outsiders' misconceptions about his people. The Chepangs were held to be many things: lazy, much given to debauchery and fearful of outside influences. The poverty of the Chepangs, said Tek, was in no way a result of an idle disposition. It was true that if Chepangs had food and money they often chose not to work; but the old man was right: they didn't want to work for the Brahmans if they could avoid it. It was simply a question of pride. There was some truth in the contention that Chepangs liked drinking; but was that surprising? Drink helped them to escape from the misery of their everyday existence. And they loved a fine wedding, a grand celebration; but didn't most people? As for the Chepangs running away from outsiders, Tek admitted that this was true of the Chepangs who lived in the higher and remoter hills. But they had good reasons for doing so – they had always been persecuted; they had grown to assume that outsiders came only with the intention of exploiting them. Many people, said Tek, described these highland Chepangs as primitive because they lived in caves and often went naked. They were missing the point: the Chepangs were simply too poor to buy clothes; too poor to construct a home. And the reason why Chepangs ate *sisnu* and *githa* was not because they were favoured foods; they ate them because if they didn't they would starve.

We made our way back to Talti a little before nightfall. Sunset was followed by supper, supper by sleep. We were up at sunrise the next day to find Tek, Krishna and a group of Chepangs from Shimthali waiting for us. Trailokya was going to approach some aid agencies in Kathmandu with the intention of organizing emergency food aid and he instructed a teacher in Talti – a Brahman who had been involved with the Chepangs – to make out a list, with the help of Tek and others, of the Chepang families in the immediate vicinity of Talti who had had little or nothing to eat over the past few weeks. There were 122 families; a total of 595 people. Before we left we gave Tek enough money to buy a hundredweight of maize, and Trailokya instructed him to give it to the ten families in direst need – 'Which doesn't include you,' he added. 'I saw you eating yesterday.' Tek seemed to find this just.

Trailokya and I had intended to make our way during the day to Dhading Besi, a town to the north of the Trisuli River where the chief project officer for *Praja Bikas* was based. However, when we reached the road at Malhaiku we heard that he was in Kathmandu, so we immediately took the bus back to the capital, having decided to visit the ministry in charge of *Praja Bikas* the next day.

The bus was full of holidaying Indians who'd come up from Birgunj, and to eyes which had had nothing more substantial to feast on than the Chepangs, they seemed an obese and portly crowd. Whenever we stopped, heavy-jowled men, fat-legged boys and flabby-bellied, big-bummed women descended from the bus and waddled about searching for tea and sweets like a shoal of ill-tempered jellyfish. Trailokya and I lounged on the roof and watched the landscape glide by. Fluffy white clouds raced across an aquamarine sky; two boys on the roof made wild grabs at the hedgehog-like fruits which hung from jackfruit trees; and we chattered. Trailokya mentioned, *à propos* of I forget what, that he had spent some time in prison, along with several thousand other members of the banned Nepali Congress Party.

'So how was prison?' I asked, expecting to hear a bitter tirade against it.

'Oh, prison was fine,' he replied.

'You weren't mistreated?'

'No, not at all. Once you get out of police custody and into prison you can be pretty sure you won't get beaten up. In fact, if I could go to prison for two months a year, then that would be fine.'

'You're joking?' I asked.

'Not entirely,' said Trailokya. 'I was surrounded by friends; we were given rice and lentils and allowed to cook for ourselves. We had plenty of good discussions and it gave me time to be quiet and reflective. Mind you, six months is too long.' He explained that when they were released they asked the prison warders why they had treated them so decently. 'Well,' they'd replied, 'in a few years' time you might be the people in power, and we'll be looking after your opponents here. We hope you'll remember us kindly.'

Trailokya talked of prison and political persecution as though they were part of everyday life. For some of his family they had been. Both his father, Shanker Man Singh, and his uncle, Ganesh Man Singh, had been jailed under the Ranas, whose rule they'd opposed, in the 1940s. His father developed TB while in prison, and its combination with meningitis killed him a few years after the Ranas had been deposed. Unlike his brother he had never been, in Trailokya's words, 'a political man'. Ganesh, on the other hand, was considered one of the country's leading revolutionary spirits. After two spells in prison in the 1940s (he was recaptured after an escape in 1945), he eventually made it to India, where he helped B. P. Koirala form the Nepali Congress Party. He was charged with the task of returning to Kathmandu to contact King Tribhuvan and organize a military uprising against the Ranas. He was caught and jailed again and released only on the conclusion of the successful revolution of

1951. Over the next nine years Ganesh Man Singh served as a minister in various governments as Nepal struggled to establish a durable democracy. In the national elections of 1959 Koirala's Nepali Congress Party was swept to power. The following year, while Koirala was away at a United Nations conference, the government was toppled in a military coup. King Mahendra assumed total power and Koirala, Singh and others were charged with corruption and one thing and another. Koirala and Singh were imprisoned from 1960 to 1968 and Singh was arrested again and imprisoned briefly in 1976. He still lives in Kathmandu, and Trailokya said he was sad I couldn't meet him: he was in Delhi getting medical treatment at the moment. I was sad too.

Dervla Murphy, I notice, admired the king for the action he took in 1960 'when he admitted that feigning to operate a democratic government in Nepal was a piece of pernicious nonsense. In the nine years since the overthrow of the Ranas in 1951 Nepal had had ten different governments, each more corrupt and cynical than the other.' This strikes me as a somewhat blithe way to dismiss a period during which the country's leaders had at least made an attempt to shake off the feudal bonds of the past. Were Dervla Murphy to return now – I wish she would, incidentally, for she could assess, far better than any other foreign writer, how the country had changed since her visit in 1965 – I suspect she would review that first decade of post-Rana history more charitably, especially when seen in the light of what has happened since then.

By the time we reached Naubise, Trailokya and I had exhausted the subject of politics, and we both sunk into our own reflections on the long climb up to the rim of the Kathmandu Valley. I experienced a mixture of sadness and elation. Sadness because I at last felt, just as I was about to leave, that I was getting to know a little about the country. At any rate, its wonderful jagged landscape was now so firmly etched on my mind that I knew the memory of it would remain with me, as vivid as it seemed now as I gazed at these blue-green receding hills, for many years to come. The reason for my elation was more prosaic: this was the last time I would be making the bus trip up this particular hillside. Before we reached the top we passed a group of people peering over a cliff: they were staring down at the remains of a car, which had just gone over the side. Nepalese bus drivers have obviously been taught that it is only safe to overtake when they see nothing coming the other way; this, needless to say, is always the case on blind corners, the sight of which can almost be guaranteed to incite the drivers to accelerate and pass whatever lies ahead. I breathed a sigh of relief when we reached the statue at the top of the hill, and I was back in the Vajra in time for dinner. The next day we set off to see Mr Promod Kumar Koirala at the Ministry of Panchayat and Local Development.

Mr Koirala, an assistant secretary to the minister and the man in charge of *Praja Bikas*, was courteous, if diffident. He was under the mis-apprehension, I soon realized, that we had yet to visit the Chepangs. 'When you go, they'll probably run away from you,' he said. 'They're even suspicious of us.' We explained that we had just returned from Talti. 'And did they run away?' he asked. We replied that we'd found them very hospitable. He seemed to assume that our visit had done little to dissipate our ignorance and proceeded to tell us what the Chepangs were like. It sounded as though he had memorized a government report and was paraphrasing it for our benefit. The king, he explained, had visited the area in 1976 and given directives to government to improve the lot of the Chepangs. *Praja Bikas Samiti* – the Chepang Development Committee – had got off the ground in 1978, since when much had been done: the Chepangs had been provided with all manner of help – drinking water facilities, fruit trees, health care, goats and chickens, irrigation schemes, mule tracks, stipends for Praja students and so forth. (The word *praja*, incidentally, means 'subject', and members of the younger generation of Chepangs prefer to be called Prajas, believing it to lack the derisory connotations of their older tribal name.) Mr Koirala admitted that the schemes set up under *Praja Bikas* had sometimes been of greater benefit to the Brahmans and other groups than to the Chepangs. 'The Brahmans are very crafty,' added Mr Koirala. Trailokya and I nodded our agreement.

As we rose to leave I asked Mr Koirala how often he visited the Chepangs. 'I haven't been to visit them yet. You see, I've only been in this post for six months.' Perhaps Mr Koirala really did believe that *Praja Bikas* was, as he claimed, 'successfully going on'; but I doubt it.

One of the projects set up by *Praja Bikas* involved the distribution of goats and chickens. On paper, it was an excellent idea. The Chepangs were given young animals with the intention that they should rear them to a decent size, then eat or sell them. It was assumed that they would breed from some and gradually build up their livestock numbers. Sadly, the project was a failure. A local teacher, himself a Brahman, described to us what happened. His account was confirmed by others.

Each Chepang family chosen for the project was given ten day-old chicks. On average about half the chicks died during the first week, and by the end of the first month only two or three of the original ten survived. Having got this far there was a reasonable chance that they would grow to maturity. The money-lenders knew this, and once the chicks were a month old they approached their owners. 'Look,' a money-lender would say to a Chepang family, 'you people are hungry; let me give you money for the chicks and in return, as interest, you look after them until they're fully grown, then I'll come and get them.' The Chepangs were given between 5 and 10 rupees for each chick – or the equivalent in maize or rice. Several months later the money-lender would return to collect them. By now each chicken was worth 60 rupees in the market. If a chick died before its time was up, the money-lender would assess his notional losses and that became a debt.

A similar thing happened with the goats, although the profits which the money-lenders made were considerably greater. They paid 50 rupees against a kid which six months later was worth 500. None of the goats which we saw at Bangarang were *Praja Bikas* goats. 'Nobody from *Praja Bikas* has ever been up here,' claimed one Chepang. 'We had to fetch the goats ourselves from Malhaiku. They were all *jamuna pari* goats from the lowlands and none survived up here – the climate was too harsh for them.' Later we heard that some Chepangs had sold their kids in Malhaiku as soon as they'd been given them.

The reluctance of the *Praja Bikas* staff to venture into the field was remarkable considering how close Talti was to the main road. A fit man could walk there in three hours. We were told that the chief project officer at Dhading Besi visited Talti only once or twice a year; and he never bothered to go any farther into the hills. 'One time, about six years ago,' said the teacher, '*Praja Bikas* sent messengers up to Talti telling the Chepangs to come down to Malhaiku the next morning. When they arrived they were given free fertilizer and milk powder. They sold their fertilizer straight away – it was even given to those without land. They kept the milk powder but they weren't told how to mix it. Their children got diarrhoea so they fed it to their animals or gave it away.'

Teaching Chepangs skills such as weaving, carpentry and basket-making had done little to improve matters in Shimthali. Since 1984 a dozen Chepangs had been given carpentry training. Once the course was over they were given no tools, so none of the trainees made use of their new skill. The weaving project has been only marginally more successful. At the time of our visit ten Chepangs had been taught how to use the looms. They were paid – or were supposed to be paid – 3 rupees 45 peisa for every metre of cloth they wove. A skilled weaver could produce seven metres in a day, thus earning him or herself about 24 rupees (a little over $1). The Chepangs had to buy the yarn in Kathmandu and sell either to *Praja Bikas* at Dhading Besi or to their supervisor. On our way back to Malhaiku we were accompanied by four Chepangs, one of whom had done the weaving course. He told us that he and his friends had recently woven 100 metres of cloth, for which they should have received 345 rupees. Instead the supervisor gave them 160 rupees. When we suggested they should have demanded what they were rightly owed he simply shrugged, as if to say, 'What could we do about it?'

The following story, told to us on three separate occasions, exemplifies the attitude of the *Praja Bikas* staff at Dhading. When the chief district officer visited Talti and Shimthali he was led to a display of beautifully made cane-and-bamboo chairs, lampshades and baskets, and told that this was the work of the Chepangs. After he left these objects were transported to Dhading, where they were put on display as examples of craftwork which *Praja Bikas* had encouraged. None of it had been made by the Chepangs; it had simply been brought from another district to impress the authorities.

Chepangs have sometimes resorted to manual labour as a means of making money. No doubt some have prospered – the term is relative, admittedly – but we heard many tales of exploitation. One man at Bangarang said he had been contracted to work on the road between Kathmandu and Pokhara and promised a wage of 20 rupees a day. Each day he was given 5 rupees by the man who had hired him. After a month the overseer disappeared, never to be seen again. He and many others, not all of them Chepangs, never received their wages. 'They're always cheating us like that,' said the Chepang despondently.

Such exploitation even occurred on projects funded by *Praja Bikas*, an example of which was the building of a canal between Talti and Malhaiku. Although it was to supply water to fields which belonged to Brahmans, *Praja Bikas* officials justified the expenditure on the grounds that its construction would provide wages for the Chepangs. It was badly designed and washed away before its completion. According to some Chepangs who worked on the project, they were paid less then two weeks' wages for four weeks' work.

Tales such as these could fill a book, but the above suffice to show how *Praja Bikas* – in the Talti area, at least – has done little to help the Chepangs, some of whom spoke more highly of the activities of a voluntary organization called the Non-formal Education Service Centre (NFESC), which began work in Talti in 1985. The NFESC has had the advantage of youth; it has observed the mistakes made by *Praja Bikas* and learnt from them. Its projects are carefully supervised to ensure that the Chepangs don't fall prey to the money-lenders and that they make the best of what help they receive. As one would expect, NFESC sees training as an important weapon in the fight against poverty. So far fifty-five adult Chepangs have been taught to read and write, and in 1987 three Chepangs were being sent to do a two-week training course at the British agricultural station at Lumle, a village to the west of Pokhara. NFESC had also set up a tree nursery at Talti and distributed goats to the poorest Chepangs. Fifteen families which previously had no goats now owned some, and although a few soon fell prey to the money-lenders, others had built up small flocks and sold their animals in the market for 500 rupees.

The foregoing may have given the impression that the problems facing the Chepangs are peculiar to them. Would that they were. The majority of Chepangs lack sufficient land to provide for themselves, but then so do millions of others in Nepal. To quote from the USAID Mission Director's report of 1981/2:

Ownership of land, the overwhelming item of wealth, and thus receipt of income, is very concentrated. Two per cent of all rural households cultivate about 27 per cent of the land. Three recent publications provide estimates for concentration of income which show Nepal as having one of the worst income concentration problems in Asia.

The land-reform law of 1964 established a limit of forty acres to what one person could own; but its effects were minimal, partly because the ceiling was set so high, and partly because those with more than forty acres could simply transfer deeds to members of their family. Over half of all farming households have less than 1.25 acres of land; about 10 per cent of rural households are landless.

As far as debt is concerned, millions of small farmers, of all tribes and castes, are virtually enslaved by it. There are no figures for national indebtedness, though isolated studies suggest it to be very high. About 70 per cent of land belonging to Limbus in the eastern hills is pledged to creditors. In another area, Palpa, a team of British academics found that one-fifth of all households were in debt, and interest rates were between 20 and 32 per cent. A study of a Terai village, Padipur, found that 35 per cent of all households owed money and 74 per cent owed food. According to Unicef:

Families are obliged to borrow money or grains to meet their needs during the 'hungry months' of April to June (when the price of grain is highest). Loans must often be repaid immediately after harvest during which time the price of grain is at its lowest. The differential constitutes an additional interest rate which accrues to the lender's profit. This also means that each year there will be less grain available in the poor farmer's store and he is thus forced into cycles of increasing borrowing and impoverishment.

Every single Chepang we spoke to was in debt to a local Brahman or Chhetri. Most said that the interest rate was 60 per cent a year. Loans were repaid either in cash, in cereals or by labour on the money-lenders' land. For a day's fieldwork the Chepangs received four kilos of maize or its equivalent in cash (which, at the time of our visit, would have been 12 rupees). One Chhetri we met at Talti told us how much he sympathised with the Chepangs; how important it was that *Praja Bikas* should do more for them. Later we learnt that he was one of the biggest money-lenders in the area, lending, it was estimated, between 30,000 and 40,000 rupees a year to Chepangs, thus making around 20,000 rupees ($1,000) in interest.

There were also poor Brahmans, Chhetris, Gurungs and Tamangs in the area and they relied, as did the Chepangs, on loans from the wealthy. As for Jairaj Senghai, the yellow-*topi*ed Brahman of Shimthali, he too must have been doing well out of usury. 'I love these people,' he'd said. 'My heart beats with their hearts.' I think he genuinely meant it, and I also believe the Chepangs looked on him with a certain affection. Debt-bondage, which is slavery under another name, kindles an odd form of reciprocal love.

10

Help and Hindrance

I‍T WAS ONLY DURING my last few weeks in the country that I discovered, and made use of, the sauna and the library in the Vajra. I was alerted to the existence of the former by an American who had been working in Kathmandu these last eight years. When he first came here on a short holiday he decided, when gazing out of the window in the sauna's changing room, that Kathmandu was a city in which he wanted to live. The same view of the city is shared by the library, and it is particularly lovely in the late afternoon, when the falling sun casts a burnished glaze across the temple roofs and the mud-brick houses. From this angle one is spared the ugliness of recent building and the city appears much as it must have done to the men and women of many centuries ago: solid, harmonious, memorable.

Sometimes I used to visit the library in the evenings when I had nothing better to do (Christoph, Marie and Charles had all gone by the time I returned from Jiri), and browsing through the shelves I would come across all manner of interesting and useless information. Every now and then I'd stumble over something which pleased me sufficiently to warrant taking a few notes, most of which have now been consigned to the dustbin. An exception are those I jotted down from a paper by Klaus T. Seeland with the unpromising title of 'The Use of Bamboo in a Rai Village in the Upper Arun Valley'. Here is a list of just some of the objects which these Rai villagers make out of bamboo:

stools	animal-muzzles
sieves for washing wool	fish-traps
trays for winnowing rice	bows
baskets	arrows
combs	hen baskets

spoons	*dokos*
pipes	flutes
chang and *tongba* straws	resonators for Jew's-harps
mats	roofs
animal-mangers	walls

Many nations have adopted trees and plants as leitmotivs, displaying them proudly on flags, stamps and government notepaper. For example, the Canadians have taken the maple; the Senegalese, the baobab; the Scots, the thistle. If I were to choose a leitmotiv for Nepal – or at any rate, for the hills of Nepal – it would be bamboo. There are few more striking sights than a grove of this bizarre grass etched on to a red-earth hillside. With its long, straight, tubular stems, often reaching up thirty feet or more, bamboo imposes a classical order upon the most anarchic of landscapes. It is as though the Arcadian god Pan had impaled in the soil handfuls of pipes, each ready to be plucked and blown whenever he wandered by. Indeed, even the softest of breezes brings music to the groves, whistling gently through the dry, brittle leaves, or singing melodiously among the whispy tufts of foliage which flutter above the stems like peacock harls on a Victorian bonnet. As the wind rises the canes jostle against one another and chatter discordantly, as though admonishing the elements for disturbing their peace. Whenever you come across a grove of bamboo, stop for a while, rest your back against the canes and close your eyes; then listen to the ancient music of time.

The prosaic mind may argue that those countries which use a plant as an emblem are doing little more than acknowledging the most conspicuous element of their vegetation (or sometimes the rarest or most beautiful). That is to deny many things, not least history. In the industrialized West, where few work on the land, we have largely forgotten, or forsaken, the intimate relationship we once had with the natural world. The industrial revolution not only drew people away from the land and into the cities, it also made redundant numerous plants, thus freeing us from a total dependency on the produce of field and forest. Certainly, we still rely on the land to produce food and timber, but the number of plants, whether wild or cropped, which we use today is but a fraction of those which our ancestors harvested. Just look, for example, at the British landscape of Elizabethan times, to which the works' of Shakespeare are an excellent introduction. From the woods came a great array of household and farming implements, a list of which would be similar to that for the Rai village in the Upper Arun today. These were made from oak, beech, hornbeam, yew, hazel, elder, ash and various other trees, some of which also provided an annual harvest of nuts or berries. For fibre the peasantry depended on such crops as flax, nettle and hemp

(Bottom and his friends in *A Midsummer Night's Dream* were dressed in 'hempen homespun'), and whatever dyes they used either came from the woods or were cultivated, as were woad and madder. One only needs to glance at *The Grete Herbal* of 1526, or *Culpeper's Herbal* of 1652, to see that there was scarcely a wild plant (or animal) which wasn't put to some medicinal use: even such things as mandrake root, spiders' web and beaver 'ballockes' were included in the old pharmacopoeias.

It seems to be an axiom of progress that the more 'advanced' or 'developed' a nation becomes, the less its populace knows about nature: time and technology have diminished our need of it. In the West timber has lost its importance, superceded in the manufacture of many goods by metals and plastics; fibres derived from oil – first rayon, later nylon – reduced our dependency on plants such as hemp, jute and sisal; artificial dyes have replaced natural ones; and the modern medicine cabinet reflects the advances of biochemistry rather than the knowledge of the herbalists.

That charismatic yet cumbersome being, the octopus of progress, is gradually pushing its tentacles into the hills of Nepal. However, it is a slow process, and one can still observe the peasantry making use of what surrounds them much as their forebears did. But as roads push farther into the hills, as Western ideas of efficient agriculture spread, as increasing numbers of people turn away from their traditional healers, the *dhamies* and *jhankris* (of whom there are some 400,000 in Nepal), in favour of modern medicines, the list of plants in everyday use will diminish. One sees this phenomenon of rejection most clearly in the case of hemp, or *Cannabis sativa;* and it is perhaps through hemp, more than any other plant, that one can establish the communality of experience which links peasants of all cultures. Bottom and his friends would have understood much better than I ever shall how the villages of Nepal work today.

Nepal is famous for its cannabis. Use of the drug is now illegal, but in the 1960s its widespread availability, and official tolerance of those who took advantage of it, was one of the country's principal attractions for the tens of thousands of hippies who made their way to Kathmandu. The legacy of that era can be seen in the streets to the south of New Road, one of which is still known as Freak Street. There are dozens of cheap hotels here, and small cafés where once upon a time you could smoke dope and eat hash-cakes. The hippies have gone, but their memory lingers in the music which drifts out on to the rickshaw-cluttered street: Pink Floyd, Genesis, Cream, Janice Jopling, Dr John, King Crimson ... It is still easy enough to buy cannabis (or any other drug you care to think of), but the vast majority of young travellers seem more interested in trekking than getting stoned.

Most Nepalese claim that only foreigners smoke cannabis now. If this is true, their own abstinence is a recent phenomenon. Colonel Kirkpatrick recorded that the cultivated fields round Kathmandu were 'skirted with Jeea, a plant that yields the drug called Cherris, for which Nepaul is so famous ... The plant would appear to differ in no respect from the hemp ... The gum is a most potent narcotic, possessing, it is said, very valuable medical qualities.' Kirkpatrick referred briefly to another use to which hemp was put: 'From the hemp the Newars of Nepaul fabricate some coarse linens, and also a very strong kind of sack-cloth.'

Hemp's long fibres have served a multitude of purposes. They were used, throughout the Old World, to make such things as shirts, smocks, bed linen, shoe-laces, halters, bridles, funeral shrouds, fishing nets, ropes and sail-cloths. During Elizabethan times the entire British fleet was fitted out in canvas and rope made from hemp, and peasants in parts of southern England were fined if they failed to grow it. Though hemp's narcotic and medicinal properties had been appreciated for many hundreds of years in the East and Asia Minor, it was not until relatively recent times that they became known to the West; Baudelaire and his friends at the *Club des Hachichins* were among the first Europeans to make use of it as a drug. And hemp was used as a medicine only after an Irish surgeon, working in Calcutta during the 1830s, brought back news of its curative properties. He found it to be particularly effective in the treatment of rheumatism and tetanus, and with its administration even 'the awful malady [of rabies] was stripped of its horrors'. Queen Victoria's physician, J. Russell Reynolds, once remarked that 'Indian hemp, when pure and administered carefully, is one of the most valuable medicines we possess.'

Hemp's golden age has passed. It is little used in the West today, except in the manufacture of cigarette papers and as a 'recreational drug', and it is no longer of such importance to the Nepalese peasantry, although its use has not entirely ceased. The Newars stopped using its fibre long ago, but I heard that in the remote far west of the country peasants still weave it into a coarse cloth with which they make shirts, trousers, dresses and many other articles. I believe it is still used in a modest way by doctors practising Ayavedic medicine and in Hindu rituals, and large quantities of hemp, much of it grown up the side valleys of the Kali Gandaki, continue to leave the country either in the form of grass or cannabis resin. Hemp, incidentally, was Rabelais's 'divine Pantagruelion', a herb which should be 'sown at the first coming of the swallows, and pulled out of the ground when the cicadas begin to get hoarse'; and if you wish to learn more about its place in Western history you must read chapters 49–52 of the *Third Book of the Heroic Deeds and Sayings of the Good Pantagruel*, which I happened to have with me in Nepal and which afforded me endless hours of entertainment.

Bamboo and hemp are two of hundreds of plants for which the Nepalese find an everyday use, or did until recently in the case of hemp. 'Green forests are the wealth of Nepal' goes one old saying; and indeed one cannot overstate the importance of forests in the scheme of things here. They provide the raw materials for building houses and for making agricultural machinery, furniture and other objects; and they provide nine-tenths of the country's fuel needs. Without forests farmers in the hills could not farm, or certainly not in the way they do at present. In the Middle Hills the number of large animals is roughly the same as the number of people. They provide draught-power, milk, meat (though not from cattle, which are sacred) and manure with which to fertilize the fields. Animal fodder is obtained largely from trees, which also provide bedding materials, and a farmer with a hectare of land needs somewhere in the region of one or two hectares of forest to supply him with his fodder and bedding requirements. Without forests there could be no domestic stock; without stock, no manure (or milk or meat); without manure, no fertile land; without fertile land, no food; without food . . .

This lengthy preamble is by way of introduction to a couple of days which I spent in the company of two Australian foresters in the vicinity of Chautara, a market town which sits on a sharp ridge about forty miles as the crow flies to the north-east of Kathmandu. It was they, more than any others, who alerted me to the remarkably complex relationship which exists between the peasant farmer and the land he works. And it was through them, and their work, that I gained the clearest insight into the ragbag of facts, ideas, myths and motives which contribute to the formulation of aid policy in Nepal.

Dr Don Gilmour was the manager of the Nepal Australia Forestry Project (NAFP); Andrew Carter, one of his assistants. Gilmour had been in charge of the project from 1981 to 1983, returning to the helm again in 1985. A short, muscular, bearded man with a gruff, direct manner, Gilmour spoke fluent Nepali and spent much of his time, as did the more ascetic-looking Carter and the other officials, out in the field with the Nepali counterparts from the Ministry of Forests and with the farmers whom the project was trying to help. The NAFP has been extensively written about – it has even been the subject of various television programmes – and consequently what I have to say about it will have less to do with the nuts and bolts of the project than the reasons which lie behind its success.

Its history, briefly, is this. Australian aid to Nepal began, in a very modest way, in 1962. Professor D. M. Griffin, whom I had met at Mohonk and who had directed operations since 1977, has written, revealingly, that:

In retrospect I believe the main significance of NAFP/1 [the forestry work conducted around Kathmandu between 1962 and 1977] lies in the opportunity it gave a number of Australian foresters to learn something of the potential nature of Nepalese forestry, *whilst being in no position to do damage through ignorance of local conditions* [my italics].

The second phase of the Australian involvement (NAFP/2) began in 1977 in two districts to the east of Kathmandu, Sindu Palchok and Kabhre Palanchok. These encompassed an area of some 390,000 hectares, within which lived over half a million people, most of whom belonged to farming households. A little over one-fifth of the land was cultivated, the rest being too steep or too high. Within the two districts there were some 200,000 hectares of forest land, one-third of which had been partially or wholly denuded of trees, and much of which was so remote that it was of little direct use to the farmers.

The aim of the project was to run the forestry business as a joint venture between the government's forestry department and the local people, with technical and financial help from the Australians. Eventually the latter would pull out and the inhabitants of the two districts, with the help of the forestry department, would look after their resources in such a way as to ensure their requirements were met in perpetuity. In Gilmour's words, the project was designed to be 'low key and low cost'. Between 1978 and 1985 Australian funding amounted to $A4.5 million (or a little over $3 million). During this period the number of tree nurseries in the two districts increased from five to 114, over 5,000 hectares of new plantations were established, and many hundreds of people were trained as forest guards, nursery foremen and professional foresters. A third phase, NAFP/3, began in 1986. It will last for five years and Australia will provide some $A7.5 million ($5 million) towards it. A further 10,000 hectares of forest will be planted and thirty-odd new nurseries created.

Many people in Nepal, and outside its borders as well, see the Nepal Australia Forestry Project as a model of excellence, worthy of emulation, but seldom emulated. Before I look at the reasons for the project's high reputation, it might be instructive to recall some of the criticisms I had heard about foreign aid before I came to Nepal. While I was at the Mohonk conference I interviewed some of the Nepalese participants, and the following are excerpts from the tapes I made.

'One of the worst things about foreign aid is that the donors – the aid agencies – have lost credibility. I've been to parts of Nepal where if you say, "We're going to do such-and-such a project", the locals will say, "Well, sod off! Go away!" You see, they've seen projects fail in the past. They've had their hopes raised, then dashed. This is one of the things which happens with aid.'

'A little while ago I was stuck for the night on the road to Pokhara.

There was a German project there – a demonstration farm – and it looked very impressive. They were raising pigs, and the pigs were nice and fat and everything was very neat and clean. That evening I was in a café and I said to the people there, "Why aren't you raising pigs?" "Pigs!" they said. "Have you seen how those pigs live? They live better than us!" If you calculate how much it costs to feed those high-tech Western pigs, it costs more than to feed a whole family. That's what they told me there.'

'You hear people saying that projects don't work because the Nepalese are too lazy, because the HMG people don't go out in the field enough. But if you talk to them they'll say: "Well, it's easy for the Western experts to say that. But they get their canned food; they have their tax-free Scotch; they have their tents and their sleeping bags and everything arranged for them by Mountain Travel; and they get their *per diem* of, say, 500 rupees. We have to live with them for 30 rupees, and the only way we can save face is by not going with them.'

'I worked on an American project in a valley which was completely cut off from the country's road system. They brought in 200 motorcycles and seventy vehicles and there wasn't even a workshop in the valley. At one time seventy cycles lay idle with simple things like punctures.'

'Many of the big irrigation and power projects are designed solely for their engineering magnificence. They are huge projects, requiring vast amounts of money and vast bureaucracies. They involve the construction of dams and barrages and canals, which means large civil engineering contracts for companies in the donor country. I know of one irrigation project in the Terai which was completed over six years ago, yet not one drop of water has gone to the farmers. Do you know why? Because the project was designed – and the money found – for the barrage and the main canals; not for the accompanying developments to supply water to the fields. It's ridiculous – you'd think this sort of thing only happened in an Abbot and Costello show. These were serious people making serious money. They went around saying, "This is the first phase; the second phase comes later." But they left after the first phase, and there still isn't any money to finish the job. People in Kathmandu aren't interested because the main work has been done and there's not much money to be made from the second phase.'

I never doubted the truth of these stories, but neither did I imagine, before I went to Nepal, that they were representative of what happened in the aid world. Unfortunately, they are; and encapsulated within them are many of the reasons which account for the failure of aid projects: among them, the 'top-down' approach to development; a failure to understand the needs of those whom the projects are supposed to benefit; an unnecessary reliance on high technology; and an obsession with creating bureaucracies.

Carter and I drove up to Chautara one morning in mid-June, stopping on the way to look at a couple of nurseries and to inspect a plantation. Soon after we arrived, Gilmour appeared, and I trust he won't be offended if I say that he looked exactly like my idea of an Australian bushwhacker. He wore a pair of shorts, heavy boots and a floppy canvas hat. The sun – it was an exceedingly hot day – had turned him lobster-pink and he dripped sweat. His first action was to sink a couple of pints of water, then he told Carter what he'd seen and done over the past three days. Much of what he said went over my head, for I knew neither the villages he'd been to, nor the people he mentioned; he also had a habit of referring to trees in Nepali and Latin. It was the nature of the conversation, rather than the substance of it, which held my attention. Any illusions I may have harboured about deforestation being a simple problem requiring a straightforward technical solution were swiftly dispelled.

Later that day, a little before sunset, Gilmour took me out to the balcony of the handsome forestry building – it had been built by Prem Dulal, now of Jiri – and he proceeded to explain the landscape which lay before us. He read it much as a pianist would a musical score. 'You see those terraces over there,' he said. 'Now, they were constructed out of a landslide a few years ago. The same goes for those ones above them, though the landslide must have happened ten or more years ago.' And gradually he worked his way round the valley, explaining why such a crop was growing here, why the farmer wouldn't grow trees there. Whereas before I had viewed the terraces – there must have been several hundred on the slope opposite – much as one would the tiles on a roof, as a gathering of individuals indistinguishable from one another, I now saw each as having a character of its own. Some were old, some young; some were fat and rich, others emaciated and poor. The Himalayan range, explained Gilmour, was young and highly mobile. Even a slight earth tremor would set off dozens of small landslides, and in any case there was a natural tendency for the soil to work its way down the hill. The farmers had adapted their activities to suit the plasticity of the environment. If a chunk of land slipped down the hill, it didn't necessarily mean it was lost to them. They simply carved new terraces out of the scar and redistributed the soil to make the best use of it again.

So how do you decide where to plant trees? 'Well, for a start,' replied Gilmour, 'you can't just come into an area and create forests within a few years. You can't just say, "Here's a denuded area, we'll plant that." Perhaps it's an area where people rest their cattle; or there may be other reasons why they don't want trees there. If you try to dictate forestry policy you will always fail.' A multiplicity of factors, he explained, had to be taken into account before you began planting. For example, who uses a particular area and what do they use it for? Who will look after the forests

– and exploit them – once they have been established? What sort of trees do they want? Perhaps they needed fodder trees rather than fuelwood; and if so, what species do they prefer?

Many people in the aid business seem to think that once they've got the *pradhan panch* on their side, the support of the villagers – his constituents – will automatically follow. (The RCUP was rumoured to have taken some *pradhan panch* from the Kali Gandaki on holiday to Hawaii in an attempt to curry local favour.) However, relying on the goodwill and support of one individual is simply not enough to guarantee the support of the whole community, and over the years the NAFP has assiduously cultivated as many different groups as possible, holding meetings not only with village leaders, but with low-caste men, high-caste men, low-caste women and so forth. 'The business of looking after forests,' said Bob Fisher, an anthropologist working with the NAFP, 'is not so much technical as managerial, so much of our effort has been geared towards establishing institutions which can successfully carry out forest management'. The emphasis has been on devolving power away from the government and down to the villages. 'What we're trying to do,' said Gilmour, 'is give back to the villagers what was taken away from them by the 1957 Nationalization Act.' Getting the villagers to trust the forest department has obviously taken time, and credit for the fact that they now do so must go, in the case of the Sindu Palchock region, to the district forestry officer at Chautara, Tej Mahat. One of the problems for the department has been its reputation. It was set up as a licensing and policing organization to control (and exploit) the forests of the Terai, and in the past it often behaved heavy-handedly: villagers were fined and imprisoned for taking wood from forests they considered ancestrally theirs, and villages were sometimes set on fire to shift their occupants.

The NAFP's success stemmed, in part, from the eagerness of the officers (both expatriate and Nepalese) to find out what the villagers actually wanted, and from their understanding of the complexity of both local politics and traditional land-use practices. What distinguished Gilmour and his colleagues from the herd was their lack of arrogance, a genuine respect for the people they were trying to help, and a willingness to learn. Their actions were not based on the latest aid theories doing the rounds among the ideologues of Washington, London or Canberra; rather they relied on observations empirically gathered, which meant that they made it their business to learn Nepali and to spend as much time in the field as possible. Their wages, when compared with those of many expatriate workers, were modest, and so were their field allowances. The Australians received 150 rupees (about $7) for each day they spent in the field. Those working for UN agencies got between $50 and $75 a day.

The Australians argued that it was too early to say whether or not the project was a success; judgment would have to wait till after they (and their money) had left. Once the villagers showed that they could manage their forests on their own, without financial assistance, then praise would be in order. Initially, the Australians controlled the financing of the project. 'This meant that the authority lay with us,' said Gilmour. 'But now we are shifting the responsibility for handling the money to the local forest committees, and it's up to them what they do with it.' Not that there is all that much of it to play with. Forest guards are paid only 10 rupees a day. 'We don't pretend this is a subsistence wage,' said Gilmour. 'We're just giving a little assistance to encourage people to look after their own resources.' And the Australians have gone out of their way to avoid introducing systems of forest management which are either costly or complicated. Most of the agencies involved in establishing forests in Nepal have endeavoured to protect them with barbed wire. From the outset the NAFP made it clear that they would provide no help to villages or individuals who wished to do likewise. 'If the forests are to survive,' said Carter, 'then local people must control their livestock; erecting fences is no solution.' In short, the NAFP has not tried to solve problems by throwing money at them. The villagers realize that there are no free lunches to be had, and that ultimately the state of the forests depends on the way they use them. Deforestation is their problem, and they must solve it themselves. The NAFP is doing no more than providing a helping hand.

In the first chapter I mentioned that there was much debate about whether or not there was an environmental crisis in the Himalaya. If you follow the news in the West you probably think there is; at least, a large number of organizations and people claim there is. A rapid growth in population during the last half-century is said to have resulted in widespread forest clearance. This has led to massive soil erosion, the loss of farmland, and serious flooding in the Terai and India. Nepal is caught in a spiral of decline, which, if not halted, will end in its total deforestation and the creation of the Himalaya's first wet desert (there are already dry ones in Ladakh and elsewhere). The cost in terms of human lives lost could make the African droughts of the past two decades seem like minor hiccups in the history of mankind.

If much of what one reads is to be believed, then the crisis is well-advanced. Here, for example, are two statements about it from British organizations:

At the rate it's going – some 1.7 million cubic metres of surface soil a year – the best part of Nepal could be in the Bay of Bengal by the end of the century. (Voluntary Service Overseas, newspaper advertisement)

38 per cent of Nepal's total land area consists of fields abandoned as a result of deforestation and soil erosion ... Every year, 240 million cubic metres of Nepalese topsoil is carried downstream to India and Bangladesh. (Earthscan, *Environmental Conflict*)

Leaving aside, for the moment, the problem of quantification (Earthscan's estimate for the loss of soil exceeds VSO's by a factor of 141), and allowing for the fact that the '38 per cent' may be a printing error (no more than 20 per cent of the country is cultivated), these statements have much in common. The facts are presented as if they *are* facts, irrefutable and of impeccable provenance. It is implied that downstream flooding has been on the increase (some would contest that), and that in any case flooding is largely, if not entirely, the result of upstream deforestation (again, some would contest that). Both agencies make it clear that a catastrophe is on the way and, without so much as saying so, they direct blame at the upland peasantry (after all, no one else is chopping the trees down).

It would be wearisome, and take far too long, to look at every aspect of the current debate about whether or not the Himalaya is steadily creeping down to Calcutta, and those who wish to study all the arguments should read Michael Thompson's admirable book, *Uncertainty on a Himalayan Scale*. The hypothesis of 'Himalayan Environmental Degradation' was promoted by scientists working in Nepal in the 1960s and early 1970s, and it was largely accepted by everyone in the development field. Among those who have recently begun to question the hypothesis are scientists who initially championed it. One of them is Dr Jack Ives, the organizer of the Mohonk conference. 'I believe,' he wrote recently, 'that [the hypothesis] may be based, at least in part, upon an element of latter-day myth – a quarter of a century of emotion and repetition of first impressions.'

Thompson and his co-authors were invited by the United Nations Environment Programme to construct a 'systems complex' for the Himalaya's environmental problems, and they immediately set about gathering all the available data for the two key variables, these being the rate at which forest was being used and the rate at which it was growing: 'If it is being used faster than it is being produced then it, and those who depend on it, are caught in a downward spiral.'

There was, they found, no shortage of data; but what did surprise them was the range of variation in the experts' estimates for the two variables. 'Depending on which pair of estimates we chose,' wrote Thompson:

we could have whatever kind of spiral we liked. To make matters even worse we found that similarly vast uncertainties enveloped the answers to such seemingly straightforward questions as: 'What is a forest?' and 'What is deforestation?' . . . Despite our convictions as to the nature of the problem, the quantitive data can give us no guidance as to whether the spiral, if indeed it exists, is upward or downward.

The experts' estimates for *per capita* fuelwood consumption varied by a factor of sixty-seven; those for the sustainable yield of forest by 150 (multiplied by the factor by which estimates for forest area varied). Depending on which pair of estimates you take, you can show that (a) the Himalaya will be washed down to the Bay of Bengal next week; (b) the mountains will sink under the weight of vegetation; (c) something between these two extremes is happening.

Thompson and others have also questioned many of the assumptions made by the doom theorists. For example, it was assumed that deforestation was a consequence of the population growth resulting from the introduction of health care programmes in the middle years of this century. Yet studies round Chautara suggest that most of the deforestation there occurred during the eighteenth and nineteenth centuries. Since then the forest area has remained roughly the same, although the *quality* of the forests has undoubtedly deteriorated. The doom theorists also assume that soil erosion and water run-off are greater on land without trees than on land with trees. This is not always the case. Erosion rates are sometimes considerably higher under forest than on grassland and terraced farmland. It should also be pointed out that three-quarters or more of all the soil washed down Nepal's rivers comes from 'mass wastage', in other words from landslides of such severity that it makes no odds whether or not there are trees on the soil.

Confronted by all this confusion, what – and whom – does one believe? The obvious thing to do is to enquire of those who work in the field – rather than those who dip in briefly to carry out one survey of one piece of ground – how they see matters. Most of those I talked to seemed to agree with Gilmour: 'The situation isn't nearly so gloomy as the gloom-and-doom merchants believe.' And most went along with Thompson's belief that:

The first part of the problem (and perhaps the most difficult part to grasp) is that there is not *a* problem. There is a plurality of contending problems – each one focused by the shared credibility it enjoys in the eyes of those who subscribe to it, and each held separate from the rest by the mutual incredibility that is the inevitable global corollary of locally focused credibilities. The reason, of course, is that if the institutions are pluralized so too will be the facts that those institutions mediate be pluralized.

No one is claiming that all is well in the hills of Nepal. 'The fact is,' says

Thompson, 'that things are very bad in some places, and absolutely fine in others.' It is clear that in some areas trees are being felled faster than they are being replaced; that in some areas there are serious problems of soil erosion; and that in some areas food production is declining while population increases. But there is no simple equation linking population growth with deforestation, deforestation with soil erosion, and soil erosion with declining food production and flooding. The Nepalese hills are astonishingly diverse, and every valley has its own unique character. Not only will it differ in terms of its climate and soils from one a few hours' walk away, it may be home to people of an entirely different culture whose social organization, religious beliefs and way of doing things differ markedly from those of their neighbours. Their problems, in terms of using the land sustainably, will differ; and so, therefore, will the solutions to them. There can be no national 'blueprint for survival', and cooking up figures which apply nationally for forest loss or erosion rates is simply a waste of time. The trick is to establish where the problems are: computer models are no substitute for looking at each area individually.

Whether or not there is an environmental crisis in the Himalaya is of more than academic interest, as much of the aid programme, which now provides two-thirds of the country's development budget, is shaped by the belief that there is. Among those keenest to promote the idea of imminent disaster have been the Nepalese government and various aid agencies. So far, they have reacted to the doubting Toms with a mixture of disdain and fury. One aid worker I met was shouted down when he suggested at an international conference that there wasn't a crisis in Nepal. So why do HMG and others persist in overstating the problem? There are, it seems, a variety of reasons. As far as HMG is concerned, the more gloomy the prognosis for the country, the greater the amount of money which flows in in the form of aid. A big problem requires a big solution, which requires big money. Even if a project fails to solve the perceived problem, those whose duty it is to see it through will benefit financially from it.

There is even an element of benign blackmail here, for if, as HMG claims, deforestation leads to downstream flooding, then those who stand to suffer include not only the Nepalese who are causing the problems, but a further 350 million people in the Ganges Basin. If you don't help us, they say, then all these innocent Indians and Bangladeshis may suffer as well. Pleas to international institutions fall on receptive ears, for such institutions are fond of international problems; indeed, to some extent, they serve as a justification for their existence.

Institutions, like the people who write newspaper leaders, like to think they understand what is going on in the world. If you ask the World Bank or the Overseas Development Administration a question, they will never reply by saying, 'Ooh, that's a tricky one, you've got me there', or 'Sorry, we haven't a clue.' They always have an answer, and they will always have figures which seem to prove what they say. Like leader-writers, institutions involved in aid are keen on self-preservation. To survive they *need* problems, and to be credible they must be able to define the problems, to dress them up in facts and figures, and thus convince their pay-masters that they have a role to play in putting right whatever is wrong. 'What you must remember,' said one expatriate aid worker, 'is that aid agencies and the big lending banks are not interested in doing small things, even when it is only small things which need to be done. What they like to fund are big schemes – roads, dams, irrigation works, large plantations. They like these things because they cost a lot of money, they require a large and expensive expatriate input and they are highly visible.'

This point – that aid agencies veer towards the grand rather than modest – is born out by much of what one sees in Nepal. Between 1976/7 and 1982/3, 25.8 per cent of the aid budget was spent on the transport sector (mostly on roads) and 23.5 per cent on the power sector (hydro-electric plants, electrification and so forth). This compares with 3.9 per cent spent on health and 2.7 per cent on drinking water projects. The proportion of the aid budget spent on forestry was also 2.7 per cent, although the figure would be greater if one included the money spent on power projects whose purpose was to provide electricity in order to reduce the consumption of fuelwood. But this simply bears out the views expressed by the aid worker: most aid goes on large projects requiring heavy inputs of capital. Even if one looks at the money allocated to projects directly concerned with growing trees (the 2.7 per cent), nearly every rupee is spent on creating new plantations – on afforestation – rather than on the better management of existing, degraded forests. 'I suppose,' said Gilmour, 'that about one per cent of the forests in the hills have been established by plantation. This is where all the effort has gone. The other 99 per cent is virtually ignored.' The agencies (and HMG) prefer to support the planting of new forests rather than the management of old because this enables them to work out targets, it gives them something to count (trees, nurseries and so on), and their actions are visible. Gilmour admits that planting trees is psychologically important: 'It gets people involved and gives them something to see for their efforts.' But what matters more is looking after the existing forests, and especially those which are in the process of being wrecked by over-grazing and lopping for fodder and fuelwood. If such areas are managed properly the trees will come back. There is no need to plant trees here; it is simply a question of controlling those activities which cause deforestation. If the forests are to be saved the skills required are managerial rather than technical.

Salvation is to be earnt rather than bought. It is high time all the aid agencies – not just a handful – realized this.

If I set out with any purpose other than to describe what I saw in Nepal, it was to supply answers to two questions: who stands to gain from all this foreign aid? And is the money – often derived from taxes in the West – well spent? Even had I seen much more than I did (there are now some forty government agencies and international institutions operating in Nepal, only a handful of which I came across), I would have had difficulty in supplying cogent answers to these questions. The one-liners might be: 'It is the rich who have gained most' and, 'No, most of the money is not well spent.' But this is altogether too trite, and indeed these two questions, once examined, throw up more questions than answers. Mulling them over during the past year, I have watched them breed like rabbits, and their progeny too have been far from celibate.

Perhaps it is true, as one Nepali friend sweepingly put it, that aid 'corrupts, distorts and destroys'. Certainly, foreign aid has led to the creation of a middle class, many of whose members are more preoccupied with feathering their own nests than anything else. Perhaps it is true that aid has induced what the French call *la mentalité assistée*. There is plenty of evidence to show that aid often induces sloth rather than industry, dependence rather than self-reliance. And perhaps it is true that the main beneficiaries of many aid programmes are those who work for, or are employed by, the donor agencies. But does all this mean that one should condemn the business of foreign aid out of hand? After all, haven't some projects – for example, the NAFP and Pakhribas – achieved what they set out to achieve? Hasn't better health care saved lives which otherwise would have been lost? Hasn't education made literate the illiterate? Haven't at least some of the poor become wealthier?

The justification for most aid projects is couched in extremely vague terms. Phrases such as 'raising the standard of living' and 'developing the local economy' abound in the prospectuses of aid agencies. Christopher Patten, Britain's minister for Overseas Development, has written that the British aid programme – it is now worth over £1,300 million a year – can be justified on four main grounds: developmental, political, commercial and humanitarian. 'Some of these are more overt than others,' states Patten, adding that 'all are inter-related and often difficult to disentangle'. However, when all is said and done, nearly all aid projects – even those which are largely determined by the donor country's political and commercial aspirations – are directly or indirectly supposed to benefit the poor. It is all too obvious that in Nepal they often do nothing of the sort.

For this and other reasons I find myself intuitively drawn to the school of thought – it has adherents of all political persuasions – which demands that we should cease interfering in the business of foreign countries (aid is a form of interference), as it costs us money and does them little good – and possibly much harm. But attractive though this idea may be, it can never be more than an idea. There are simply too many vested interests whose well-being hinges on the continuance of an aid programme. Nepal's ruling élites would strenuously resist any withdrawal of foreign aid, and in any case none of the large donor countries would be prepared to sacrifice the political advantages of being there. Were the United States to leave, then the USSR would be only too glad to fill the lacuna. Political considerations will always override the humanitarian.

What Nepal will be like twenty, fifty or a hundred years hence none can tell. The future, like the Plains of Heaven, is imponderable. I hope, incidentally, that the latter are liberally interspersed with great mountains, and the more like the Himalaya the better. The great thing about mountains – or at least about those of the non-celestial variety – is that they cannot be tamed in the way that plains can. The flat land of the Terai could be cultivated by exactly the same sort of machinery one finds on the American prairies or the corn fields of eastern England, and I imagine that before long tractors will replace ox and buffalo as the main beasts of burden in the fields round Birgunj and Biratnagar. Up in the hills there will be changes too over the coming years. Television will reach into areas where roads never can, and so will electricity; the hill people will be introduced to new ideas, a broader vision of the world, and possibly the Kenwood mixer. But wherever the land lies mid-way between the horizontal and the vertical, wherever its exploitation depends on the existence of terraces, traditional methods of ploughing, sowing and harvesting will persist. Whatever else happens in the Himalaya, the buffalo will always pull the plough, and behind the buffalo will be a man, or sometimes a woman or young boy, following on foot, often without shoes and nearly always with a stick. Change here can never be absolute; this alone fills me with hope.

Epilogue

I AM WRITING THESE LAST few pages some eight months after leaving Nepal. No doubt many things have changed already, especially in and around Kathmandu. During the winter of 1987–8 a few snippets of news reached me, though little of it through our national press, which, as always, has been too concerned with the goings-on in India to bother reporting affairs in its small neighbour. The news I have, coming mostly from friends or travellers, is sketchy and idiosyncratic, reminding me of those lines in Eliot's 'Portrait of a Lady':

> An English countess goes upon the stage.
> A Greek was murdered at a Polish dance,
> Another bank defaulter has confessed.

Apparently 250 Nepalese civil servants were sacked recently; some were guilty of corrupt practices, others of inefficiency. The man responsible for running the milk board was sacked too; he was said to have been behind the powdered milk mischief. And a senior police officer has been imprisoned – for twenty years, I believe – for the part he played in the heroin-smuggling trade. The *Independent* recently carried a little item reporting that Bangladesh had returned 1,600 tons of radiated milk powder to Poland, though it didn't say how much, if any, had been distributed or whether any had reached Nepal. And a week later *The Times* ran a long editorial poking fun at the Nepalese royal family for putting a stop to a performance of *Hamlet* in Kathmandu.

A while ago a card arrived from Brot, telling me that he had just finished installing a hydro-electric scheme for the monastery at Tyangboche in Sagarmatha National Park. Along with the card came two headlines from *Rising Nepal*. 'Winners Come Out In Various Sports Events' read one enigmatically; 'Man-Eater Leopard Kills Woman' said the other. Brot also had some sad news from the Dudh Kosi: 'Yes, believe it or not a dead body was found in the river at the bridge below Namche. People believe he was "sucked into the abyss" by the sheer breath-bating exposure of that awesome, unforgiving and unrepenting cliff face. I looked to see if he bore a resemblance to you ...'

Reading through what I have written, I am struck now by the many things I have missed out. For example, I have said little about the shrines which are found at every street corner, or bedded into crumbling brick walls, or strangled and broken by the roots of trees. And nearly always they were stained with *tika* and in front of them would be the detritus of offerings, some limp leaves and some broken rice, and perhaps a glob of wax, the funerary remains of a candle that had flickered and shone for a little while. Neither have I written about the trees in the Terai with flowers the colour of blood-oranges, nor about the blue-tailed bee-eaters and golden-backed woodpeckers in Chitwan, not about the television programmes they get in Kathmandu, most people's favourite being *Yes, Minister*. And I forgot to mention the elaborate paintwork on the lorries, the beggar with elephantiasis in Pokhara, the black drongos near Karkineta whose long tails fluttered tremulously as they swooped on insects; and there are a thousand and one other things which might equally well have gone into this book but haven't. Not just things, but people too.

One might think, from much of what I have written, that what I saw in Nepal left me with a feeling of sadness and despondency. I almost feel it should have done. But it hasn't. It hasn't for the simple reason that what is genuinely good and uplifting and admirable about Nepal far outweighs what is wrong with it. I know that in a few years' time my memories of the country will have nothing to do with the business of aid or with the problems of development. The things I shall remember belong to all times and many places: the pleasures of friendship; men and women labouring in the fields under a hot sun; the sound of people laughing and hooves clattering on dry cobbles; the moist breath of whiskery buffaloes; the heavy musk of a perfumed woman passing, her hips swinging, her calloused toes splayed in the dust ...

Bibliography

Having browsed through the shelves of many of London's larger bookshops, I concluded, before departing to Nepal, that virtually everything written about the country came from the pens of either climbers or anthropologists. This is far from being the case: there are scores of books on Nepal, and they cover a wide range of subjects. Many are hard or impossible to obtain in Britain, though most can be found in Kathmandu, whose best bookshop is on Darbar Marg, near the junction with Bagh Bazaar. Otherwise, try the shops in Thamel. (The best map of Kathmandu, and the prettiest, is the one drawn by Didi Thunder and published by 'American Women of Nepal'.) The books listed below are just a fraction of those available, but they are the ones which I found instructive or entertaining, and sometimes both. I particularly recommend those by Coburn, Downs and Murphy. I have made no attempt to sort the books into categories, but from their titles their bent should be obvious.

I also read dozens of documents about the aid projects I visited, but I can see no good reason to list them here. Anyone wishing to learn more about the development business should thumb through past issues of *Mountain Research and Development*, a journal produced at the University of Colorado and edited by Dr Jack Ives and his wife. The International Centre for Integrated Mountain Development (ICIMOD, P. O. Box 3226, Kathmandu) has published an excellent series of 'Occasional Papers' on a range of pertinent topics. If you visit Nepal you should read the English-language daily, *Rising Nepal*, whose cricket coverage is rivalled, in that part of world, only by the *Times of India*.

Armington, Stan, *Trekking in the Nepal Himalaya*, South Yarra, Lonely Planet, 1985.
Bezruschka, Stephen, *A Guide to Trekking in Nepal*, Seattle, The Mountaineers, 1981.

Bibliography

Bista, Dor Bahadur, *People of Nepal*, Kathmandu, Ratna Pustak Bhandar, 1980. First published 1967.

Coburn, Broughton, *Nepali Aama: Portrait of a Nepalese Hill Woman*, Santa Barbara, Ross-Erikson, 1982.

Day, J. Wentworth, *King George V as a Sportsman*, London, Cassell, 1935.

Downs, Hugh R., *Rhythms of a Himalayan Village*, San Francisco, Harper & Row, 1979.

Farwell, Byron, *The Gurkhas*, Harmondsworth, Penguin, 1985.

Gajurel, C.L. and Vaidya, K.K., *Traditional Arts and Crafts in Nepal*, New Delhi, S. Chand, 1984.

Hagen, Toni, *Nepal*, New Delhi, Oxford and IBH, 1980.

Herzog. Maurice, *Annapurna*, London, Triad/Paladin, 1986.

Hodgson, Brian H., *Essays on the Languages, Literature and Religion of Nepal and Tibet*, London, Trubner & Co, 1974.

Hunter, W.W., *The Life of Brian Hodgson*, London, John Murray, 1896.

Integrated Development Systems, *Foreign Aid and Development in Nepal*, Kathmandu, IDS, 1983.

Jefferies, Margaret, *The Story of Mount Everest National Park*, Auckland, Cobb/Horwood, 1986.

Joshi, B.C. and Rose, Leo E., *Democratic Innovations in Nepal*, Berkeley, University of California Press, 1966.

Kirkpatrick, Col. F., *An Account of the Kingdom of Nepaul*, New Delhi, Biblioteca Himalaya, 1969. First published 1800.

Matthiessen, Peter, *The Snow Leopard*, London, Chatto & Windus, 1979.

Murphy, Dervla, *The Waiting Land: A Spell in Nepal*, London, John Murray, 1967, and Century Hutchinson, 1987.

National Planning Commission Secretariat, *Nepal: Statistical Pocket Book of 1986*, Kathmandu, NPCS, 1986.

Peissel, Michel, *Tiger for Breakfast*, London, Hodder, 1966.

Peissel, Michel, *Mustang: A Lost Tibetan Kingdom*, London, Collins Harvill, 1968.

Rai, Navin K., *People of the Stones: the Chepangs of Central Nepal*, Kathmandu, Centre for Nepal and Asian Studies, Tribhuvan University, 1985.

Sanday, John, *Monuments of the Kathmandu Valley*, Paris, Unesco, 1979.

Seddon, David, *Nepal: A State of Poverty*, New Delhi, Vikas, 1987.

Thapa, Netra B., *A Short History of Nepal*, Kathmandu, Ratna Pustak Bhandar, 1981.

Thompson, M., Warburton, M. and Hatley, T., *Uncertainty on a Himalayan Scale*, London, Milton Ash, 1986.

Tüting, Ludmilla and Dixit, Kunda (eds), *Bikas-Binas: the change in life and environment of the Himalaya*, Munich, Geobuch, 1986.

Bibliography

Unicef, *Children and Women in Nepal: A Situation Analysis*, Kathmandu, Unicef, 1987.

van Gruisen, Lisa (ed.), *Insight Guide to Nepal*, Singapore, Apa Productions, 1985.

von Fürer-Haimendorf, Christoph, *The Sherpas Transformed: Social Change in a Buddhist Society of Nepal*, New Delhi, Sterling, 1984.

Wright, David (ed.), *Vamsuvali: History of Nepal, with an Introductory Sketch of the Country and People*, Calcutta, Susil Gupta, 1958. First published 1877.

Index

Index

Index

READ MORE IN PENGUIN

In every corner of the world, on every subject under the sun, Penguin represents quality and variety – the very best in publishing today.

For complete information about books available from Penguin – including Puffins, Penguin Classics and Arkana – and how to order them, write to us at the appropriate address below. Please note that for copyright reasons the selection of books varies from country to country.

In the United Kingdom: Please write to *Dept. EP, Penguin Books Ltd, Bath Road, Harmondsworth, West Drayton, Middlesex UB7 ODA*

In the United States: Please write to *Consumer Sales, Penguin USA, P.O. Box 999, Dept. 17109, Bergenfield, New Jersey 07621-0120*. VISA and MasterCard holders call 1-800-253-6476 to order Penguin titles

In Canada: Please write to *Penguin Books Canada Ltd, 10 Alcorn Avenue, Suite 300, Toronto, Ontario M4V 3B2*

In Australia: Please write to *Penguin Books Australia Ltd, P.O. Box 257, Ringwood, Victoria 3134*

In New Zealand: Please write to *Penguin Books (NZ) Ltd, Private Bag 102902, North Shore Mail Centre, Auckland 10*

In India: Please write to *Penguin Books India Pvt Ltd, 706 Eros Apartments, 56 Nehru Place, New Delhi 110 019*

In the Netherlands: Please write to *Penguin Books Netherlands bv, Postbus 3507, NL-1001 AH Amsterdam*

In Germany: Please write to *Penguin Books Deutschland GmbH, Metzlerstrasse 26, 60594 Frankfurt am Main*

In Spain: Please write to *Penguin Books S. A., Bravo Murillo 19, 1° B, 28015 Madrid*

In Italy: Please write to *Penguin Italia s.r.l., Via Felice Casati 20, I–20124 Milano*

In France: Please write to *Penguin France S. A., 17 rue Lejeune, F–31000 Toulouse*

In Japan: Please write to *Penguin Books Japan, Ishikiribashi Building, 2–5–4, Suido, Bunkyo-ku, Tokyo 112*

In South Africa: Please write to *Longman Penguin Southern Africa (Pty) Ltd, Private Bag X08, Bertsham 2013*

READ MORE IN PENGUIN

A CHOICE OF NON-FICTION

The Time Out Film Guide   Edited by Tom Milne

The definitive, up-to-the minute directory of over 9,500 films – world cinema from classics and silent epics to reissues and the latest releases – assessed by two decades of *Time Out* reviewers. 'In my opinion the best and most comprehensive' – Barry Norman

The Remarkable Expedition   Olivia Manning

The events of an extraordinary attempt in 1887 to rescue Emin Pasha, Governor of Equatoria, are recounted here by the author of *The Balkan Trilogy* and *The Levant Trilogy* and vividly reveal unprecedented heights of magnificent folly in the perennial human search for glorious conquest.

Skulduggery   Mark Shand

Mark Shand, his friend and business partner Harry Fane and world-famous but war-weary photographer Don McCullin wanted adventure. So, accompanied by a fat Batak guide, armed only with a first-aid kit and with T-shirts, beads and tobacco for trading, they plunged deep into the heart of Indonesian cannibal country . . .

Lenin's Tomb   David Remnick

'This account by David Remnick, Moscow correspondent for the *Washington Post* from 1988 to 1992, of the last days of the Soviet Empire is one of the most vivid to date' – *Observer*

Roots Schmoots   Howard Jacobson

'This is no exercise in sentimental journeys. Jacobson writes with a rare wit and the book sparkles with his gritty humour . . . he displays a deliciously caustic edge in his analysis of what is wrong, and right, with modern Jewry' – *Mail on Sunday*

READ MORE IN PENGUIN

A CHOICE OF NON-FICTION

Stones of Empire Jan Morris

There is no corner of India that does not contain some relic of the British presence, whether it is as grand as a palace or as modest as a pillar box. Jan Morris's study of the buildings of British India is as entertaining and enlightening on the nature of imperialism as it is on architecture.

Bitter Fame Anne Stevenson

'A sobering and salutary attempt to estimate what Plath was, what she achieved and what it cost her ... This is the only portrait which answers Ted Hughes's image of the poet as Ariel, not the ethereal bright pure roving sprite, but Ariel trapped in Prospero's pine and raging to be free' – *Sunday Telegraph*

Here We Go Harry Ritchie

From Fuengirola to Calahonda, *Here We Go* is an hilarious tour of the Costa del Sol ... with a difference! 'Simmering with self-mocking humour, it offers a glorious celebration of the traditions of the English tourist, reveals a Spain that Pedro Almodovar couldn't have conjured up in his worst nightmare, and character-assassinates every snob and pseud' – *Time Out*

Children First Penelope Leach

Challenging the simplistic nostalgia of the 'family values' lobby, Leach argues that society today leaves little time for children and no easy way for adults – especially women – to be both solvent, self-respecting citizens and caring parents.

Young Men and Fire Norman Maclean

On 5 August 1949, a crew of fifteen airborne firefighters, the Smokejumpers, stepped into the sky above a remote forest fire in the Montana wilderness. Less than an hour after their jump, all but three were dead or fatally burned. From their tragedy, Norman Maclean builds an unforgettable story of courage, hope and redemption.

READ MORE IN PENGUIN

A CHOICE OF NON-FICTION

My Secret Planet Denis Healey

'This is an anthology of the prose and poetry that has provided pleasure and inspiration to Denis Healey throughout his life ... pleasurable on account of the literature selected and also for the insight it provides of Denis Healey outside the world of politics ... a thoroughly good read' – *The Times*

The Sun King Nancy Mitford

Nancy Mitford's magnificent biography of Louis XIV is also an illuminating examination of France in the late seventeenth and early eighteenth centuries. It covers the intrigues of the court and the love affairs of the king, with extensive illustrations, many in full colour.

This Time Next Week Leslie Thomas

'Mr Thomas's book is all humanity, to which is added a Welshman's mastery of words ... Some of his episodes are hilarious, some unbearably touching, but everyone, staff and children, is looked upon with compassion' – *Observer*. 'Admirably written, with clarity, realism, poignancy and humour' – *Daily Telegraph*

Against the Stranger Janine di Giovanni

'In her powerfully written book Janine di Giovanni evokes the atmosphere of the Palestinian refugee camps in the Gaza Strip ... The effect of the Palestinians' sufferings on the next generation of children is powerfully documented' – *Sunday Express*

Native Stranger Eddy L. Harris

Native Stranger is a startling chronicle of the author's search for himself in Africa, the land of his ancestors. 'Since Richard Wright's *Black Power*, there has been a dearth of travel narratives on Africa by black Americans. *Native Stranger* picks up where Wright left off, and does so with both courage and honesty' – Caryl Phillips in the *Washington Post*

READ MORE IN PENGUIN

THE TRAVEL LIBRARY – A SELECTION

Hindoo Holiday	J. R. Ackerley
The Innocent Anthropologist	Nigel Barley
South from Granada	Gerald Brenan
The Road to Oxiana	Robert Byron
An Indian Summer	James Cameron
Granite Island	Dorothy Carrington
The Hill of Devi	E. M. Forster
Journey to Kars	Philip Glazebrook
A Little Tour in France	Henry James
Mornings in Mexico	D. H. Lawrence
The Stones of Florence *and* Venice Observed	Mary McCarthy
They Went to Portugal	Rose Macaulay
Calcutta	Geoffrey Moorhouse
Spain	Jan Morris
Aspects of Provence	James Pope-Hennessy
Travels in Nepal	Charlie Pye-Smith
The Marsh Arabs	Wilfred Thesiger
Journey into Cyprus	Colin Thubron
City of Gold	Gillian Tindall
Ninety-Two Days	Evelyn Waugh
Third-Class Ticket	Heather Wood

BY THE SAME AUTHOR

Barcelona
A Celebration and a Guide

For its nightlife, turbulent history, fabulous artistic heritage and architecture from Gothic to Gaudi, Barcelona is one of the liveliest cities in Europe. Charlie Pye-Smith's book is more than an indispensable introduction to the city's glorious medieval past and avant-garde present. It is also an informative guide to getting around the city, offering suggestions on where to stay, where to eat and even where to dance.

A brief history, from Roman times to the present, is followed by a detailed tour of the city: of its gardens and galleries, its stately palaces and seedy backstreets. Its core is a description of the medieval, Gothic and other main districts. Other chapters give information on where to find the city's nightlife, on the delights of Catalan cuisine and Catalonia's other attractions. Highly informative and immensely practical, this book is a marvellous celebration of this superbly stylish city and region.